The Film Reader

Classic Readings
in American Film History

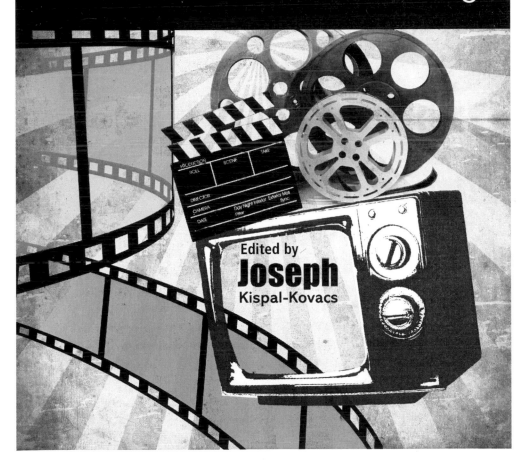

Edited by
Joseph
Kispal-Kovacs

Kendall Hunt
publishing company
4050 Westmark Drive • P O Box 1840 • Dubuque IA 52004-1840

Cover images used under license from Shutterstock, Inc.

Kendall Hunt
publishing company

www.kendallhunt.com
Send all inquiries to:
4050 Westmark Drive
Dubuque, IA 52004-1840

Printed in the United States of America
10 9 8 7 6 5 4 3 2

Contents

Introduction

Joseph Kispal-Kovacs

This film reader collects together excerpts from a number of important books about American film. The emphasis is on work that is historical in nature but there is also attention given to works dealing with narrative structure and those providing an explanation of the political context in which American movies were made and viewed.

The first reading is from Stephen J. Ross' *Working-Class Hollywood: Silent Film and the Shaping of Class in America* (1998). This book played a significant role in increasing our understanding of the early film industry in the United States. A discussion of the overall importance of Ross' contribution to film historiography can also be found in Chapter 1 of the companion volume to this collection: *Film, Television and American Society: Lectures on The Media and On Empire* (2010).

This reading originally made up Chapter 1 of the Ross book. It provides us with an account of movie exhibition in the US between 1905 (when the first nickelodeons appeared) and April 1917 (when the US entered World War I). The chapter explores the class character of the entertainment industries in early twentieth century US and why the working class made up the vast majority of the film audience before World War I.

As the American economy embraced industrialization in the late 19th century the very nature of work changed. Mechanization, combined with long working hours, made work even less appealing than it had been prior to this. Leisure activities in the few hours available to people after working in the factories, warehouses, mines and other places, increasingly took on a prominence. Rather than creating their own culture and leisure activities as had happened in pre-industrial societies, America's workers, like their sisters and brothers in other industrialized and industrializing countries, turned to the offerings of a new segment of the business class, the "cultural entrepreneurs" (Ross 13).

These businessmen created a whole range of activities that varied widely in accessibility because of cost. The entertainment industries were class stratified. At the bottom of this constellation of leisure activities were the ones that America's workers could afford—the odd trip to a circus, amusement park or ball game and by 1905, entrance to rudimentary movie houses that charged its patrons five cents for the possibility of being amused for a time by watching a program of short films. These nickelodeons could eventually be found in all of the major cities and towns of America within a few years and admissions quickly numbered in the millions.

The existence of this institution and its mass appeal was the source of fear and hysteria for the self appointed moral guardians of society—clergymen, politicians and others. Films that portrayed working class people and the institutions that advocated on their behalf in a positive light alarmed many of them. Trade unions and left-wing political organizations saw in the movies a new way of getting their message out and hurried to use the medium to communicate with their target audiences. Feminists, in the form of the suffragette movement of the late nineteenth and early twentieth century, also saw in the movies a potential vehicle for helping their cause (27).

Equally alarming was the tendency of many early movies to mock the established political and economic order. The movies also pushed the boundaries of what was then acceptable and non-acceptable sexual behavior. All these factors put pressure on both filmmakers and theatre owners to "clean up" their act. The first response was to try to change the class character of the movie audience. More expensive movies in luxurious picture palaces began to attract a middle class and upper class audience. The movies became more respectable. The second response was to promote the idea of censoring the movies. This will be addressed in the discussion of Richard Maltby's essay in this anthology.

David Bordwell's essay in this collection originally appeared in an anthology edited by Philip Rosen (1986). It is an adaptation of some of the ideas that Bordwell has explained in greater detail in his *Narration in the Fiction Film* (1985) and in a book he co-authored entitled *The Classical Hollywood*

Cinema: Film Style & Mode of Production to 1960 (1985). These are works of what is sometimes referred to as "neoformalist" analysis. Put simply, Bordwell and others in this intellectual current are trying to uncover and describe the deep structures of commercial film narrative, particular that body of work labeled the "Classical Hollywood Cinema." Bordwell has adopted the method of the Russian formalist scholar, Vladimir Propp. Propp's famous analysis of the Russian folktale and his attempt to discern its most basic elements becomes the model for Bordwell's account of Hollywood narrative.

This account of the deep structures of Hollywood narrative, its recurring patterns and its dependence on repetitive formulae complements our understanding of the institutions that were making these films. The Hollywood studio system, a factory-like entity employing thousands of workers, was a hierarchical culture industry organized around the continuity script. The script, the basis for the plot and story of a film to be made, also becomes the blueprint for the discrete tasks that the film workers had to carry out to bring a project to completion (Staiger 20).

This mode of film production became the dominant form of film narrative production not just in the United States but in many other countries as well who were trying to imitate the success of the American model. Even as the film industry in the US changed after the breakup of the studio system after 1960, the basic forms of storytelling have remained largely unchanged. Bordwell's article reminds of how compelling and influential this narrative model remains.

Richard Maltby's essay on film censorship in the United States covers the period from the early twentieth century until the 1950s. While most countries in the world relied on some form of state censorship to regulate the content of the movies, the history of censorship in the United States is somewhat different.

Early attempts at censoring the content of movies in the US were haphazard. At the beginning municipalities sometimes used fire regulations to close down theatres showing films found to be offensive. Later various states tried to implement prior-censorship of the movies shown in their jurisdictions. The result of all this was a patchwork of uneven and inconsistent censorship institutions. Hollywood, in the mid 1920s began thinking about ways that they might forestall this kind of external censorship by doing it themselves.

The Motion Picture Producers and Distributors of America (MPPDA) founded in 1922 and led by Will Hays tried various strategies to get the industry to regulate itself. At first a voluntary code was devised but was not always followed by the members of the organization. Organizations like the Catholic Church and the Legion of Decency began to lobby governments to change the behavior of the studios and they also began to organize boycotts of offending movies. Hollywood became alarmed that they would lose control over the regulation of the industry. So in 1934, the MPPDA founded the Production Code Administration (PCA) which was able to implement a form of self-censorship with teeth.

The PCA followed a list of dos and don't (which weren't always followed in the 1920s) and had a mechanism for enforcing it. Films that weren't submitted for approval would not be shown in the theatres of any of the companies belonging to the MPPDA. A fine of $25,000 for showing a film that wasn't approved also provided a strong incentive to follow the rules. This system lasted until 1966 but it already began to unravel in the 1950s. Richard Maltby's short piece traces these developments.

The reading from Michael Ryan and Douglas Kellner's book, *Camera Politica*, covers the issues related to the American film industry's response to the Vietnam War and its aftermath. The book is an ambitious work that tries to trace the developments in mainstream American film in the period between the late 1960s and the early 1980s. It is also an account of how the film industry both documented and sometimes anticipated the major changes that were talking place in American society during this period.

The liberal political consensus that characterized the American political scene since the 1930s began to unravel in the late 1960s. In the 1970s, American institutions experienced a crisis of legitimacy following the Watergate scandal, an economic crisis and the military defeat in Vietnam. Liberals were unable to address this crisis and this lead to the resurgence of conservative political ideas in the late 1970s and early 1980s. The movies of this period seem to follow this development closely. This is not to say that all the movies in the beginning of this period were liberal in outlook and then turned conservative later. Films from both perspectives were made throughout this entire period. What is evident, though, is that conservative films began to figure more prominently by the time the 1980s rolled around.

Hollywood films took on the major social issues of the day from a variety of political perspectives. Films like *The Godfather* (1972) are identified as conservative because they seemed to be glorifying the return to strong and violent male leadership in a society were patriarchy was under attack from a number of sources. Liberal films like *Norma Rae* (1979) suggest that women can take leadership roles in their communities and that black and white workers can join together to struggle against employers who would hold both groups back.

Chapter 7 of this book (reprinted here) addresses the contradictory ways in which Hollywood addressed the war in Vietnam. While the war was on, the commercial film industry ignored the war. There were many documentaries made but few fictional films. A pro-war film made by John Wayne, *The Green Berets* (1968) was a critical and financial failure. Despite the fact that this war dominated the nightly news on television, Hollywood decided to avoid the issue altogether. However, after the war ended and the US-backed government of South Vietnam collapsed, dozens of movies about it were made about it.

Fictional films about the Vietnam War took a number of different forms including combat films as well returning veteran narratives. Combat films could be conservative and pro-war in outlook (although these were in a minority) or liberal and anti-war. What unites both conservative and liberal films about Vietnam is the exclusive focus on the soldiers themselves. Very little screen time is devoted to the people of Vietnam (who were presumably the object of the US concern about their welfare). This kind of "imperial narcissism" is also a feature of more recent combat films dealing with the two wars in Iraq. Returning veteran films tended to focus on the problems faced by former soldiers who have been abandoned by the military, the government and the rest of society.

The second part of this chapter examines the exhaustive efforts by the US military to rehabilitate its image after the fiasco in Vietnam. Public confidence in the leadership of the armed forces was at an all-time low. In addition to the creation of an all-volunteer force (in response to the morale problems created by the draft and its uneven application), the military began to enlist the help of Hollywood in its recruitment strategies. The result was a number of pro-military films released in the 1980s. In return for free access to military equipment, bases and other assets, filmmakers agreed to allow the military to vet scripts before they went into production.

The third part of the chapter deals with the effects of the re-emergence of the Cold War in 1979 and after. Movies that had a distinctly anti-Russian and anti-Communist outlook were encouraged. Also evident was the popularity of films that prompted aggressive militarism as a solution to the "Vietnam

Syndrome." The lesson was not to avoid mistakes like the intervention in Vietnam but to rewrite history to suggest that the problem wasn't a failure of policy but a lack of nerve to finish the job.

The collection of essays in the book, *Conglomerates and the Media* (1997), brings together contributions from some of American's top media scholars. The purpose of the book is to examine the characteristics and consequences of a concentrated corporate media system in the US. The 1980s and 1990s saw the emergence of an oligopolistic structure across all of the media industries and not just in a single industry (like the film industry in the 1930s and 1940s or the television industry between the 1940s and 1970s). No longer is it the case that a small number of companies control an entire industry but rather that a small number of companies dominate numerous industries.

Thomas Schatz's contribution addresses the ways in which the film industry fits into these larger media corporations. Companies like Time-Warner and Disney make films, own television networks, own book and magazine publishing firms, and are involved in numerous other entertainment industries. The film industry has increasingly become reliant on "franchises". A successful film makes money at the box office, then it goes to home video, and then to cable and broadcast television. It may also be spun off into novelizations, comic books, video games and so on. The company that owns the franchise collects revenues at each stage. The film divisions of these corporations effectively become the launch pad for these multi-media franchises. Schatz's essay traces the beginnings of this development. Subsequently this process has continued and has become more firmly entrenched in the media industries. Disney's recent purchase of Marvel Comics and its large stable of superheroes is further evidence of this phenomenon.

It may be a little premature to call Stephen Prince's recent book, *Firestorm: American Film in the Age of Terrorism* (2009) a classic. However, it is one of the better attempts (among many) to analyze the response of the Hollywood film industry to the terror attacks of 2001 and the subsequent "War on Terror." Also recommended is Douglas Kellner's, *Cinema Wars: Hollywood Film and Politics in the Bush-Cheney Era* (2010).

This anthology includes the first Chapter of *Firestorm*, which is entitled, "Theatre of Mass Destruction". The focus of this reading is on the pre-history of September 11, 2001. Prince points outs that many American action films with their focus of explosive spectacle actually pre-figured the media spectacle that was made of the tragic events of that September day in New York City, Washington, D.C. and the fields of rural Pennsylvania. Eyewitnesses to the tragedy sometimes spoke of the experience as being like watching a movie.

Movies about terrorism go back quite a few decades. Examples from the 1930s are discussed as well as the many disaster movies of the 1970s, which anticipate the more contemporary action spectacles. The long history of other terrorist attacks in the United States going back a century is also detailed in this first chapter. The rest of the book examines the response of the film industry to these events. There are discussions about the movies that deal with the wars in Afghanistan and Iraq, the movies about domestic security and the movies about possible future terror attacks.

This collection is not meant to be exhaustive but rather meant to give students a sample of some of the outstanding work that has been done by scholars of American film to help us better understand the movies and their place in our society. It is this editor's hope that students will go on to read the entirety of the books from which these readings were taken.

Works Cited

Bordwell, David. *Narration in the Fiction Film.* Madison: University of Wisconsin Press, 1985.

——. "Classical Hollywood Cinema: Narrational Principles and Procedures." Narrative, *Apparatus, Ideology: A Film Theory Reader.* Edited by Philip Rosen. New York: Columbia University Press, 1986, pp. 17-34.

Bordwell, David; Thompson, Kristin and Staiger, Janet. *The Classical Hollywood Cinema: Film Style & Mode of Production to 1960.* New York: Columbia University Press, 1985.

Kispal-Kovacs, Joseph. *Film, Television and American Society: Lectures On the Media and On Empire.* Dubuque, IA: Kendall Hunt, 2010.

Kellner, Douglas. *Cinema Wars: Hollywood Film and Politics in the Bush-Cheney Era.* Chichester, UK: Wiley-Blackwell, 2010.

Maltby, Richard. "Censorship and Self-Regulation." *The Oxford History of World Cinema.* Edited by Geoffrey Nowell-Smith. Oxford: Oxford University Press, 1996, pp. 235–247.

Prince, Stephen. "Theater of Mass Destruction." *Firestorm: American Film in the Age of Terrorism.* New York: Columbia University Press, 2009, pp.17–70.

Ross, Steven J. "Going To the Movies: Leisure, Class, and Danger in the Early Twentieth Century." *Working Class Hollywood: Silent Film and The Shaping of Class In America.* Princeton, NJ: Princeton University Press, 1998, pp. 11–33.

Ryan, Michael and Kellner, Douglas. "Vietnam and the New Militarism." *Camera Politica: The Politics and Ideology of Contemporary Hollywood Film.* Bloomington: Indiana University Press, 1988, pp. 194–216.

Schatz, Thomas. "The Return of the Studio System." *Conglomerates and the Media.* Barnouw, Erik, et.al. New York: The New Press, 1997, pp. 73–103.

Staiger, Janet. "Dividing Labor for Production Control." *Cinema Journal.* Spring 1979, v18, n2, pp. 16–25.

Going to the Movies: Leisure, Class, and Danger in the Early Twentieth Century

Steven J. Ross

On a warm spring night in 1910, millions of excited Americans set out for an evening of entertainment. In San Francisco, an elegantly dressed couple stepped out of their carriage and entered the luxurious lobby of the Columbia Theater, where they had come to hear *Tosca*. In Boston, a middle-aged merchant and his wife journeyed to the Shubert Theater, bought two orchestra seats for one dollar each, and prepared to be amused by the musical comedy *The Midnight Sons*. In Kansas City, a group of less well-heeled clerical workers met downtown at the Orpheum Theater, paid their forty-five cents, and settled in to enjoy ten acts of vaudeville. In New York City, thousands of working people—native born and foreign born, black and white, young and old—made their way to neighborhood movie theaters where, after paying five or ten cents, they proceeded to cheer, boo, and sing along with the images that flickered across the screen.

The desire for fun is timeless, but the ways in which people have amused themselves are not. The early years of the twentieth century witnessed the dramatic appearance of a variety of new commercial recreations. As the average work week decreased and wages rose, Americans looked for new ways to spend their increased time and money. An emerging generation of entrepreneurs quickly discovered that a population willing to buy their food rather than grow it, and buy their clothing rather than make it, would also buy their entertainment rather than create it. In large cities, small towns, rural hamlets, and mining camps the thirst for fun sparked the unprecedented proliferation of dance halls, billiard parlors, vaudeville and burlesque houses, amusement parks, and professional sports. Yet none of these activities was more popular than the movies. By 1910, 26 million people, nearly 30 percent of the nation's population, flocked to the movies each week. Ten years later, 50 million Americans, half the population, went weekly to one of the 15,000 theaters or 22,000 churches, halls, and schools that screened movies.[1]

Going to the movies is not an activity most Americans today associate with danger or transgressive behavior. But this was not always the case. No early amusement created greater fear—and pleasure—than the movies. From the appearance of the first nickelodeons in 1905 until the early 1920s, when star-studded features and lavish picture palaces gave the industry a patina of respectability, movies and movie theaters were often arenas of turmoil and contention. The political content of films and the places in which they were shown were far more open and unpredictable during the first two decades of the new century than at any subsequent time. Often located in working-class areas where few "respectable" folks dared enter, movie theaters were fluid social spaces over which audiences exerted considerable control, places where anything might happen and where boisterous patrons frequently transgressed middle-class boundaries of acceptable behavior. Romance, fantasy, sex, adventure, and politics could all be found at the movies.

An activity that most working-class patrons saw as simple fun, others viewed as a dangerous enterprise fraught with untold political consequences. At a time when the country was repeatedly rocked by bitter strikes and deadly incidents of class violence, the growth of a powerful medium that appealed directly and primarily to working-class audiences proved frightening to local and national leaders. Far from being harmless diversions, many early films presented poignant stories of immigrants and workers suffering at the hands of employers, politicians, and hypocritical clergy and civic leaders. More frightening still, the victims of injustice in films often fought back—and won.

By creating a common link between millions of working people who were often divided by ethnicity, religion, race, and gender, movies emerged as a vehicle capable of expressing a new public identity dominated by working-class sensibilities. Reformers such as Frederic C. Howe wrote worriedly about films that "tended to excite class feelings," and warned of the day when movies would become "the daily press of industrial groups, of classes, of Socialism, syndicalism, and radical opinion."[2] Concerned with what they perceived as the multiple political, moral, and physical dangers posed by movies and movie theaters, politicians, clergy, reformers, and civic leaders struggled to alter their forms or shut them down completely.

The years between 1905 and April 1917, between the rise of nickelodeons and American entry into World War I, mark a critical era in the evolution of the movie industry and the class character of its films and audience. This was a time when Hollywood was simply a place and not yet a powerful institution; when audiences, critics, and industry leaders fought over the political direction the fledgling industry would take. To understand why movies could fire the imagination of millions of people and cause consternation among so many others, we need to understand the myriad ways in which they were experienced and the class dangers they appeared to pose. This chapter tells the story of what it was like to go to the movies in the years before the first World War: who went, what they saw, and what they did at this most favored of all amusements.[3]

WORKING-CLASS LEISURE AND THE RISE OF COMMERCIAL RECREATION

"Living for the weekend," a concept so ingrained in modern times, was foreign to the world of the 1800s. Work, not leisure, dominated the daily lives of ordinary Americans. For much of the nineteenth century, wage earners labored ten, twelve, or fourteen hours a day, six days a week. Opportunities for enjoying oneself on Sunday, the one day most workers had off, were often restricted by local blue laws that prohibited commercial amusements from operating on the Sabbath. Consequently, in large cities like New York and small towns like Winona, Minnesota, picnics, sports, church activities, and family outings were among the main forms of popular entertainment.[4]

The leisure revolution of the twentieth century was built upon the industrial revolution of the nineteenth century. The rise of large impersonal factories, the greater reliance on machinery, and the ever-accelerating pace of production created unprecedented increases in output. But they came at the cost of making work more tedious and unsatisfying for the worker. Walter Wyckoff, who left the Princeton Theological Seminary in 1891 and tramped across the country working as an unskilled laborer, spoke sadly about the changing character of work: "There is for us in our work none of the joy of responsibility, none of the sense of achievement, only the dull monotony of grinding toil, with the longing for the signal to quit work, and for our wages at the end of the week.[5]

As work grew less creative and fulfilling, people looked to leisure to provide their lives with new meaning. Rallying around the cry of "Eight Hours for Work, Eight Hours for Rest, and Eight Hours for What We Will," the nation's wage earners succeeded in reducing their labor—largely through strikes and union bargaining—from a seventy-two-hour, six-day work week common before 1860 to a sixty-hour, five-and-a-half-day work week in 1890 (with Saturday afternoons off) and a fifty-one-hour week in 1920. Men and women not only went home earlier, but they also went home with increasingly fatter pay checks. Real wages for nonfarm employees rose by 35 percent between 1890 and 1920.[6]

With more money in their pockets and more time to spend it, working people sought new outlets for amusement in order to gain a sense that work, however oppressive, was at least buying them some measure of life. Enterprising businessmen, "cultural entrepreneurs," as they were often called, were only too happy to satisfy their yearnings—for a modest price. The rapid growth of cities between 1870 and 1920, a remarkable 447 percent increase, created vast new markets for commercial recreations. Massive waves of immigrants, whose numbers rose from 5.6 million in 1870 to 13.9 million in 1920, accounted for much of this dramatic urban growth.[7] With so many potential customers living in such close proximity, it was no surprise that business people—many of them immigrants themselves—rushed in to sell cheap amusements to the masses.

Selling entertainment, however, proved far more complicated than most entrepreneurs imagined. The rise of new commercial recreations in the late nineteenth century was paralleled by the reshaping of class identities and by the growing separation of leisure into "respectable" high culture and "suspect" low culture. When French writer Alexis de Tocqueville traveled through America in 1831–1832, he was struck by the absence of a conspicuous elite culture. "Inequality both of wealth and education is certainly found in private life," he observed. "But for the outsider these inequalities are not noticeable." During the 1870s and 1880s, however, a new generation of wealthy citizens began forging a highly visible American elite. They did so by erecting mansions in exclusive areas like Newport, Rhode Island, and along elegant streets like New York's Fifth Avenue and Chicago's Lake Shore Drive; by publishing "blue books" that listed a city's elite families; and by building exclusive cultural institutions for the rich and respectable.[8]

As the upper ranks of American society grew more visible, the composition of the middle class grew more ambiguous. During the early decades of the nineteenth century, workers, manufacturers, farmers, and merchants spoke of themselves as belonging to a common "producing class"—people who, whether employer or employee, performed productive labors that contributed to the nation's wealth. The growth of industrial capitalism and the rapid expansion of corporations in the latter part of the century precipitated dramatic changes in occupational structures and perceptions of class identity. By 1910, several groups were laying claim to the title "middle class." Farmers, manufacturers, and small businessmen comprised what scholars call the "old middle class," a group generally "committed to prudence and self-restraint." Their numbers and power were rivaled by the rise of a "new middle class" of professionals and salaried corporate managers who "tended to have a less than total allegiance to traditional moralism."[9]

The boundaries between working class and middle class also grew more problematic. Rising alongside the "old" and "new" middle class was a third group of low-level white-collar and service-sector employees whose class status remained unclear. Although today white-collar workers are assumed to be middle class, that was not the case during the early decades of the new century. Many of these young clerks, office workers, and salespeople were the gum-chewing offspring of blue-collar parents who had pushed them to take safer, more secure white-collar jobs. Working among the self-professed middle class but often living in working-class households and neighborhoods, these young men and women moved between two worlds. Whether they thought of themselves as middle class or working class was crucial to capitalists and labor leaders alike. Both understood that a united, self-conscious working class composed of blue and white-collar employees could use their numerical superiority as voters to dominate American political life. Consequently, as leisure joined work as an arena in which different classes came to define themselves and each other, controlling the class character of amusements became an important element in controlling the class consciousness of American society.[10]

Although the barriers between classes or between high and low culture were never completely impenetrable, leisure at this time was often stratified by class, ethnicity, race, gender, age, and physical space. Historian Lawrence Levine observes how, under the control of wealthy patrons, cultural activities once widely attended by all classes—opera, theater, symphony—were increasingly "performed in isolation from other forms of entertainment to an audience that was far more homogeneous than those which had gathered earlier." The "prohibitive price" of "our best theatres," Indianapolis social surveyor James Sizer explained in 1917, "practically excludes all except the wealthy and those who are willing to brave public opinion by taking a cheap seat." Moreover, added Sizer, "if you wish to be respectable, you must take a taxicab and wear a dress suit." Opera- and theater-loving immigrants and workers continued attending performances, but they generally did so in less costly and spatially removed neighborhood venues—which were often segregated and patronized by specific ethnic groups.[11]

With millions of people effectively excluded from expensive entertainments, cultural entrepreneurs created an alternative world of cheaper amusements aimed largely at blue-collar audiences and the rapidly expanding ranks of low-level white-collar workers. Although vaudeville, burlesque, dance halls, amusement parks, and professional sports teams all attracted devoted groups of revelers, none were as cheap or as popular as the movies. People in Cincinnati, San Francisco, Detroit, and Waltham (Mass.) went to the movies so often that weekly attendance in 1913 equaled, respectively, 193 percent, 90 percent, 86 percent, and 72 percent of the city's total population.[12]

Statistics alone cannot reveal the excitement that movies generated among countless men, women, and children. Cultural conservatives spoke of movie theaters as places "of darkness, physical and moral," but for working-class audiences they were exhilarating spaces where fantasies could he lived out and where anything could happen.[13] It was the unpredictability of these experiences that made moviegoing so appealing to the masses and so frightening to elites. Although the nation's elite was composed of a variety of groups (businessmen, financial magnates, major land owners, politicians, and civic leaders), many shared a common dread of what might happen if an untamed working class was exposed to the same kinds of entertainments at roughly the same time. To understand the joy and fear elicited by this new form of mass culture we need to enter the world of its participants and reconstruct what going to the movies was like from the point of view of the moviegoer.

EARLY MOVIE THEATERS

The era of commercial moving pictures began in New York City on Saturday, April 14, 1894, when the Holland brothers opened the nation's first kinetoscope parlor. Excited customers bent over a kinetoscope (what we might call today a peep show), placed their eye on a small viewing port, and saw one of ten brief action scenes produced by at Thomas Edison's laboratory in West

Orange, New Jersey. New Yorkers were given an even bigger thrill on April 23, 1896, when Koster and Bial's Music hall offered the debut of the country's first successful large-screen motion pictures. Audiences gazed in awe at scenes of waves breaking against a Dover pier, a burlesque boxing bout, a group of soldiers marching to the strains of a military band, and a serpentine dancer who undulated across the screen. Most of these films were no more than 150 feet long, and in the course of fifteen minutes vaudeville patrons might see ten or twelve of them. Nevertheless, moving pictures proved so popular that over the next decade they became fixtures in the nation's better vaudeville houses and among traveling shows, which exhibited them at fairgrounds, churches, and local opera houses.[14]

The age of the modern movie theater began in Pittsburgh on June 19, 1905, when vaudeville magnate Harry Davis and his brother-in-law John P. Harris opened the first site devoted exclusively to showing moving pictures. The Nickelodeon, whose name combined the slang word for the cost of admission (nickel) with the Greek word for theater (odeon), was little more than a remodeled storeroom fitted up with a "white linen sheet, some [ninety-six] opera chairs, a crude phonograph, a lot of stucco, burlap and paint, and a myriad of incandescent light." The opening performance, which consisted of fifteen minutes of film, was greeted with such enthusiasm that it ran from eight in the morning until midnight and purportedly attracted over six thousand customers.[15]

The success of this initial venture led Davis and other entrepreneurs to open nickelodeons in cities and villages across the country. By 1913, every community with a population of five thousand had at least one movie theater and most averaged four. Running a nickelodeon proved especially appealing to immigrants with lots of ambition but little cash. Greeks, Hungarians, Italians, Norwegians, Germans, Irishmen, and especially Jews were attracted to a venture with low start-up costs and high customer demand. Modest capital requirements and lack of an established male hierarchy in the new business also enabled many women to open their own movie houses. For $200, one could convert a plain storefront into a magical Bijou Dream or Good Time Theater. Future movie industry moguls Adolph Zukor and Marcus Loew (both furriers), William Fox and Harry Warner (clothiers), and Lewis Selznick (a jeweler) all began their ascent to power by switching into the nickelodeon business. When asked what prompted his decision to change trades, Harry Warner, who sold clothing in a store near

Davis' Nickelodeon, replied: "I looked across the street and saw the nickels rolling in."[16]

During the next several years, the variety movie theaters expanded to include small storefronts (often known as "nickel dumps") that seated one hundred people; large legitimate theaters or vaudeville houses that were converted into movie theaters; neighborhood theaters built especially to show movies; and, after 1914, opulent movie palaces. Of all these early venues, the nickelodeon was the first to capture the public's imagination. Initially clustered in downtown commercial districts and soon after along densely populated streets in immigrant and working-class neighborhoods, the nickelodeon was designed to attract the eye of the casual passerby. The front of the building was covered in pressed tin or stamped metal that made it shimmer during the day, and bright neon lights spelled out the theater's alluring name—Idle Hours, Dreamland, Happy Times—and lit its exterior at night. Flashy banners and gaudy color posters were plastered across the wall, while barkers or musicians stood next to the box office making loud noises that promised excitement inside. For the ordinary passerby reminisced one hyperbolic old-timer, these "twinkling, tungsten facades, the apotheosis of pressed tin and light bulb," were "effulgent, wild, and imaginative."[17]

Although contemporary commentators often cringed at the ostentatious exteriors of nickelodeons, they also marveled at their "democratic" interiors. Unlike legitimate theaters or vaudeville houses, where audiences were separated according to their ability to pay, the nickelodeon admitted all customers for a single price and allowed them to sit wherever they wished. Recreational democracy was not, however, desired by all. "In many neighborhoods," *Variety* reported in 1913, "the better class of citizens kept away from the movies because of the strange seat fellows that a nickel made possible." Nickelodeons were, however, warmly embraced by workers and immigrants. Why spend a dime at a "fancy" theater, they reasoned, when you could see a movie for five cents? One Chicago theater lured cost-conscious patrons by charging only two or three cents a show, and exhibitors in Harrison, Arkansas, accepted payment in eggs: two eggs for adults, one for children.[18]

Movie theaters were not the only places people went to see movies. Thousands of churches, schools, unions, factories, settlement houses, and numerous voluntary associations screened carefully selected movies as a means of bolstering attendance. Showing films in church, one Congregational minister discovered, proved an effective way of "reaching out to interest those who remain away from religious service and attend the movies on Sunday."[19]

Avid moviegoers discovered they did not need four walls and a roof to see their favorite films. Bill Edwards, a Los Angeles native and member of Hollywood's first costumers' union, remembers spending evenings with dozens of area residents seated in an open field on Vermont and Jefferson Avenues. The impromptu "theater" was surrounded by a ten-foot high canvas fence and featured a pianist who accompanied the images that flashed on the huge sheet that served as a screen. New Yorker Peggy Nolan recounts a similar experience of packing crackers and dill pickles on Friday nights and going to Chelsea Park to watch movies under the stars. Outdoor screenings in public parks and in open-air theaters called "airdromes" became a regular part of summer life in many of the nation's cities.[20]

EARLY AUDIENCES

Movie theaters attracted a wide range of patrons. Young and old, black and white, native-born and foreign-born, men and women, poor and well-to-do, Protestants, Catholics, and Jews could all be found at the cinema. Yet few were so passionately devoted to picture shows as the nation's blue-collar workers. Contemporary writers repeatedly referred to movies as the "academy of the working man," the "poor man's amusement," the "Workingman's Theater," and a medium supported by "the nickels of the working class."[21] It was in the "densely populated foreign and labor quarters of the industrial cities," observed film publicist-turned-historian Terry Ramsaye, that movies found their greatest audience. In Manhattan, where Jews, Italians, Poles, and other immigrant wage earners religiously flocked to the movies, a survey conducted in 1910 found that 72 percent of audiences came from the blue-collar sector, 25 percent from the clerical workforce, and 3 percent from what surveyors called the "leisure class." Even in small towns such as Winona, Minnesota, where entrepreneurs hoped to build a middle-class following, movies drew a largely "working-class audience."[22]

Film scholars have debated when middle-class people first started going to the movies, but it is clear that workers and their families composed the bulk of the moviegoing population before World War I. Certainly, some adventurous members of the "old" and "new" middle class attended movies before the war, and especially after the appearance of the first movie palaces in 1914. Confusion over how many went stems from the flawed assumption held by many social surveyors of the time (and by some scholars today) that white-collar workers could be unproblematically classified as middle class.

This is a premise that not all white-collar workers shared. We must not read back into the past current assumptions about class identity. It was not until the early 1920s, as we shall see in Chapter 7, when hundreds of luxurious movie palaces were built and when many white-collar and some blue-collar workers came to see themselves as "middle class" that moviegoing became a regular activity for all sectors of the middle class.[23]

The appeal of movies was simple: they were cheap, convenient, easily understood, and, most important, fun. For five cents, any man, woman, or child could escape the crowded slums or dismal tenement flats by walking into a nearby theater and find themselves magically transported to another place and time. "If I ever go to Berlin or Paris I will know what the places look like," a Harlem cigar-store clerk gushed in 1907. "I have seen runaways in the Boys de Boulong [sic] and a kidnapping in the tinter der Linden. I know what a fight in an alley in Stamboul looks like. . . . I know a lot of the pictures are fakes, but what of it? It costs only five cents."[24]

Movies offered millions of hard-working men and women a quick fix of pleasure to ease the pain and tedium of the daily work grind. Audiences could forget their problems and allow fantasy to take over—so much so that they occasionally forgot where they were. Film director King Vidor tells of visiting a theater in Texas where a cowboy (and obvious movie neophyte), seeing that his hero "was about to be hung unjustly for cattle rustling," pulled out his "six-shooter and put several shots in the screen." Even more experienced patrons could momentarily lose touch with reality. Such was apparently the case at one Pittsburgh theater in 1914 when a house fly inadvertently flew into the projector lens and was magnified several hundred times. The audience, engrossed in a "thriller," panicked when on the screen there suddenly appeared "a monster with legs like the limbs of a big tree, eyes as big as saucers, and a huge body covered with hair that looked like standing wheat."[25]

Watching movies was easily integrated into the rhythms of a worker's day. Since most neighborhood and downtown theaters had continuous performances that played the same brief films over and over, customers could drop in at any time and stay for several minutes or several hours. White-collar workers were particularly fond of frequenting movies during lunchtime breaks—"nooning" as the practice was popularly known. Likewise, harried wage earners who found themselves "still nervously rushing" at the end of the day could stop at a theater for twenty minutes before heading home and, as one contemporary observer noted, "thus feel that they are getting something out of life."[26]

Immigrants were especially drawn to an entertainment that required little knowledge of English. "The Russian Jew, the German, the Austrian, or the Italian who has not been in this country a week and cannot understand English," explained one socialist daily, "goes to the motion picture theaters because what he sees on the screen is very real to him, and he understands as well as the American." The widespread popularity of movies also helped break down long-standing patterns of ethnic isolation among immigrant groups. Walking into a nickelodeon along the Bowery in New York City, one was likely to see a diverse audience of "Chinamen, Italians, and Yiddish people, the young and old, often entire families, crowded side by side." At the Alhambra Theater in Lowell, Massachusetts, you could find "a dozen different nationalities being represented in the audience."[27]

Movies could educate as well as entertain. It is doubtful, as some contemporary observers feared, that immigrants believed everything they saw on the screen. Traveling across the ocean did not cause people to lose all common sense. Yet by watching movies, recently arrived men, women, and children did get a vision of the kinds of fashions, values, and politics that producers portrayed as typifying American life. The desire to read intertitles (dialogue cards that were flashed on the screen), which were often translated by a *spieler* hired by the exhibitor, may have encouraged many immigrants to achieve English-language skills and prepare them to participate in political life. Indeed, movies could teach immigrants what it meant to belong to a particular class, and whether strikes, labor unions, and radical organizations were needed in their new land. For this reason, movies were both embraced and feared by reformers, radicals, and conservatives.[28]

Although movie audiences were predominantly working class, they did not all attend theaters in the same ways or for the same reasons. Children were among the medium's most ardent devotees. Movies offered boys and girls a chance to see many of the "naughty" things in life that their parents warned them against. Chicago police reported that children comprised 75 percent of the nickel movie audience in 1912, and authorities in one Connecticut mill town discovered that 90 percent of the youngsters surveyed in 1910 went at least once a week. Moviegoing was perhaps more class-specific among children than in any other group. Offspring of wealthy and cultured families, such as Rose Hobart, whose father played cello for the New York Symphony and whose mother sang opera, were often forbidden to enter the workingman's theater. It was simply not a place for "respectable" girls.[29]

Movies were especially important in transforming the gendered uses of public space and expanding the limited range of public amusements available to women. Throughout the nineteenth century, men were free to spend their evenings roaming the streets and participating in any entertainment they desired. Women, however, were expected to remain at home or, if they did venture out, to do so in the company of a proper escort. Single women who walked the city streets at night were often taken for prostitutes, and going to saloons, burlesque houses, or dance halls unchaperoned was unthinkable for "respectable" women of any class.[30]

The explosion of movie theaters after 1905 helped redefine public space by transforming city streets into hustling recreational thoroughfares that were open to everyone, day and night. Working-class women were greatly heartened by these changes. "Tied to her home, with infrequent opportunities after marriage for the balls and dances she loves," settlement house director Mary Simkhovitch observed in 1917, "what social life she has is within a short radius of her home." Neighborhood nickelodeons expanded social possibilities by offering nearby places where mothers and older sisters entrusted with the care of their siblings could go to escape from the drudgery of domestic chores and daily routines. The casual nature of moviegoing fit well into the natural rhythm of their work day. "Mothers do not have to 'dress' to attend them," noted one reporter, "and they take the children and spend many restful hours in them at very small expense." Movie theaters also served as female enclaves where, as the *Jewish Daily Forward* explained in 1908, large crowds of women "gossip, eat fruit and nuts, and have a good time."[31]

Local exhibitors aggressively wooed female patrons by advertising their theaters as day-care centers where busy mothers might leave their youngsters. Pittsburgh's movie houses were often used as a "convenience nursery for children" where, for the "small outlay of the admission price, parents may be free from the responsibility of supervising and taking care of noisy infants." Exhibitors in other cities encouraged harried mothers to "Bring the Children" and assured them that boys and girls in their theaters "are just as safe as they would be in their own homes."[32]

For young single males and females, movie theaters were places to have fun and enjoy romance away from the scrutiny of bosses, parents, and nosy siblings. Working women who lived at home and gave most of their earnings to their parents claimed that movies were among the few affordable entertainments that provided the "stimulus of exciting pleasures" and the possibility of social freedom. For daughters raised in strict immigrant households, movies were one of the rare amusements they could attend without a chaperone. "My parents wouldn't let me go out anywhere else," recounted Italian garment worker Filomena Ognibene, "even when I was twenty-four." Movies were particularly popular with young couples. Men could treat their dates to a night at the cinema for considerably less than it cost to attend a dance hall or vaudeville show. The dark, close quarters of theaters pleased young couples who lacked private space for courting, but worried parents and reformers. "These young people," warned one midwestern investigator, "begin by slight familiarities and are soon embracing each other in the dark during the progress of the entertainment." Insisting that "promiscuous contact of the lips is especially dangerous," authorities in Camden, New Jersey, then in the midst of a flu epidemic, passed an ordinance in 1915 banning kissing in movie theaters.[33]

Come weekends, theater owners usually drew their greatest business from families. "Where a family had only from 15 cents to 25 cents a week for recreation," the *Saturday Evening Post* noted in 1917, "it went into motion pictures." Reformers who were critical of so many aspects of movie culture praised its ability to strengthen family life by luring men away from the saloon and adolescents from disreputable dance halls. "The workingman can afford to take his family to the picture show," observed the Reverend Charles Stelze, "because it usually costs no more than if he spent the evening in a saloon. And he feels a lot better for it the morning after." Neighborhood houses cultivated family trade by providing bargain weekend rates for children and offering special promotional evenings. "You can pay a nickel or a dime," recounted one jubilant Lower East Side resident, "and go home with a whole chicken."[34]

Movies crossed racial lines as easily as they did state lines. The "moving picture theater craze has developed a wonderful stampede among the Negro," the *Chicago Defender* reported in 1910. Yet the "democratic" nature of movie theaters praised in so many newspapers and magazines did not extend to most black audiences. Large theaters in northern cities often forced African-Americans to sit in segregated balconies, while many smaller houses in the North and South excluded them entirely. At Hurtig and Seamon's in New York, which later became the Apollo Theater, Francis "Doll" Thomas, one of the city's first black movie operators, remembered how "you had to go 'round 126th Street and go up the back stairway. They tried to get fancy with it and call it the upper mezzanine, but everybody knew it as 'nigger heaven,' and it was built for that." Some angry patrons protested against such blatant discrimination. When a Bayshore, Long Island, exhibitor refused to allow George Queen to sit in the theater's reserved section, Queen took him to court in 1915 and won $200 in damages.[35]

Excluded from white theaters, black movie fans spent their time and money at one of the nation's "colored" neighborhood houses, many of which were owned by black businessmen. In Lexington, Kentucky, the owners of the Frolic Theater (1907) invited the city's African Americans to watch movies where they are welcome and can mingle with their fellows unhampered." People patronizing the black entertainment area on Chicago's South Side, known as The Stroll, could drop in at one of twelve movie theaters clustered along the four-block stretch. By 1913, over 200 "colored" houses were catering to the entertainment needs of the nation's black citizenry.[36]

Asian and Mexican immigrants also encountered racism in many local theaters. At Los Angeles' popular Hippodrome Theater, Japanese patrons were forced to sit in undesirable balcony areas, even if seats were available downstairs, "In those days," recounted shoe merchant Mitsuhiko Shimizu, "they insulted us at will. The best thing was not to go outside Little Tokyo at all." Consequently Shimizu and his friends watched movies at the Japanese-owned Bankoku-za and Toyo-za theaters. In Chicago, Mexican movie fans who were unwelcome in most white and ethnic theaters tended to patronize the friendly confines of the Olympia Theater.[37]

Regardless of the problem, be it encountering racist theater owners or sitting in crowded, uncomfortable nickelodeons, the desire to see moving pictures and the pleasure experienced inside the movie theater succeeded in drawing millions of people to the movies week after week. The twenty or thirty minutes spent at the movies made the fifty or sixty hours spent at work seem almost worthwhile. And yet, once inside the movie theater, audiences did not always try to escape from their problems or indulge in harmless fantasies. Gathered among their own kind, workers and immigrants often talked and fantasized about challenging the dominant political order and creating a very different kind of America. Movies had the power to move the masses— a prospect that did not sit well with the bastions of law and order.

AT THE MOVIES: WHAT AUDIENCES SAW, HEARD, AND DID

Early reformers and social surveyors generally characterized moviegoing as a passive, homogeneous experience in which people plopped themselves down in front of the screen and spent their time in what was at best mindless entertainment and at worst a perversion that fostered crime, sexual profligacy, and class conflict. Social worker Mary Simkhovitch echoed this point of view in 1917 when she insisted that movies were simply "fed out to the auditors, whose reaction is but slight." These critics were wrong. Had they attended shows in immigrant and working-class neighborhoods (which many were afraid to do), they would have discovered that life inside these theaters was filled with talking, yelling, fighting, singing, and lots of laughter. Movie theaters were places where people could recapture the sense of aliveness that had been lost in the regimented factories of the era. As Olga Marx's Uncle Igel told her: "When you go to a movie, you get so exhausted that when you get home you fall asleep like a bleeze."[38]

Early movie theaters were fluid social spaces in which working people were able to shape moviegoing experiences to serve their own ethnic, class, gender, racial, and political needs. Neighborhood theaters were not like churches or museums where people spoke in hushed whispers. They were boisterous social centers in which multiple messages could be heard. Audience interaction was as much a part of the moviegoing experience as the movies themselves. As historian Roy Rosenzweig observes: "Whatever the degree of control of the middle and upper classes over movie content, the working class was likely to determine the nature of behavior and interaction within the movie theater."[39]

The first "movies" were little more than a series of several short subjects that lasted a total of twenty or thirty minutes. The standard show at Chicago's Family Electric Theater, and most other early nickelodeons, was "three reels of film and an 'illustrated song' [slides featuring the lyrics to popular tunes] for a nickel." Each of these reels included two or more dramas, comedies, or travelogues, and news films. As the novelty of watching moving pictures wore off, producers began turning out longer, more complex narrative films. By 1910, many theater owners ran programs that might include a two-reel drama or adventure film, a one-reel western, a Keystone Mops comedy, and several reels of "historical and geographical subjects, current events, scenes of commercial and industrial life, and occasionally literary subjects."[40]

Films of this era were silent, but the movie theaters were not. Moviegoing was as much an aural experience as a visual one. Actions on the screen were accompanied by a variety of sounds, some produced by theater personnel and some by audiences. Nickelodeon owners often played phonographs during performances or purchased special sound effects equipment that, for a modest $30, allowed them to enhance visual images with an array of sounds that featured lion roars, car crashes, howling winds, horse trots, steam whistles, and ocean noises. More prosperous exhibitors hired piano players, organists, drummers, and occasionally small orchestras to play during the film and between reel changes. Music-loving wage earners who could not afford local operas or symphonies might hear good music at the movies. Boston theater orchestras, for example, entertained audiences with excerpts from *La Boheme, Tosca, Madame Butterfly,* and other "songs of popular and musical appeal."[41]

Moviegoing was a participatory experience in which audiences became an important part of the show. Drawing upon old music hall and vaudeville traditions, exhibitors hired comics or crooners who urged patrons to join in as "illustrated songs" were flashed on the screen. Local theaters also sponsored amateur nights in which those eliciting popular approval received cheers and prizes, while less talented performers met "with jeers and a long hook" that pulled them off stage.[42]

Phonographs, pianos, orchestras, sing-alongs, and amateur acts all contributed to the melodious and cacophonous sounds that characterized a typical visit to the movies. But the loudest noises came from the audience itself. Unlike today's theaters, where patrons are urged not to talk during the film, silent theaters maintained a communal atmosphere in which audiences regularly booed, cheered, or applauded scenes that reflected harshly or kindly on their lives and politics. The New York League of Motion Picture Exhibitors complained in 1913 of "losing its most desirable element because of the continuous talkfests of certain classes of movie fans," and suggested that managers hand out slips asking patrons to refrain from loud conversations. Yet any neighborhood exhibitor who dared do this would undoubtedly lose his patrons. The working-class movie fan, explained one Los Angeles labor daily, enjoys putting "into the mouths of the silent actors the exclamations, words and lines that he himself would use under the circumstances." Although audiences in upscale movie palaces might do this in silence, neighborhood fans preferred to share their thoughts with everyone around them.[43]

Local theaters also doubled as neighborhood social centers where people went to meet their friends, gossip, flirt, vent frustrations, and discuss politics. They served as living rooms for tens of thousands of wage earners who dwelled in dark, vermin-infested tenements. They were places where men and women might entertain and be entertained. One New York reporter described the casual atmosphere of local houses where "regulars stroll up and down the aisles between acts and visit friends." Although large theaters in downtown commercial districts drew diverse crowds, local houses were frequently dominated by a specific ethnic or racial group. A stranger could determine the ethnic composition of a neighborhood by listening to the languages spoken in its local theaters.[44]

Like other social centers, the character of the movie theater was shaped by the class, ethnicity, race, gender, and politics of the community surrounding it. There was a reciprocal process at work in these neighborhood houses: different groups wanted different kinds of entertainment and exhibitors anxious to build a regular clientele gave them what they wanted. Theaters in African-American neighborhoods of Chicago, Atlanta, Memphis, and Lexington, Kentucky offered customers black vaudeville acts and, after 1913, movies with all-black casts ("race films" as they were called) made specifically for black audiences. Ethnic exhibitors on New York's Lower East Side screened Yiddish films and Yiddish acts for Jewish audiences, and select Kalem comedies for Irish patrons. Theater owners in the Little Tokyo sections of Los Angeles and Sacramento showed features produced for Japanese moviegoers, while their Chicago counterparts often supplemented their programs with Polish playlets.[45]

Movie theaters also maintained an active political life rarely seen in today's entertainment world. Neighborhood houses served as political centers that existed outside the control and norms of middle-class life and, unlike other contemporary political institutions, included women as well as men. Local exhibitors catered to the political tastes of their patrons, even when those tastes ran counter to the dominant values of society. Although women did not win a constitutional amendment granting full suffrage until 1920, New York exhibitor Perry Williams made "voting by women in his [seven theater] lobbies a permanent feature of election day performances" beginning in 1908. Women's rights advocates frequently persuaded theater managers to run suffragist films, such as *Votes For Women* (1912) or *Eighty Million Women Want—?* (1913), and to permit one of their members to speak to audiences during reel changes. Socialists in large cities like New York and Chicago and small towns like Aurora, Illinois, and Yolo, California, were equally successful in bringing radical speakers and films such as *From Dusk to Dawn* (1913) and *The Jungle* (1914) to their local houses.[46]

Public space was transformed into political space as activities previously confined to union halls and street demonstrations became a regular part of neighborhood theater life. Exhibitors allowed unions to show slides publicizing some particular cause or to use theaters to raise funds for needy strikers.

Socialist party candidates gave speeches and showed campaign films at neighborhood theaters prior to election day. Indeed, certain houses developed reputations based largely on the political character of their patrons. Theater owners in heavily unionized areas of Long Beach, Los Angeles, and Cleveland encouraged this process by hanging signs in box offices that proclaimed "Concerns Friendly to Organized Wage Earners," and placing newspaper advertisements that read "a staunch friend and in sympathy with the cause of Labor." In Brooklyn, socialists enjoyed gathering with like-minded friends at the Gotham Theater, a house known to welcome radicals.[47]

Not everyone loved the movies, however. As working-class passions for film heated up, so too did the fears of conservative civic leaders. They were concerned that oppositional movements seen on the screen or discussed in the theater might inspire similar working-class movements outside the theater, and felt they had to take action against this "dangerous" mix of politics and pleasure.

MOVIES UNDER ATTACK

"Crusades have been organized against these low-priced moving-picture theatres," *Harpers Weekly* reported in August 1907, "and many conservators of the public morals have denounced them as vicious and demoralizing." These crusades continued for several decades as reformers, clergy politicians, and concerned parents questioned a wide range of real and perceived dangers posed by the new medium. Congress considered the possibility of regulating the movie industry; municipal authorities investigated the types of films being shown and the theaters that showed them; and civic leaders called for censorship boards that would expunge the deleterious content of films. These early critics were not a single elite speaking with a single voice. Rather, they were a diverse group of citizens who tended to divide into two camps. There were those who saw movies as politically dangerous and morally degraded, and fought to exert tighter control over what one group referred to as the "pernicious moving picture abomination." There were also "uplifters," as they were popularly known, who strived to improve a medium they saw as holding great potential for good or evil.[48]

Most of these critics feared that impressionable children, the nation's future leaders, would absorb and mimic the incessant examples of crime, violence, and indecent sexuality that appeared on the screen. Children went to the movies "hoping to find a clue to life's perplexities," social worker Jane

Addams asserted in 1909, and what they saw, "flimsy and poor as it often is, easily becomes their actual moral guide." Genuinely concerned about the welfare of minors, critics such as Addams rarely credited children with the ability to separate right from wrong, fantasy from reality Instead, police reports, newspaper articles, and sermons were filled with accounts of wayward youths whose passion for movies led them to steal money in order to raise the price of admission. The propensity to commit crimes was further hastened by the allegedly immoral films shown inside the theater. "Amateur burglars have robbed houses exactly as portrayed by the pictures," insisted the Society for Prevention of Cruelty to Children in November 1911.[49]

Sexuality on the screen and in the theater were equally troublesome to cultural conservatives. Films that revealed women's undergarments, featured scenes of partially nude women, or told stories of premarital sex were deemed scandalous by more prudish men and women of the time. In Lowell, Massachusetts, citizens voiced fears that movies "teach false ideas of love and tend to destroy the sacredness of marriage." Dimly lit movie theaters were criticized as breeding grounds for sexual delinquency. Countless reports warned of darkened theaters where "boys and men slyly embrace the girls and offer cheap indignities"; where girls "who had always been known as decent" started on a "downward path." Sexual dangers also lurked outside the movie theater where, as a Brooklyn judge warned a grand jury, "young girls are seized by young ghouls and vultures" and sold into "white slavery."[50]

But even more frightening to many critics were the class dangers posed by movies. The politicization of neighborhood houses, the frequent appearance of oppositional values on the screen and in the theater, and the markedly working-class composition of movie audiences raised fears that the new medium would intensify class divisions. In a 1915 article entitled "Class-Consciousness and the 'Movies,'" drama critic Walter Eaton wrote of the dire consequences that might arise from the continued fragmentation of leisure along class lines. "Already the spoken drama and the silent drama are far apart. Each is the amusement, the pastime, of a separate and antagonistic class. . . . From the Syndicalist's point of view, then, surely, the movies should be regarded as a blessing, as an aid in the growth of class consciousness." Although such class divisions were confined to large cities, Eaton warned of the day when movies would reach into smaller towns and foster similar cleavages between "the proletariat . . . and capitalist class."[51]

Class fears were further exacerbated by the decidedly foreign-born character of early audiences and movie producers. Rather than see class violence as rooted in the inequalities bred by industrial capitalism, conservative politicians, manufacturers, and civic leaders repeatedly portrayed strikes and labor conflicts as the work of foreign-born agitators who imported European "isms"—socialism, communism, anarchism—to our shores. The massive influx of millions of eastern, central, and southern Europeans at the turn of the century intensified these xenophobic fears. By 1910, immigrants and their American-born children composed more than 70 percent of the population of New York, Chicago, Boston, Cleveland, Detroit, Buffalo, and Milwaukee, and more than 50 percent in six other cities. The presence of so many foreigners sparked frenzied Americanization campaigns aimed at teaching these "gross aliens," as Henry James called them, traditional "American" values and absorbing them into the mainstream of American life.[52] In this climate of anxiety, it is understandable why a medium that attracted the devoted support of so many immigrants engendered such great suspicion among the nation's largely Protestant cultural and political elite. Here was a business in which foreign-born exhibitors, many of them Jews, showed films made in Catholic countries like France to foreign audiences in foreign-dominated American cities.

Such concerns about the consequences of unregulated working-class leisure activities were certainly not new. Well before the nickelodeon, many of the nation's leaders spoke worriedly about what they perceived as the steady erosion of their public authority and the decline of traditional values of hard work, thrift, and self-restraint. Whether or not this was true, the "guardians of public morality," as one historian called them, acted as if it was, and sought to preserve these values wherever possible. The rapid growth of a powerful new medium that bypassed "the traditional, accepted socializing institutions such as the family, the school, and the church," and spoke directly to millions of immigrants and laborers presented them with a grave new threat. Revolution, explained novelist and radical Jack London, was unlikely so long as a fragmented working class "groped for ways to express the dim and formless thoughts against oppression that grew in their consciousness." Movies hastened that possibility by distributing "knowledge in a language that all may understand." Conservative fears concerning the radical potential of film were raised to new levels in December 1909 and again in September 1911, when socialists in Chicago and Los Angeles, respectively, announced their plans to open movie theaters that would be used to introduce "Socialist propaganda . . . [to] the thousands of people who attend 5 and 10c theaters."[53]

Middle-class anxieties were further heightened by the fact that many early films undermined the power of the dominant culture by mocking strict Victorian sexual codes and attacking the traditional authority of police, employers, clergy, and politicians. Although some reformers responded to these perceived threats by trying to improve the moral character of movies and movie theaters, others reacted by censoring films, raising license fees for exhibitors, enforcing Sunday closing laws, and tightening theater safety standards. Both groups, however, undoubtedly agreed with Cincinnati civic leaders that "healthy recreation in individual and community life" demanded that movies and the movie industry "must submit to social control."[54]

MAKING MOVIES RESPECTABLE

Film producers and exhibitors responded to their critics by attempting to transform movies from a cheap amusement for the masses into a respectable entertainment for all classes. Although they would not fully succeed until the early 1920s, industry personnel began the process by making quality films and building elegant theaters. Farsighted showmen such as Adolph Zukor, George Kleine, and Vitagraph's James Stuart Blackton believed they could keep censors at bay and attract a more prosperous clientele (and thereby charge higher admission) by producing longer films of more artistic merit. The success of imported "photoplays" such as the four-reel *Queen Elizabeth* (1912) and the eight-reel, two-hour Italian spectacle *Quo Vadis* (1912), which Kleine showed on Broadway, led American producers to adapt popular novels, plays, biblical stories, and narrative poems to the screen. By 1914, the one-reel "short" of earlier years was increasingly replaced by three- or four-reel "features" and even longer "photoplays" that included the first generation of movie stars. The financial and critical success of D. W. Griffith's *The Birth of a Nation* in 1915, a two-and-a-half-hour epic film that was often shown at the astounding price of two dollars ($26 in 1990 dollars), brought national respectability to the medium (except among those offended by the film's blatant racism), and ensured the preeminence of the feature-length film.[55]

The creation of a better class of films that would, in Zukor's words, "kill the [movies'] slum tradition" was paralleled by the construction of a better class of theaters for a better class of patrons. Early movie theaters failed to attract large numbers of "old" and "new" middle-class audiences in part because they were often plagued by poor ventilation, inadequate lighting, filthy interiors, and unsafe facilities. The greatest danger, however, came from the threat of fire. Early films were made on highly flammable nitrate stock and, unless carefully tended to by a skilled operator, could easily catch on fire—especially since patrons and operators smoked in theaters. But owners of nickelodeons and converted theaters frequently showed little regard for fire safety. Their houses lacked adequate fire escapes, fire extinguishers, and metal projection booths that would help contain conflagrations. In New York, one socialist daily worried about the nine hundred "'nicolettes' existing in stores beneath the tenement houses, where . . . if a fire should start, the loss of life would be appalling." By 1910 municipal governments, often with widespread neighborhood support, began passing bills tightening fire safety standards and requiring licenses for all motion picture projector operators.[56]

Innovative exhibitors such as Samuel "Roxy" Rothapfel, a former Marine who began his movie career by running a nickel theater in the back room of a Pennsylvania saloon, succeeded in luring a more prosperous clientele by showing films in safe and comfortable surroundings. In 1911, he converted Minneapolis' Lyric Theater into an elegant movie house that featured the latest releases, an array of singers, and an orchestra whose members were drawn from the city's symphony. In Los Angeles, Thomas Clune opened an equally stylish structure that seated nine hundred and featured an eight-piece orchestra plus an hour and a half of first-class entertainment. Over the next few years, similarly impressive theaters appeared in cities and small towns across the nation.[57]

The transition from elegant movie theaters to opulent movie palaces began on April 11, 1914, when the Strand Theater opened on Broadway and 47th Street. Broadway capital of the legitimate stage, had been invaded several months earlier when Vitagraph studios converted the Criterion Theater into a movie palace. But the Strand was designed and built exclusively to show movies, and it offered audiences the kind of surroundings most had seen only in films. The socialist *New Pork Call* declared the 3,500-seat theater the "most imposing and impressive institution of its kind in existence," and marveled at how every "modern device for public comfort and safety has been incorporated and the promoters have sought in every way possible to avoid the beaten tracks everywhere providing novelty." "Roxy" Rothapfel, who was lured to New York to run the Regent Theater and then the Strand, adopted as his motto: "Don't 'give the people what they want'—give them something better." And he did. For 10, 15, 25, or 50 cents for box seats, patrons could enjoy ornate lobbies, opulent interiors, royal-sized restrooms, and uniformed ushers who escorted them to plush seats. The opening program was equally elaborate: an overture played by a fifty-piece orchestra, a quartet singing parts of Rigoletto, a Pathé newsreel, a Keystone comedy, and finally, a photoplay, *The Spoilers.*[58]

The Strand was an immediate success. "Great crowds have taxed the capacity of the large auditorium at every performance since the opening of the house last week," observed one reporter. And great crowds continued to pour into the movie palaces that soon opened in Pittsburgh, Seattle, Boston, and other major cities.[59]

By offering the public better films and theaters, industry leaders began attracting greater numbers of white-collar and middle-class patrons. "In Atlanta, Georgia," the *Atlantic Monthly* observed in 1915, "you may often see automobiles packed two deep along the curb in front of a motion-picture theater, which hardly suggests an exclusively proletarian patronage." Even the usually staid theater critics of the *New York Times* were impressed by the changing composition of movie audiences. "If anyone had told me two years ago that the time would come when the finest looking people in town would be going to the biggest and newest theater on Broadway for the purpose of seeing motion pictures," wrote Victor Watson, "I would have sent them down to my friend, Dr. Minas Gregor, at Bellevue Hospital. The doctor runs the city's bughouse, you know."[60]

The opening of elegant theaters and movie palaces did not signal the demise of neighborhood theaters, nor did the middle class suddenly supplant the working class as the medium's dominant audience. Movie palaces accounted for only 1 percent of the nation's theaters in 1915, and New York City, the country's exhibition capital, had only ten luxury houses in 1916. Nickelodeons and small storefront theaters slowly disappeared, but moderately sized neighborhood houses continued to do well. The average theater in 1916 contained 502 seats—larger than the first nickelodeons but considerably smaller than luxury houses. And workers and immigrants continued to fill the bulk of those seats. Even as late as 1924, the Motion Picture Theater Owners' Association insisted that "80 percent of the movie patrons were either poor or only moderately well off."[61]

Luxury theaters and feature films did, however, change the ways in which people went to the movies. The casual and often raucous atmosphere that characterized many neighborhood theaters was missing from the more highly regulated movie palace. It was the palace manager, not the audience, who set the social and political tone of the theater. People now rarely just dropped into a movie palace on the way home from work, for most folks wanted to watch lengthy feature films and the various entertainments that accompanied them from the beginning—especially if they were paying movie palace prices. Many large theaters abandoned the practice of continuous performances and instituted set times for their shows. Audiences were now expected to adjust to the theater's time and not vice versa. The emphasis on time discipline that characterized so much of work life, and which wage earners bitterly protested against, slowly came to dominate the movies.

By April 1917, on the eve of American entry into a war that would change world history and reshape the movie business, industry leaders had achieved a partial victory in their efforts to uplift the movies. Exhibitors worked hard to make theaters safe and respectable. They succeeded in luring all classes to their most luxurious houses. Making the movies themselves safe and respectable, however, proved a far more difficult task. At the same time that exhibitors were downplaying class differences, producers were turning out politically contentious films that dealt with highly divisive themes of class conflict. The diversity of producers and easy access to the screen during the prewar years meant that anyone, from socialists to capitalists, could reach mass audiences with their interpretation of contemporary problems. For many critics, the greatest danger posed by the new medium lay not with what went on in the theater, but with what appeared on the screen. What dangers, then, did audiences see when they looked up at the screen? Could cinematic fantasies actually affect life outside the theater? Answering these questions demands that we shift our attention from movie theaters and their audiences to films and their politics.

Classical Hollywood Cinema: Narrational Principles and Procedures

David Bordwell

Three aspects of narrative can, at least provisionally, be kept distinct. A narrative can be studied as *representation,* how it refers to or signifies a world or body of ideas. This we might call the "semantics" of narrative, and it is exemplified in most studies of characterization or realism. A narrative can also be studied as a *structure,* the way its components combine to create a distinctive whole. An example of this "syntactic" approach would be Vladimir Propp's morphology of the magical fairy tale.[1] Finally, we can study a narrative as an *act,* a dynamic process of presenting a story to a perceiver. This would embrace considerations of source, function, and effect; the temporal progress of information or action; and concepts like the "narrator." This is the study of *narration,* the "pragmatics" of narrative phenomena. What follows concerns itself with narration in classical Hollywood cinema between 1917 and 1960, but it does not singlemindedly stick to this aspect. It is common for any one narrative analysis to focus on one aspect but to bring in others as needed. Lévi-Strauss, for instance, uses a concept of narrative structure to disclose deeper levels of meaning, what the myth represents: syntax is a tool for revealing semantics. In this essay; I introduce issues of representation (especially denotative representation) and structure (especially dramaturgical structure) in order to highlight how classical Hollywood narration constitutes a particular configuration of

Adapted from David Bordwell, *Narration in the Fiction Film* (Madison: University of Wisconsin Press, 1985), reprinted by permission of the University of Wisconsin Press.

normalized options for representing the story and manipulating composition and style. Since this is a précis of an extensive body of research, it will have an unfortunately programmatic, *ad hoc* air about it, but the readers can refer to the end of the article for the evidence upon which these claims are based.[2] Unusual nomenclature is glossed below.*

THE STRAIGHT CORRIDOR

The classical Hollywood film presents psychologically defined individuals who struggle to solve a clear-cut problem or to attain specific goals. In the course of this struggle, the characters enter into conflict with others or with external circumstances. The story ends with a decisive victory or defeat, a resolution of the problem and a clear achievement or nonachievement of the goals. The principal causal agency is thus the character, a distinctive individual endowed with an evident, consistent batch of traits, qualities, and behaviors. Although the cinema inherits many conventions of portrayal from theater and literature, the character types of melodrama and popular fiction get fleshed out by the addition of unique motifs, habits, or behavioral tics. In parallel fashion, the star system has as one of its functions the

---

* *Fabula:* Russian formalist term for the narrative events in causal chronological sequence. (Sometimes translated as "story.") A construct of the spectator.

Syuzhet: Russian formalist term for the systematic presentation of fabula events in the text we have before us. (Sometimes translated as "plot.")

Narration: the process of cueing a perceiver to construct a fabula by use of syuzhet patterning and film style.

Knowledgeability: the extent to which the narration lays claim to a range and depth of knowledge of fabula information.

Self-consciousness: the degree to which the narration acknowledges its address to the spectator.

Communicativeness: the extent to which the narration withholds or communicates fabula information.

Compositional motivation: justifying the presence of an clement by its function in advancing the syuzhet.

Realistic motivation: justifying the presence of an element by virtue of its conformity with some extratextual reality.

Artistic motivation: justifying the presence of an element by its calling attention to itself as a distinct device.

Transtextual motivation: justifying the presence of an element by reference to the category of texts to which this one belongs (e.g., by appealing to genre conventions).

creation of a rough character prototype which is then adjusted to the particular needs of the role. The most "specified" character is usually the protagonist, who becomes the principal causal agent, the target of any narrational restriction, and the chief object of audience identification. These features of the syuzhet come as no surprise, though already there are important differences from other narrational modes (e.g., the comparative absence of consistent and goal-oriented characters in art-cinema narration).

Of all such modes, the classical one conforms most closely to the "canonic story" which story-comprehension researchers posit as normal for our culture. In fabula terms, the reliance upon character cause and effect and the definition of the action as the attempt to achieve a goal are salient features of the canonic format.[3] At the level of the syuzhet, the classical film respects the canonic pattern of establishing an initial state of affairs which gets violated and which must then be set right. Indeed, Hollywood screenplay-writing manuals have long insisted on a formula which has been revived in recent structural analysis: the plot consists of an undisturbed stage, the disturbance, the struggle, and the elimination of the disturbance.[4] Such a syuzhet pattern is the inheritance not of some monolithic construct called the "novelistic" but of specific historical forms: the well-made play, the popular romance, and, crucially, the late nineteenth-century short story.[5] The characters' causal interactions are thus to a great extent functions of such overarching syuzhet/fabula patterns.

In classical fabula construction, causality is the prime unifying principle. Analogies between characters, settings, and situations are certainly present, but at the denotative level any parallelism is subordinated to the movement of cause and effect.[6] Spatial configurations are motivated by realism (a newspaper office must contain desks, typewriters, phones) and, chiefly, by compositional necessity (the desk and typewriter will be used to write causally significant news stories, the phones form crucial links among characters). Causality also motivates temporal principles of organization: the syuzhet represents the order, frequency, and duration of fabula events in ways which bring out the salient causal relations. This process is especially evident in a device highly characteristic of classical narration—the deadline. A deadline can be measured by calendars (*Around the World in Eighty Days*), by clocks (*High Noon*), by stipulation ("You've got a week but not a minute longer"), or simply by cues that time is running out (the last-minute rescue). That the climax of a classical film is often a deadline shows the structural power of defining dramatic duration as the time it takes to achieve or fail to achieve a goal.

Usually the classical syuzhet presents a double causal structure, two plot lines: one involving heterosexual romance (boy/girl, husband/wife), the other line involving another sphere—work, war, a mission or quest, other personal relationships. Each line will possess a goal, obstacles, and a climax. In *Wild and Wooly* (1917), the hero Jeff has two goals—to live a wild western life and to court Nell, the woman of his dreams. The plot can be complicated by several lines, such as countervailing goals (the people of Bitter Creek want Jeff to get them a railroad spur, a crooked Indian agent wants to pull a robbery) or multiple romances (as in *Footlight Parade* and *Meet Me in St. Louis*). In most cases, the romance sphere and the other sphere of action are distinct but interdependent. The plot may close off one line before the other, but often the two lines coincide at the climax: resolving one triggers the resolution of the other. In *His Girl Friday,* that reprieve of Earl Williams precedes the reconciliation of Walter and Hildy, but it is also the condition of the couple's reunion.

The syuzhet is always broken up into segments. In the silent era, the typical Hollywood film would contain between 9 and 18 sequences; in the sound era between 14 and 35 (with postwar films tending to have more sequences). Speaking roughly, there are only two types of Hollywood segments: "summaries" (compromising Metz's third, fourth, and eighth syntagmatic types) and "scenes" (Metz's fifth, sixth, seventh, and eighth types.)[7] Hollywood narration clearly demarcates its scenes by neoclassical criteria— unity of time (continuous or consistently intermittent duration), space (a definable locale), and action (a distinct cause-effect phase). The bounds of the sequence will be marked by some standardized punctuations (dissolve, fade, wipe, sound bridge.[8] Raymond Bellour points out that the classical segment tends also to define itself microcosmically (through internal repetitions of style or story material) and macrocosmically (by parallels with other segments of the same magnitude).[9] We must also remember that each film establishes its own scale of segmentation. A syuzhet which concentrates on a single locale over a limited dramatic duration (e.g., the one-night-in-a-haunted-house film) may create segments by character entrances or exits, a theatrical *liaison des scènes.* In a film which spans decades and many locales, a series of dissolves from one small action to another will not necessarily create distinct sequences.

The classical segment is not a sealed entity. Spatially and temporally it is closed, but causally it is open. It works to advance the causal progression and open up new developments.[10] The pattern of this forward momentum is quite codified. The montage sequence tends to function as a transitional summary, compressing a single causal development, but the scene of character action—the building block of classical Hollywood dramaturgy—is more intricately constructed. Each scene displays distinct phases. First comes the exposition, which specifies the time, place, and relevant characters—their spatial positions and their current states of mind (usually as a result of previous scenes). In the middle of the scene, characters act toward their goals: they struggle, make choices, make appointments, set deadlines, and plan future events. In the course of this, the classical scene continues or closes off cause-effect developments left dangling in prior scenes while also opening up new causal lines for future development. At least one line of action must be left suspended, in order to motivate the shifts to the next scene, which picks up the suspended line (often via a "dialogue hook"). Hence the famous "linearity" of classical construction—a trait not characteristic of Soviet montage films (which often refuse to demarcate scenes clearly) or of art-cinema narration (with its ambiguous interplay of subjectivity and objectivity).

Here is a simple example. In *The Killers* (1946), the insurance investigator Riordan has been hearing Lieutenant Lubinsky's account of Ole Anderson's early life. At the end of the scene, Lubinsky tells Riordan that they're burying Ole today. This dangling cause leads to the next scene, set in the cemetery. An establishing shot provides spatial exposition. While the clergyman intones the funeral oration, Riordan asks Lubinsky the identity of various mourners. The last, a solitary old man, is identified as "an old-time hoodlum named Charleston." Dissolve to a pool hall, with Charleston and Riordan at a table drinking and talking about Ole. During the burial scene, the Lubinsky line of inquiry is closed off and the Charleston line is initiated. When the scene halts, Charleston is left suspended, but he is picked up immediately in the exposition of the next scene. Instead of a complex braiding of causal lines (as in Rivette) or an abrupt breaking of them (as in Antonioni, Godard, or Bresson), the classical Hollywood film spins them out in smooth, careful linearity.

The linkage of localized causal lines must eventually terminate. How to conclude the syuzhet? There are two ways of regarding the classical ending. We can see it as the crowning of the structure, the logical conclusion of the

string of events, the final effect of the initial cause. This view has some valid-
ity not only in the light of the tight construction that we frequently encounter
in Hollywood films but also given the precepts of Hollywood screenwriting.
Rule books tirelessly bemoan the pressures for a happy ending and emphasize the need for a logical wrap-up. Still, there are enough instances of unmotivated or inadequate plot resolutions to suggest a second hypothesis: that
the classical ending is not all that structurally decisive, being a more or less
arbitrary readjustment of that world knocked awry in the previous eighty
minutes. Parker Tyler suggests that Hollywood regards all endings as "purely
conventional, formal, and often, like the charade, of an infantile logic.[11]
Here again we see the importance of the plot line involving heterosexual
romance. It is significant that of too randomly sampled Hollywood films,
over 60 ended with a display of the united romantic couple—the cliché
happy ending, often with a "clinch"—and many more could be said to end
happily. Thus an extrinsic norm, the need to resolve the plot in a way that
provides "poetic justice," becomes a structural constant, inserted with more
or less motivation into its proper slot, the epilogue. In any narrative, as Meir
Sternberg points out, when the syuzhet's end is strongly precast by convention, the compositional attention falls on the retardation of outcome accomplished by the middle portions; the text will then "account for the necessary
retardation in quasi-mimetic terms by placing the causes for delay within
the fictive world itself and turning the middle into the bulk of the represented action."[12] At times, however, the motivation is constructed to be
inadequate, and a discordance between preceding causality and happy
denouement becomes noticeable as an ideological difficulty; such is the case
with films like *You Only Live Once, Suspicion, The Woman in the Window,*
and *The Wrong Man.*[13] We ought, then, to be prepared for either a skillful
tying up of all loose ends or a more or less miraculous appearance of what
Brecht called bourgeois literature's mounted messenger. "The mounted messenger guarantees you a truly undisturbed appreciation of even the most
intolerable conditions, so it is a sine qua non for a literature whose sine qua
non is that it leads nowhere."[14]

The classical ending may be a sore spot in another respect. Even if the
ending resolves the two principal causal lines, some comparatively minor
issues may still be left dangling. For example, the fates of secondary characters may go unsettled. In *His Girl Friday* Earl Williams is reprieved, the corrupt administration will be thrown out of office, and Walter and Hildy are
reunited, but we never learn what happens to Molly Malloy, who jumped

out a window to distract the reporters. (We know only that she was alive after the fall.) One could argue that in the resolution of the main problem we forget minor matters, but this is only a partial explanation. Our forgetting is promoted by the device of closing the film with an *epilogue,* a brief celebration of the stable state achieved by the main characters. Not only does the epilogue reinforce the tendency toward a happy ending; it also repeats connotative motifs that have run throughout the film. *His Girl Friday* closes on a brief epilogue of Walter and Hildy calling the newspaper office to announce their remarriage. They learn that a strike has started in Albany, and Walter proposes stopping off to cover it on their honeymoon. This plot twist announces a repetition of what happened on their first honeymoon and recalls that Hildy was going to marry Bruce and live in Albany. As the couple leave, Hildy carrying her suitcase, Walter suggests that Bruce might put them up. The neat recurrence of these motifs gives the narration a strong unity; when such details are so tightly bound together, Molly Malloy's fate is more likely to be overlooked. Perhaps instead of "closure" it would be better to speak of a "closure effect," or even, if the strain of resolved and unresolved issues seems strong, of "pseudo-closure." At the level of extrinsic norms, though, the most coherent possible epilogue remains the standard to be aimed at.

Commonplaces like "transparency" and "invisibility" are on the whole unhelpful in specifying the narrational properties of the classical film. Very generally, we can say that classical narration tends to be omniscient, highly communicative, and only moderately self conscious. That is, the narration knows more than any or all characters, it conceals relatively little (chiefly "what will happen next"), and it seldom acknowledges its own address to the audience. But we must qualify this characterization in two respects. First, generic factors often create variations upon these precepts. A detective film will be quite restricted in its range of knowledge and highly suppressive in concealing causal information. A melodrama like *In This Our Life* can be slightly more self-conscious than *The Big Sleep,* especially in its use of acting and music. A musical will contain codified moments of self-consciousness (e.g., when characters sing directly out at the viewer). Second, the temporal progression of the syuzhet makes narrational properties fluctuate across the film, and these too are codified. Typically the opening and closing of the film are the most self-conscious, omniscient, and communicative passages. The credit sequence and the first few shots usually bear traces of an overt narration. Once the action has started, however, the narration becomes more covert, letting the characters and their interaction take over the transmission of information. Overt narrational activity returns at certain conventional moments: the beginnings and endings of scenes (e.g., establishing shots, shots of signs, camera movements out from or in to significant objects, symbolic dissolves), and that summary passage known as the "montage sequence." At the very close of the syuzhet, the narration may again acknowledge its awareness of the audience (musical motifs reappear, characters look to the camera or close a door in our face), its omniscience (e.g., the camera retreats to a loner shot), and its communicativeness (now we know all). Classical narration is thus not equally "invisible" in every type of film nor throughout any one film; the "marks of enunciation" are sometimes flaunted.

The communicativeness of classical narration is evident in the way that the syuzhet handles gaps. If time is skipped over, a montage sequence or a bit of character dialogue informs us; if a cause is missing, we will typically be informed that something isn't there. And gaps will seldom be permanent. "In the beginning of the motion picture," writes one scenarist, "we don't know anything. During the course of the story information is accumulated, until at the end we know everything.[15] Again, these principles can be mitigated by generic motivation. A mystery night suppress a gap (e.g., the opening of *Mildred Pierce*), a fantasy might leave a cause still questionable at the end (e.g., *The Enchanted Cottage*). In this respect, *Citizen Kane* remains somewhat "unclassical": the narration supplies the annswer to the "Rosebud" mystery, but the central traits of Kane's character remain partly undetermined, and no generic motivation justifies this.

The syuzhet's construction of time powerfully shapes the fluctuating overtness of narration. When the syuzhet adheres to chronological order and omits the causally unimportant periods of time, the narration becomes highly communicative and unselfconscious. On the other hand, a montage sequence compresses a political campaign, a murder trial, or the effects of Prohibition into moments, and the narration becomes overtly omniscient. A flashback can quickly and covertly fill a causal gap. Redundancy can be achieved without violating the fabula world if the narration represents each story event several times in the syuzhet, through one enactment and several recountings in character dialogue. Deadlines neatly let the syuzhet unselfconsciously respect the durational limits that the fibula world sets for its action. When it is necessary to suggest repeated or habitual actions, the montage sequence will again do nicely, as Sartre noted when he praised *Citizen Kane's* montages for achieving the equivalent of the "frequentative" tense: "He made his wife sing in every theater in America."[16] When the syuzhet uses a newspaper headline to cover gaps of time, we recognize both the narration's omniscience and its relatively low profile. (The public record is less self-conscious than an intertitle "coming straight from" the narration.) More generally classical narration reveals its discretion by posing as an *editorial* intelligence that selects certain stretches of time for full-scale treatment (the scenes), pares down others a little, presents others in highly compressed fashion (the montage sequences), and simply scissors out events that are inconsequential. When fabula duration is expanded, it is done through crosscutting.

Overall narrational qualities are also manifested in the film's manipulation of space. Figures are adjusted for moderate self-consciousness by angling the bodies more or less frontally but avoiding to-camera gazes (except, of course, in optical point-of-view passages). That no causally significant cues in a scene are left unknown testifies to the communicativeness of narration. Most important is the tendency of the classical film to render narrational omniscience through spatial *omnipresence*.[17] If the narration plays down its knowledge of effects and upcoming temporal developments, it does not hesitate to reveal its ability to change views at will. Cutting within a scene and crosscutting between various locales testify to the narration's omnipresence. Writing in 1935, a critic claims that the camera is omniscient in that it "stimulates, through correct choice of subject matter and set-up, the sense within the percipient of 'being at the most vital part of the experience—at the most advantageous point of perception' throughout the picture."[18] Whereas Miklos Jancso's long takes create spatial patterns that refuse omnipresence and thus drastically restrict the spectator's knowledge of story information, classical omnipresence makes the cognitive schema we call "the camera" into an *ideal* invisible observer, freed from the contingencies of space and time but then discreetly confining itself to codified patterns for the sake of story intelligibility.

By virtue of its handling of space and time, classical narration makes the fabula world an internally consistent construct into which narration seems to step from the outside. Manipulation of mise-en-scène (figure behavior, lighting, setting, costume) creates an apparently independent profilmic event, which becomes the tangible story world framed and recorded from without. This framing and recording tends to be taken as the narration itself, which can in turn be more or less overt, more or less "intrusive" on the posited homogeneity of the story world. Classical narration thus depends upon the notion of the "invisible observer."[19] Bazin, for instance, portrays the classical scene as existing independently of narration, as if on a stage.[20] The same quality is named by the notion of "concealment of production": the fabula seems not to have been constructed but appears to have preexisted its narrational representation. (In production, in some sense, it often did: for major films of the 1930s and thereafter, Hollywood set designers created three-dimensional tabletop mockups of sets within which models of cameras, actors, and lighting units could be placed to predetermine filming procedures.)[21]

This invisible-observer narration is itself often fairly effaced. The stylistic causes of this I shall examine shortly, but we can already see that classical narration quickly cues us to construct story logic (causality, parallelisms), time, and space in ways that make the events "before the camera" our principal source of information. For example, it is obvious that Hollywood narratives are highly redundant, but this effect is achieved principally by patterns attributable to the story world. Following Susan Suleiman's taxonomy,[22] we can see that the narration assigns the same traits and functions to each character on her or his appearance; different characters present the same interpretive commentary on the same character or situation; similar events befall different characters; and so on. Information is for the most part repeated by characters' dialogue or demeanor. There is, admittedly, some redundancy between narrational commentary and depicted fibula action, as when silent film expository intertitles convey crucial information or when nondiegetic music is pleonastic with the action (e.g., "Here Comes the Bride" in *In This Our Life*). Nevertheless, in general, the narration is so constructed that characters and their behavior produce and reiterate the necessary story data. The Soviet montage cinema makes much stronger use of redundancies between narrational commentary and fibula action. Retardation operates in analogous fashion: the construction of the total fabula is delayed principally by inserted lines of action (e.g., causally relevant subplots, interpolated comedy hits, musical numbers) rather than by narrational digressions of the sort found in the "God and Country" sequence of *October*. Similarly, causal gaps in the fabula are usually signaled by character actions (e.g., the discovery of clues in detective films). The viewer concentrates on constructing the fibula, not on asking why the narration is representing the fibula in this particular way—a question more typical of art-cinema narration.

The priority of fibula causality and an integral fabula world commits classical narration to unambiguous presentation. Whereas art-cinema narration can blur the lines separating objective diegetic reality, characters' mental states, and inserted narrational commentary, the classical film asks us to assume clear distinctions among these states. When the classical film restricts knowledge to a character, as in most of *The Big Sleep* and *Murder My Sweet,* there is nonetheless a firm borderline between subjective and objective depiction. Of course, the narration can set traps for us, as in *Possessed* (1947), when a murder that appears to be objective is revealed to have been subjective (a generically motivated switch, incidentally); but the hoax is revealed immediately and unequivocally. The classical flashback is revealing in this connection. Its *presence* is almost invariably motivated subjectively, since a character's recollection triggers the enacted representation of a prior event. But the *range of knowledge* in the flashback portion is often not identical with that of the character doing the remembering. It is common for the flashback to show us more than the character can know (e.g., scenes in which s/he is not present). An amusing example occurs in *Ten North Frederick.* The bulk of the film is presented as the daughter's flashback, but at the end of the syuzhet, back in the present, she learns for the first time information we had encountered in "her" flashback! Classical flashbacks are typically "objective": character memory is a pretext for a nonchronological syuzhet arrangement. Similarly optically subjective shots become anchored in an objective context. One writer notes that a point-of-view shot "must be motivated by, and definitely linked to, the objective scenes [shots] that precede and follow it."[23] This is one source of the power of the invisible-observer effect: the camera seems always to include character subjectivity within a broader and definite objectivity.

Classical Style

Even if the naive spectator takes the style of the classical Hollywood film to be invisible or seamless, this is not much critical help. What makes the style so self-effacing? The question cannot be answered completely until we consider the spectator's activity, but we may start with Yuri Tynyanov's suggestion: "Pointing to the 'restraint' or 'naturalism' of the style in the case of some film or some director is not the same as sweeping away the role of style. Quite simply, there are a variety of styles and they have various roles, according to their relationship to the development of the syuzhet."[24] Three general propositions, then.

(1) On the whole, classical narration treats film technique as a vehicle for the syuzhet's transmission of fabula information.

Of all modes of narration, the classical is most concerned to motivate style compositionally, as a function of syuzhet patterning. Consider the very notion of what we now call a shot. For decades, Hollywood practice called a shot a "scene," thus conflating a material stylistic unit with a dramaturgical one. In filmmaking practice, the overriding principle was to make every instantiation of technique obedient to the character's transmission of fabula information, which would invariably make bodies and faces the focal points of attention. Given the recurrent causal structure of the classical scene (exposition, closing off of an old causal factor, introduction of new causal factors, suspension of a new factor), the filmmaker can deploy film techniques isomorphically with respect to this structure. The introduction phase typically includes a shot which establishes the characters in space and time. As the characters interact, the scene is broken up into closer views of action and reaction, while setting, lighting, music, composition, and camera movement enhance the process of goal formulation, struggle, and decision. The scene usually closes on a portion of the space—a facial reaction, a significant object—that provides a transition to the next scene.

While it is true that sometimes a classical film's style becomes "excessive," decoratively supplementing denotative syuzhet demands, the use of technique must be minimally motivated by the characters' interactions. "Excess," such as we find in Minnelli or Sirk, is often initially justified by generic convention. The same holds true for even the most eccentric stylists in Hollywood, Busby Berkeley and Josef von Sternberg, each of whom required a core of generic motivation (musical fantasy and exotic romance, respectively) for his experiments.

(2) In classical narration, style typically encourages the spectator to construct a coherent, consistent time and space of the tabula action.

Many other narrational norms value disorienting the spectator (albeit for different purposes). Only classical narration favors a style which strives for utmost denotative clarity from moment to moment. Each scene's temporal relation to its predecessor will be signaled early and unequivocally (by intertitles, conventional cues, a line of dialogue). Lighting must pick out figure from ground; color must define planes; in each shot, the center of story interest will tend to be centered in relation to the sides of the frame. Sound recording is perfected so as to allow for maximum clarity of dialogue. Camera movements aim at creating an unambiguous, voluminous space. "In dollying," remarks Alan Dwan, "as a rule we find its a good idea to *pass* things. . . . We always noticed that if we dollicd past a tree, it became solid and round, instead of flat."[25] Hollywood makes much use of the *anticipatory* composition or camera movement, leaving space in the frame for the action or tracking so as to prepare for another character's entrance. Compare Godard's tendency to make framing wholly subservient to the actor's immediate movement with this comment of Raoul Walsh's: "There is only one way in which to shoot a scene, and that's the way which shows the audience what's happening next."[26] Classical editing aims at making each shot the logical outcome of its predecessor and at reorienting the spectator through repeated setups. Momentary disorientation is permissible only if motivated realistically. Discontinuous editing, as in Slavko Vorkapich's sequence of the earthquake in *San Francisco,* is motivated by the chaos of the action depicted. Stylistic disorientation, in short, is permissible when it conveys disorienting story situations.

(3) Classical style consists of a strictly limited number of particular technical devices organized into a stable paradigm and ranked probabilistically according to syuzhet demands.

The stylistic conventions of Hollywood narration, ranging from shot composition to sound mixing, are intuitively recognizable to most viewers. This is because the style deploys a limited number of devices, and these devices are regulated as alternative depictive options. Lighting offers a simple example. A scene may be lit "high-key" or "low-key." There is three-point lighting (key, fill, and backlighting on figure, plus background lighting) versus single-source lighting. The cinematographer also has several degrees of diffusion available. Now in the abstract all choices are equiprobable, but in a given context, one alternative is more likely than its mates. In a comedy, high-key lighting is more probable; a dark street will realistically motivate single-source lighting; the closeup of a woman will be more heavily diffused than that of a man. The "invisibility" of the classical style in Hollywood relies not only on highly codified stylistic devices but also upon their codified functions in context.

Or recall the ways of framing the human figure. Most often, a character will be framed between *plan-american* (the knees-up framing) and medium closeup (the chest-up framing); the angle will be straight-on, at shoulder or chin level. The framing is less likely to he an extreme long-shot or an extreme closeup, a high or low angle. And a bird's eye view or a view from straight below are very improbable and would require compositional or generic motivation (e.g., as an optical point of view or as a view of a dance ensemble in a musical).

Most explicitly codified into rules is the system of classical continuity editing. The reliance upon an axis of action orients the spectator to the space, and the subsequent cutting presents clear paradigmatic choices among different kinds of "matches." That these are weighted probabilistically is shown by the fact that most Hollywood scenes begin with establishing shots, break the space into closer views linked by eyeline-matches and/or shot/reverse shots, and return to more distant views only when character movement or the entry of a new character requires the viewer to be reoriented. Playing an entire scene without an establishing shot is unlikely but permissible (especially if stock or location footage or special effects are employed); mismatched screen direction and inconsistently angled eyelines are less likely; perceptible jump cuts and unmotivated cutaways are flatly forbidden. This paradigmatic aspect makes the classical style, for all its "rules," not a formula or a recipe but a historically constrained set of more or less likely options.[27]

These three factors go some way toward explaining why the classical Hollywood style passes relatively unnoticed. Each film will recombine familiar devices within fairly predictable patterns and according to the demands of the syuzhet. The spectator will almost never be at a loss to grasp a stylistic feature because s/he is oriented in time and space and because stylistic figures will be interpretable in the light of a paradigm.

When we consider the relation of syuzhet and style, we can say that the individual film is characterized by its obedience to a set of extrinsic norms which govern both syuzhet construction and stylistic patterning. The classical cinema does not encourage the film to cultivate idiosyncratic intrinsic norms; style and syuzhet seldom enjoy prominence. A film's principal innovations occur at the level of the fabula—i.e., "new stories." Of course, syuzhet devices and stylistic features have changed over time. But the fundamental principles of syuzhet construction (preeminence of causality goal-oriented protagonist, deadlines, etc.) have remained in force since 1917. The stability and uniformity of Hollywood narration is indeed one reason to call it classical, at least insofar as classicism in any art is traditionally characterized by obedience to extrinsic norms.[28]

THE LOGIC OF CLASSICAL SPECTATORSHIP

The stability of syuzhet processes and stylistic configurations should not make us treat the classical spectator as passive material for a totalizing machine. The spectator performs particular cognitive operations which are no less active for being habitual and familiar. The Hollywood fabula is the product of a series of particular schemata, hypotheses, and inferences.

The spectator comes to a classical film very well prepared. The rough shape of syuzhet and fabula is likely to conform to the canonic story of an individual's goal-oriented, causally determined activity. The spectator knows the most likely stylistic figures and functions. The spectator has internal-ized the scenic norms of exposition, development of old causal line, and so forth. The viewer also knows the pertinent ways to motivate what is pre-sented. "Realistic" motivation, in this mode, consists of making connec-tions recognized as plausible by common opinion. ("A man like this would naturally . . .") Compositional motivation consists of picking out the impor-tant links of cause to effect. The most important forms of transtextual moti-vation are recognizing the recurrence of a star's persona from film to film and recognizing generic conventions. Generic motivation, as we have seen, has a particularly strong effect on narrational procedures. Finally, artistic motivation—taking an element as being present for its own sake—is not unknown in the classical film. A moment of spectacle or technical virtuos-ity, a thrown in musical number or comic interlude: the Hollywood cinema intermittently welcomes the possibility of sheer self-absorption. Such moments may be highly reflexive, "baring the device" of the narration's own work, as when in *Angels Over Broadway* a destitute playwright reflects, "Our present plot problem is money."

On the basis of such schemata the viewer projects hypotheses. Hypotheses tend to be probable (validated at several points), sharply exclu-sive (rendered as either/or alternatives), and aimed at suspense (positing a future outcome). In Phil Rosen's *Roaring Timber* (1937), a landowner enters a saloon in which our hero is sitting. The owner is looking for a tough fore-man. Hypothesis: he will ask the hero to take the job. This hypothesis is probable, future-oriented, and exclusive (either the man will ask our hero or he won't). The viewer is helped in framing such hypotheses by several processes. Repetition reaffirms the data on which hypotheses should be grounded. "State every important fact three times," suggests scenarist Frances Marion, "for the play is lost if the audience fails to understand the premises on which it is based."[29] The exposition of past fabula action will characteris-tically be placed within the early scenes of the syuzhet, thus supplying a firm basis for our hypothesis-forming. Except in a mystery film, the exposition neither sounds warning signals nor actively misleads us; the primacy effect is given full sway. Characters will be introduced in typical behavior, while the star system reaffirms first impressions. ("The moment you see Walter Pidgeon in a film you know he could not do a mean or petty thing."[30] The device of the deadline asks the viewer to construct forward-aiming, all-or-nothing causal hypotheses: either the protagonist will achieve the goal in time or s/he will not. And if information is unobtrusively "planted" early on, later hypotheses will become more probable by taking "insignificant" foreshadohwing material for granted.

This process holds at the stylistic level as well. The spectator constructs fabula time and space according to schemata, cues, and hypothesis-framing. Hollywood's extrinsic norms, with their fixed devices and paradigmatic organization, supply the viewer with firm expectations that can be measured against the concrete cues emitted by the film. In making sense of a scene's space, the spectator need not mentally replicate every detail of the space but need only construct a rough relational map of the principal dramatic factors. Thus a "cheat cut" is easily ignored because the spectator's cognitive processes rank cues by their pertinence to constructing the ongoing causal chain of the tabula, and on this scale, the changes in speaker, camera position, and facial expression are more noteworthy than say, a slight shift in hand positions.[31] The same goes for temporal mismatches.

What is rare in the classical film, then, is Henry James's "crooked corridor" the use of narration to make us jump to invalid conclusions.[32] The avoidance of disorientation we saw at work in classical style holds good more broadly as well. Future-oriented "suspense" hypotheses are more important than past-oriented "curiosity" ones, and surprise is less important than either. In *Roaring Timber,* imagine if the landowner had entered the bar seeking a tough foreman, offered the job to our hero, and he had replied in a fashion that showed he was not tough. Indeed, one purpose of foreshadowing and repetition is exactly to avoid surprises later on. Of course, if all hypotheses were steadily and immediately confirmed, the viewer would quickly lose interest. Several factors intervene to complicate the process. Most generally, schemata are by definition abstract prototypes, structures, and procedures, and these never specify all the properties of the text. Many long-range hypotheses must await confirmation. Retardation devices, being unpredictable to a great degree, can introduce objects of immediate attention as well as delay satisfaction of overall expectation. The primacy effect can be countered by what psychologists call a "recency effect" which qualifies and perhaps even appears to negate our first impression of a character or situation. Furthermore, the structure of the Hollywood scene, which almost invariably ends with an unresolved issue, insures that an event-centered hypothesis carries interest over to the next sequence. Finally, we should not underestimate the role of rapid rhythm in the classical film; more than one practitioner has stressed the need to move the construction of story action along so quickly that the audience has no time to reflect—or get bored. It is the task of classical narration to solicit strongly probable and exclusive hypotheses and then confirm them while still maintaining variety in the concrete working out of the action.

The classical system is not simpleminded. Recall that under normal exhibition circumstances the film viewer's rate of comprehension is absolutely controlled. The cueing of probable, exclusive, and suspense-oriented hypotheses is a way of adjusting dramaturgy to the demands of the viewing situation. The spectator need not rummage very far back into the film, since his or her expectations are aimed at the future. Preliminary exposition locks schemata into place quickly, and the all-or-nothing nature of most hypotheses allows rapid assimilation of information. Redundancy keeps attention on the issue of immediate moment, while judicious lacks of redundancy allow for minor surprises later. In all, classical narration manages the controlled pace of film viewing by asking the spectator to construe the syuzhet and the stylistic system in a single way: construct a denotative, univocal, integral fibula.

IMPLICATIONS AND AVENUES

By virtue of its centrality within international film commerce, Hollywood cinema has crucially influenced most other national cinemas. After 1917, the dominant forms of filmmaking abroad were deeply affected by the models of storytelling presented by the American studios. Yet the Hollywood cinema cannot be identified with classicism *tout court*. The "classicism" of 1930s Italy or 1950s Poland may mobilize quite different narrational devices. (For instance, the happy ending seems more characteristic of Hollywood than of other classicisms.) But in most such cinemas classical narration's *principles* and *functions* can be considered congruent with those outlined here. A group of Parisian researchers has come to comparable, if preliminary, conclusions about French films of the 1930s.[33] Noël Burch has shown that in the German cinema, a mastery of classical style is displayed as early as 1922, in Lang's *Dr. Mabuse Der Spieler.*[34] As a narrational mode, classicism clearly corresponds to the idea of an "ordinary film" in most cinema-consuming countries of the world.

The many variants of classicism make any overall periodization of the mode very difficult. Even the history of Hollywood norms is notoriously hard to delineate with any precision. This is partly because significant periods in the history of studios or technology will not necessarily coincide with changes in stylistic or syuzhet processes. Broadly speaking, we could periodize classical Hollywood narration on three levels. With respect to *devices,* we could trace changes within classical narrational paradigms, according to what options come into favor at certain periods. Here we should look not only for innovations but for normalization, patterns of majority or customary practice. Connecting scenes by dissolves is possible but rare in the silent cinema, yet it is the favored transition between 1929 and the late 1950s. On the dimension of narrational *systems,* we could study the principles that constitute narrative causality, time, and space. Spatial continuity within a scene can be achieved by selecting from several functionally equivalent techniques, but such continuity rests on broader principles, such as the positing of the 180°-line, or axis of action; and changes in this postulate can be traced across the history of cinema. We could also study the fluctuations of the more abstract narrational *properties* over time. For instance, narration in the 1920–1923 American silent cinema tends to be somewhat more self-conscious than in the later 1920s, chiefly because of a greater use of expository intertitles in the earlier period. Similarly, an insistently overt suppressiveness emerges in many films associated with the grouping known as *film noir.* I can here only hint at the manifold possibilities; we await a thorough history of classical storytelling and style.

Where, we might finally ask, does all this leave two important critical issues: authorship and ideology? In this space, only sketchy answers can be suggested. It seems evident that an auteur's work can be identified by its characteristic narrational principles and patterns. Hitchcock and Fuller's films are more selfconscious than, say, those of Hawks and Preminger. Moreover, we can associate consistent stylistic choices with directorial signatures: Ophuls' preference for tracking shots over cut-ins, Lubitsch's use of closeups. Most important is the fact that any distinct authorial approach to narration typically remains within classical bounds, creating extrinsic norms that conform to or amplify intrinsic ones. Authorial difference in Hollywood thus dramatizes the range and limits of the classical paradigm. As for the ideological significance of classical narration, all the principles and procedures I have considered could be analyzed in this regard. The goal-oriented hero, the appeal to principles of unity and realism, the functions of temporal and spatial coherence, the centrality of the invisible observer, the arbitrariness of closure—each bears the traces of social-historical processes of production and reception. The predominance of three-point lighting appeals to canonized conceptions of glamor and beauty; the treatment of heterosexual romance links Hollywood classicism to dominant conceptions of sexual relations. The 180-degree system not only bears the traces of a mode of production seeking speedy and economical filmmaking; it also continues a tradition of spatial representation at work since the Greek theater. Each film works with, or with and against, ideological and economic protocols.

What is important, however, is that even in this most ordinary cinema, the spectator constructs form and meaning according to a process of knowledge, memory, and inference. No matter how routine and "transparent" classical film viewing has become, it remains an activity Any alternative or oppositional cinema will mobilize narration to call forth activities of a different sort.

ENDNOTES

1. V. Propp, *Morphology of the Folktale* (Austin: University of Texas Press, 1968).
2. This essay refers to material discussed at length in chapters 1 to 7 of David Bordwell, Janet Staiger, and Kristin Thompson, *The Classical Hollywood Cinema: Film Style and Mode of Production to 1960* (New York: Columbia University Press, 1985). A general background for the discussion is David Bordwell and Kristin Thompson, *Film Art: An Introduction* (Reading MA: Addison-Wesley, 1979).
3. Perry W. Thorndyke, "Cognitive Structures in Comprehension and Memory of Narrative Discourse," *Cognitive Psychology* (1977), 9:84–96. For an example of an approach to a different narrative cinematic mode, see my article "The Art Cinema as a Mode of Film Practice," *Film Criticism* (Fall 1979), 4(1):56–64.
4. Eugene Vale, *The Technique of Screenplay Writing* (New York: Grosser and Dunlap, 1972), pp. 135–60; Stephen Heath, "Film and System: Terms of Analysis," *Screen* (Spring 1975), 16(1):48–50.
5. See Bordwell, Staiger, and Thompson, *The Classical Hollywood Cinema,* chapters 14–18.
6. Rick Altman stresses the need to consider the importance of character parallels as "paradigmatic" relations in the classical text. It is true that analogies and contrasts of situation or character occur in classical films, but these relations are

typically dependent upon logically prior causal relations. Rick Altman, "The American Film Musical: Paradigmatic Structure and Mediatory Function," in Altman, ed., *Genre: The Musical* (London: Routledge and Kegan Paul, 1981), pp, 197–207.

7. Christian Metz, "Problems of Denotation in the Fiction Film," in *Film Language,* tr. Michael Taylor (New York: Oxford University Press, 1974), pp. 108–46 [included in this anthology—ED.].

8. Raymond Bellour, "The Obvious and the Code," *Screen* (Winter 1974–75), 15(4):7–8 [included in this anthology—ED.). See also Alan Williams, "Narrative Patterns in 'Only Angels Have Wings,'" *Quarterly Review of Film Studies* (November 1976), 1(4):357–72.

9. Raymond Bellour, "To Analyze, to Segment," in Altman, ed., *Genre* pp. 107–16 [included in this anthology—ED.]

10. Thierry Kuntzel, "The Film-Work II," *Camera Obscura* (1980), 5:25.

11. Parker Tyler, *The Hollywood Hallucination* (New York: Simon and Schuster, 1970), p. 177.

12. Meir Sternberg, *Expositional Modes and Temporal Ordering in Fiction* (Baltimore: Johns Hopkins University Press, 1978), p. 178.

13. See Richard Dyer, *Stars* (London: British Film Institute, 1979), p. 65, and David Bordwell, "Happily Ever After, Part II," in *The Velvet Light Trap* (1982), no. 19, pp. 2–7.

14. Benoit Brecht, *Collected Plays,* ed. Ralph Manheim and John Willett (New York: Vintage, 1977), 2:331.

15. Vale, *Technique of Screenplay Writing,* p. 81.

16. Jean-Paul Sartre, "Quand Hollywood veut faire penser," L'Écran français (3 August 1945), no. 5, p. 3.

17. I borrow the term from Seymour Chatman, *Story and Discourse: Narrative Structure in Fiction and Film* (Ithaca: Cornell University Press, 1978), p. 103.

18. A. Lindsley Lane, "The Camera's Omniscient Eye," *American Cinematographer* (March 1935), 16(3):95.

19. The clearest statement of the "invisible observer" notion is to be found in V. I. Pudovkin, *Film Technique* (New York: Grove, 1960), pp. 67–71.

20. André Bazin, *What Is Cinema?* trans. Hugh Gray (Berkeley: University of California Press, 1966), p. 32.

21. See Hal Herman, "Motion Picture Art Director," *American Cinematographer* (November 1947), 28(11):396–97, 416–17; Herman Blumenthal, "Cardboard Counterpart of the Motion Picture Setting," *Production Design* (January 1952), 2(1):16–21.

22. Susan Rubin Suleiman, *Authoritarian Fictions: The Ideological Novel as a Literary Genre* (New York: Columbia University Press, 1983), pp. 159–71.

23. Herb Lightman, "The Subjective Camera," *American Cinematographer* (February 1946), 27(2):46, 66–67.
24. Yury Tynyanov "Fundamentals of the Cinema," in Christopher Williams, ed., *Realism in the Cinema* (London: Routledge and Kegan Paul, 1980), p. 149. I have modified the translation slightly.
25. Peter Bogdanovich, *Alan Dwan* (Berkeley: University of California Press, 1970), p. 86.
26. Quoted in Thomas Elsaesser, "Why Hollywood," *Monogram* (April 1971), no. 1, p. 8.
27. Because norms are guidelines that rank options probabilistically, we ought not to be too quick to disclose "transgressions" of classical style. For instance, Peter Lehman claims that subjective framings of a character's to-camera stare in *Dr. Jekyll and Mr. Hyde* (1932) are "quite at odds with the usual Hollywood paradigm." Yet optical point-of-view shots are not forbidden by classical protocols; they are just less likely than other alternatives. Similarly, Lehman points out a discontinuity when Jekyll leaves an establishing shot and supposedly turns his back; cut to Ivy looking at the camera and tossing a garter at it. I would suggest three things here. First, the cues seem ambiguous as to whether Jekyll in fact turns his back; he could still be watching offscreen. A later shot, of his feet turned toward Ivy as the garter lands before him, reinforces some such spatial hypothesis. Second, the playfulness of the point-of-view pattern is not unlike the whimsical play with space in Lubitsch and other innovative classical directors. Finally, we should recall that *Dr. Jekyll and Mr. Hyde* begins with a lengthy traveling shot from Jekyll's optical point of view, before we have been introduced to the character. Optical subjectivity thus constitutes an important part of the films intrinsic norm. One could argue that Ivy's glance into an ambivalent offscreen eye simply amplifies the film's narrational norm. See Peter Lehman, "Looking at Ivy Looking at Us Looking at Her: The Camera and the Garter," *Wide Angle* (1983), 5(3):59–63.
28. "There are, of course, periods tending toward maximally attainable harmony and stability; they are usually called periods of classicism." Jan Mukarovsky, "The Aesthetic Norm," in Structure, Sign, and Function: Selected Essays by Jan Mukarovsky, trans. and ed. by John Burbank and Peter Steiner (New Haven: Yale University Press, 1978), p. 54.
29. Frances Marion, *How to Write and Sell Film Stories* (New York: Covici-Friede, 1937), p. 144.
30. Richard Mealand, "Hollywoodunit," in Howard Haycraft, ed., *The Art of the Mystery Story* (New York: Grosset and Dunlap, 1946), p. 300.
31. It is thus somewhat misleading for Vance Kepley to assert that the restaurant scene in *His Girl Friday* creates "a shifting cinematic space not unlike what

Burch finds in *Ivan the Terrible* and what other theorists find in such non-classical directors as Ozu." Eisenstein and Ozu make mismatches more prominent than does Hawks. The point is not that Hawks's scene has no spatial incompatibilities, but the classical spectator is simply cued to overlook them. See Vance Kepley, Jr., "Spatial Articulation in the Classical Cinema: A Scene From *His Girl Friday*," *Wide Angle* (1983), 5(3):50–58.

32. Sternberg, *Expositional Modes*, p. 71.

33. Michèle Lagny, Marie-Claire Ropars, and Pierre Sorlin, "Analyse d'un ensemble filmique extensible: Les Films français des années 30," in Théorie du film, ed. J. Aumont and J. L. Leutrat (Paris: Albatros, 1980), pp. 132–64.

34. Noël Burch, "Fritz Lang: German Period," in Richard Roud, *Cinema: A Critical Dictionary*, ed. (New York: Viking, 1980), 2:583–88.

Censorship and Sel-

Richard Maltby

When applied to cinema, the term 'censorship' often conflates
two distinct practices: governmentally administered systems of
control over the expression of political ideas in film; and systems of self-regulation operated by entertainment cinema industries to ensure that the content of films conforms to the moral,
social, and ideological mores of their national culture. Except
in periods of national emergency, such as wartime, authoritarian forms of censorship, exercised through the monopoly power
of the State, have not been prominent features of twentieth-
century liberal democracies, and the explicit, routine supervision of film content by state institutions—censorship as a form
of official criticisms—has been largely the preserve of totalitarian regimes. Self-regulation, on the other hand, can be understood as a form of market censorship, in which those forces in
control of the production process determine what may and may
not be produced. The most effective form of market censorship
prevents movies from being made rather than suppressing them
after production, but in either guise, censorship is a practice of
power, a form of surveillance over the ideas, images, and representations circulating in a particular culture. Because cinema
has been an international industry almost from its inception,
the two forms of censorship have constantly interacted to reinforce each other. But Hollywood's international dominance
has also meant that its form of self-regulation has been the most
important censorship practice in cinema history.

ORIGINS OF FILM CENSORSHIP

Although film has always been more closely regulated than other forms of communication, cinema censorship cannot be directly equated with censorship of the press or other publications, because, for most of their history, films have not been granted a legally protected status as speech. In a 1915 decision that established the legal status of cinema in the United States, the US Supreme Court declared the exhibition of motion pictures to be 'a business pure and simple, originated and conducted for profit', and not to be regarded 'as part of the press of the country or as organs of public opinion'. They were thus not protected by the First Amendment's guarantee of free speech, but liable to prior censorship by state and municipal authorities. This legal definition of cinema as outside the spheres of politics and art is itself an implicit form of censorship. As a result debates over the regulation of cinema have been primarily concerned with questions of whether the entertainment it provided had harmful effects on its individual viewers. In practice, the great majority of film censorship, at least in the English-speaking world, has been concerned more with the cinema's representations, particularly of sex and violence, than with its expression of ideas or political sentiments.

Both the basis on which the censorship of cinema was justified and the mechanisms by which it would be practised were already well established by the time of the Supreme Court's judgement. Although the details of censorship procedures varied from nation to nation, there was a striking similarity in the evolution of those mechanisms in the countries of Europe, the Americas, and Australasia. In the nineteenth century most of these countries divided public entertainment performances into two categories for regulative purposes. What was often called 'legitimate theatre' was distinguished from what was known in France as *spectacles de curiosité*, a category of commercialized amusement that included marionettes, *cafés-concerts*, magic shows, panoramas, animal exhibitions, and 'all travelling shows which lack either a permanent site or a solid structure'. In France, for example, theatrical censorship ceased in 1906, but because cinema was classed as a spectacle, its performances were still subject to the control of local authorities.

By 1906, as cinema exhibition began to move into dedicated buildings, municipal governments determined that it was necessary to license the 'nickelodeons' or 'penny gaffs' on grounds of public safety, since they were seen as firetraps and health hazards. The regulation of content was something of an afterthought to these environmental concerns. The principal anxieties were created by the fact that nickelodeons were hot, dark places, where children in particular might be 'influenced for evil by the conditions surrounding some of these shows'.

The proliferation of local controls over cinema exhibition led to the establishment of national institutions of industrial self-regulation in the United States, Britain, and other European countries. By 1908, municipal public safety regulations were being widely used as the pretext for local film censorship, a practice which was strongly opposed by the emerging national distribution industries, because such regulations interfered with the circulation of their product. The symbiotic relationship between the regulation of film content and the development of monoopoly structures within the industry is best illustrated by the creation of the American National Board of Censorship (NBC) in 1909.

Just before Christmas 1908, New York's Mayor George B. McClellan closed all New York's movie theatres because of alleged fire hazard. In response, New York exhibitors formed an association to protect themselves from both the closures and the Motion Picture Patents Company (MPPC), whose formation had been announced only days before McClellan's action. In alliance with anti-monopoly reformers (and in the hope of displacing the reform movement's concern with the 'movie problem' from the theatres themselves to the movies shown in them), they called for censorship to 'protect them from the film manufacturers who foisted improper pictures' on them, and for the establishment of a Board of Censorship. The MPPC, however, saw in the Board an instrument for the imposition of a nationally standardized product over which it could have control, and the trade press and reform journals alike advocated that the Board become a national organization, to obviate the need for local censorship.

The institutional function of the National Board was to develop standardized formulas of acceptable content: not only prohibiting the representation of particular actions but encouraging the construction of narratives relying on a regulated set of conventions. For example, the Board's Standards on Crime declared:

> The results of the crime should be in the long run disastrous to the criminal, so that the impression carried is that crime will inevitably find one out, soon or late, and bring on a catastrophe which causes the temporary gain from the crime to sink into insignificance. The results should spring logically and convincingly from the crime, and the results should take a reasonable proportion of the film.

Such narrative strategics demonstrated the 'respectability' of moving pictures as an instrument for both ordering and explaining a dominant ideology, and there was an implicit political censorship in insisting on the triumph of virtue. *Moving Picture World* objected to a 1912 movie that ended with 'the villain unrepentant and unpunished and the poor in their same, sad situation', because 'subjects of this character are calculated to arouse class prejudices unless treated in the most delicate manner and it is open to question if good can result from accentuating the social differences of the people'.

Although the NBC lost its authority after the outcry over *The Birth of a Nation,* by 1915 the industry had developed its essential strategy for avoiding external censorship: a system of containment, overseen by an internal regulation more subtly compulsory and pervasive than any legal prior censorship might be.

The American pattern was repeated elsewhere. In Britain the 1909 Cinematograph Act required local authorities to issue licences to cinemas as evidence that they met safety standards, but this power was rapidly used as the basis for local censorship. In 1912 representatives of the industry asked the government to approve the establishment of the British Board of Film Censors (BBFC), which, like the NBC, had no statutory power of enforcement. These industry bodies did not replace local censorship, but their purpose was to make it unnecessary by anticipating its prescriptions, and in this they were generally successful. A different pattern evolved in France, where in 1916 the Ministry of the Interior established a Commission to examine and regulate films shown throughout the country, by issuing a visa to films that had been approved French constitutional law, however, determined that the visa did not pre-empt local authorities from taking further censorship action.

Most of the countries of Europe, South America, and the French and British Empires enacted censorship legislation between 1911 and 1920, and extended government control on grounds of national security during the First World War. The Soviet Union abolished film censorship in 1917, but reinstated it in 1922, in order to exercise ideological control over films imported from abroad. In Germany, the national censorship established by the imperial administration collapsed in November 1918, but it was re-established by the Weimar government in 1920, when two censor boards were set up in Berlin and Munich.

The justification for censorship was invariably paternalist. Cinema was held to exert a powerful influence over its viewers, particularly over those susceptible groups which comprised the bulk of its audience: children, workers, and those described by colonial rhetoric as 'subject races' (or, in the USA, immigrants). Legislation usually regulated the attendance of children, but only in Belgium were censors restricted to determining which films were 'calculated to trouble the imagination of children, to upset their equilibrium and moral well-being'. From its inception. British censorship classified the films it approved, initially either as 'U' (suitable for universal exhibition), or 'A' (restricted to adults only). The BBFC classifications served only as guidelines, but after 1921 most local authorities accepted the London County Council rules that banned children under 16 from 'A' movies unless they were accompanied by a guardian. In 1932 the BBFC added a further category, 'H' (for horror), from which children were excluded altogether. State-enforced schemes followed similar procedures, prohibiting children's attendance at certain films. Exhibitors, however, resisted such arrangements when they could, in part because they were themselves usually required to police the law while also being liable for any breaches of it. Moreover, they objected to the loss of custom, and to the way in which the classification of the movie being shown randomly changed the public space that their cinema provided, from a family environment to one for adults only. In the United States, these arguments were sufficient to outweigh the demands of reformers for classification, and the occasional argument from producers that classification would improve the quality or sophistication of the movies they could make. The American industry's machinery of self-regulation resisted introducing classification until 1968.

In the early days, the preoccupations of censors varied: the Dutch and Scandinavian boards were more concerned by violence than by sexual themes, while Australian and South African censors tended to be noticeably more puritanical than the British Board. Agendas of cultural or political nationalism operated more or less overtly. In 1928 France required its Commission to take 'national interests' into consideration, 'especially the interest in preserving the national customs and traditions, as well as (in the case of foreign films) the facilities given to French films in the countries of origin'. In countries with a substantial indigenous production industry, censorship legislation was frequently used as a form of protectionism, particularly after the American industry achieved its global hegemony. In general, censors' decisions showed a greater degree of sensitivity to matters of foreign policy—in seeking to avoid offence to other nations, for instance—than they did to domestic issues. While France banned all Soviet films in 1928, the Weimar government actively encouraged their exhibition as a way of promoting German-Soviet relations.

HOLLYWOOD AND SELF-REGULATION

Although in most countries the function of censorship was undertaken by a government-appointed agency, there was invariably a large element of industry participation in the process. The aim of censorship was to police exhibition rather than to prohibit it, and both distributors and exhibitors recognized that it was in their economic interest to co-operate with established censorship practices. Self-regulation was thus justified as an anticipatory form of co-operation, as well as a means of circumventing demands for more extensive governmental regulation of the industry.

Between 1911 and 1916 Pennsylvania, Kansas, Ohio, and Maryland established state censor boards, and in the early 1920s almost every state legislature considered a censorship bill. The increased vigour of this pro-censorship campaign had less to do with the more explicit sexuality of movies such as Cecil B. DeMille's *Why Change your Wife?* (1920) than it did with larger social factors: the establishment of prohibition, and the post-war depression, which intensified middle-class anxieties about the potentially disruptive condition of the working class.

In 1921 the National Association of the Motion Picture Industry (NAMFI) unsuccessfully attempted to prevent the passage of the New York state censorship bill. Discussions began about replacing NAMPI with a more effective body to serve the mutual interests of the major companies, which were then under attack from anti-trust reformers. In August 1921 the Federal Trade Commission charged Famous Players-Lasky with monopolizing first-run exhibition, and there were calls for the Senate Judiciary Committee to conduct an investigation into the political activities of the motion picture industry. These events led to the creation, in March 1922, of the Motion Picture Producers and Distributors of America, Inc. (MPPDA), with former Postmaster-General Will Hays as its president.

Resisting the spread of state censorship and regulating movie content was only one aspect of the MPPDA's overall task of internally reorganizing the industry's affairs. The disputes between distributors and exhibitors during the process of vertical integration had been exploited by reform groups and had also undermined the confidence of Wall Street in the competence of industry management. The Hollywood scandals of 1920 and 1921 led

the industry to be regarded as a site of moral as well as economic extravagance. Hays persuaded industry leaders that they needed a much more effective public relations operation to reorient the industry's image, and he
constructed the MPPDA as the instrument to resolve the contradictions of
efficiently restricting Hollywood's extravagance.

Hays sought to persuade his employers that they could not 'ignore the
classes that write, talk, and legislate': their movies had not merely to provide
a satisfactory level of entertainment for their diverse audiences, but also to
offend as small a proportion of the country's cultural and legislative leadership as possible. His public relations policy affiliated the MPPDA with
nationally federated civic and religious organizations, women's clubs, and
parent-teacher associations, aiming to contain the legislative threat posed by
their political lobbying power. To establish self-regulation as a form of industrial self-determination, the industry had to demonstrate that, as Hays put
it, 'the quality of our pictures is such that no reasonable person can claim
any need of censorship'. In part he achieved this by conceding that there was
no dispute over the need to regulate entertainment or over the standards by
which it should be regulated, only over who possessed the appropriate
authority to police the apparatus of representation.

In addition to municipal censorship, state censor boards now operated
in seven of the forty-eight states, and the MPPDA estimated that more than
60 per cent of domestic exhibition, together with virtually the entire foreign
market, was affected. This meant that the Association's self-regulation comprised an additional, rather than a replacement, censorship structure.

In 1924 Hays established a mechanism for vetting source material,
known as 'the Formula', in order 'to exercise every possible care that only
books or plays which are of the right type are used for screen presentation'.
In 1927, the Association published a code to govern production, administered by its Studio Relations Committee (SRC) in Hollywood. The 'Don'ts
and Be Carefuls', as this code was familiarly known, was compiled by a committee chaired by Irving Thalberg, and synthesized the restrictions and elim-
inations applied by state and foreign censors. Films were modified after
production but before release in order to assuage the concerns of civic, religious, or manufacturing interests, but until 1930 the SRC's function was
only advisory.

The technological complexities of sound production necessitated a more
exact arrangement. Unlike silent film, talkies could not be altered by local
censors, regional distributors, or individual exhibitors without destroying

Will Hays

(1879–1954)

Will Hays's name is perpetuated in cinema history through the Hays Code, the popular name for the Motion Picture Production Code. But censorship was only the most conspicuous aspect of Hays's role. As the industry's most prominent public representative, he exercised a determining influence over the organization and products of Hollywood.

As chairman of the Republican National Committee Hays organized Warren Harding's presidential campaign in 1920, and became Postmaster General. He was then approached by film industry leaders looking for a prominent figure to become president of their new trade association, the Motion Picture Producers and Distributors of America (MPPDA). The financial scandals that discredited the Harding administration ended Hays's chances of gaining high elective office, but he remained influential in the Republican Party throughout the 1920s and 1930s.

Hays was selected for the job partly because he was the most respectable Protestant politician industry leaders could buy, but also because of his political connections and organizational skills. *Variety* gave Hays the grandiloquent title of 'czar of all the Rushes', but Hays presented the MPPDA as an innovative trade association at the forefront of corporate development, largely responsible for the industry's maturation into respectability, standardizing trade practices and stabilizing relationships between distributors and exhibitors through Film Boards of Trade, arbitration, and the Standard Exhibition Contract. Its stated object, to establish 'the highest possible moral and artistic standards of motion picture production', was in one sense simply an extension of this practice, but it also implicitly accepted that 'pure' entertainment—amusement that was not harmful to its consumer—was a commodity comparable to the pure meat guaranteed by the Food and Drug Administration.

The MPPDA's central concern was that legislation or court action might impose a strict application of the anti-trust laws on the industry, and force the major vertically integrated companies to divorce production, distribution, and exhibition from each other. Throughout the 1920s and 1930s, the industry was subject to a constant barrage of municipal and state legislation, proposed by politicians who saw the fabled riches of Hollywood as a potential source of local revenue. The MPPDA maintained an extensive network of local political alliances to prevent the passage of such legislation. as well as conducting the industry's dealings with the federal government and its foreign policy in negotiations over treaties and quotas with other countries.

Hays's political influence secured the industry's favourable treatment by the Coolidge administration, permitting the smooth expansion of the 1920s. Although the Association was attacked by Protestant religious groups who viewed its manipulation of public opinion as symptomatic of the crimes of the 1920s 'business civilization', Hays's gift for the resonant plaitude and his adept political organization piloted the industry through the legislative uncertainties of the early Depression. One of Hays's great political skills was his ability to stage-manage and manipulate a crisis such as that created by the Legion of Decency in 1934.

Although the MPPDA was initially implicated in the Department of Justice's 1938 anti-trust suit, which did eventually break up the vertically integrated structure of the industry, Hays helped to engineer the consent decree that postponed resolution of the case until 1948. He also ensured that the federal government recognized Hollywood as an 'essential indus try' during the Second World War. He retired two weeks after the end of the war, and was replaced by Eric Johnston, who changed the MPPDA's name to the Motion Picture Association of America.

Will Hays was a conventional man. Small with large cars, a Presbyterian Church elder who neither smoked nor drank, to many he seemed a Babbitt in Babylon on a 'Charlie Chaplin salary', an easy figure to caricature. But he had a gift for compromise, a faith in the principle or arbitration, and an enthusiasm for communicating; he was rumoured to have the largest telephone bill in the United States. His 'deepest personal convictions', he averred, were 'faith in God, in folks, in the nation, and in the Republican party'. Paradoxically, his profoundly conventional public persona has almost effaced him from most histories as other more flamboyant figures, including Production Code Administration director Joseph Breen, have been accorded greater prominence. But Hays did more than any other individual to preserve Hollywood for oligopoly capital, and his comment on his role in bringing the Production Code into being might summarize his career achievement of maintaining the industry's status quo: 'I give Providence the glory, but I did the engineering.'

RICHARD MALTBY

Bibliography

Hays, Will H. (1955), *The Memoirs of Will H. Hays*.
Gomery, Douglas (ed.) (1986), *The Will Hays Papers*.

Don'ts and Be Carefuls

Hollywood's First Self-regulating Code, 1927

It is understood that those things included in the following list shall not appear in motion pictures irrespective of the manner in which they are treated:

1. Pointed profanity—this includes the words, God, Lord, Jesus Christ (unless they be used reverently in connection with proper religious ceremonies), S.O.B., Gawd, and every other profane and vulgar expression.
2. Any licentious or suggestive nudity—in fact or in silhouette; and any lecherous or licentious notice thereof by other characters in the picture.
3. The illegal traffic in drugs.
4. Any inference of sexual perversion.
5. White slavery.
6. Miscegenation (sex relationships between the white and black races).
7. Sex hygiene and venereal diseases.
8. Scenes of actual childbirth—in fact or in silhouette.
9. Children's sex organs.
10. Ridicule of the clergy.
11. Willful offense to any nation, race, or creed.

It is also understood that special care be exercised in the manner in which the following subjects are treated, to the end that vulgarity and suggestiveness may be eliminated and that good taste may be emphasized:

1. The use of the Flag.
2. International relations (avoid picturing in an unfavorable light another country's religion, history, institutions, prominent people and citizenry).
3. Religion and religious ceremonies.
4. Arson.
5. The use of firearms.
6. Theft, robbery, safe-cracking and dynamiting trains, mines, buildings, et cetera (having in mind the effect which a too-detailed description of these may have upon the moron).
7. Brutality and possible gruesomeness.
8. Technique of committing murder by whatever method.
9. Methods of smuggling.
10. Third degree methods.
11. Actual hangings or electrocutions as legal punishments for crime.
12. Sympathy for criminals.

13. Attitude toward public characters and institutions.
14. Sedition.
15. Apparent cruelty to children or animals.
16. Branding of people or animals.
17. The sale of women, or a woman selling her virtue.
18. Rape or attempted rape.
19. First night scenes.
20. Man and woman in bed together.
21. Deliberate seduction of girls.
22. The institution of marriage.
23. Surgical operations.
24. The use of drugs.
25. Titles or scenes having to do with law enforcement or law enforcement officers.
26. Excessive or lustful kissing, particularly when one character or the other is a 'heavy'.

synchronization. Producers began to demand something firmer than advice from the SRC, but at the same time they wanted to establish a more permissive code for sound. But their desire to 'bring Broadway to Main Street' ran counter to the hostility of an increasingly insecure Protestant provincial middle class. Combining opposition to monopoly with a barely concealed anti-Semitism, provincial Protestantism saw movies threaten the ability of small communities to exercise control over the cultural influences they tolerated.

In the autumn of 1929 the Association was the subject of heavy criticism for reasons only tangentially connected to movie content. Its relationship with the federal government had been strained by a wave of mergers and theatre-buying among the major companies. At the same time, the public relations edifice Hays had constructed disintegrated in the wake of the Association's failure to establish a co-operative relationship with the Protestant churches similar to that they enjoyed with organized Catholicism. In the aftermath of the Wall Street Crash, the movie industry provided a highly conspicuous target for critics of the business culture of the 1920s, and the Protestant campaign gave independent exhibitors the chance to combine their attack on the majors' trade practices with a morals charge. Confronted with criticism about the moral standards of the movies they showed, small exhibitors defended themselves by arguing that the majors'

Marlene Dietrich

(1901–1992)

An aura of sexual fascination surrounds the star persona of Marlene Dietrich. More than half a century after she sprang to prominence in the films directed by her mentor Josef von Sternberg her image continues to circulate as a cinematic fetish for gay and straight fans alike, and the androgynous glamour and sexual ambiguity that marked her star persona are more fashionable than ever.

Her career began on the German stage of the 1920s, with small parts in dramas and musical reviews. She rapidly became a figure of adoration in Berlin's raucous post-war cabaret scene. Within that enclave, she was renowned for stylish donning of male evening wear and her ability to attract a myriad assortment of lovers of both sexes. In her professional life, Dietrich became a promising performer with film, recording, and stage experience, but she possessed no definitive screen image until Sternberg hired her to play Lola Lola in the Ufa/Paramount co-production *Der blaue Engel/The Blue Angel* (1930). It was the 'Sternberg touch' and Dietrich's performance in the film as a *femme fatale* insolently indifferent to male sexual debasement that would bring her instant international fame and suggest the beginnings of the Dietrich legend.

With a two-film contract with Paramount Pictures, Dietrich went to Hollywood in 1930 as Sternberg's protégée. The Paramount publicity machine promoted her as an alluring Continental rival to MGM's Greta Garbo. *Morocco* (1930), co-starring Gary Cooper and Adolphe Menjou, was a hit even before *The Blue Angel* was released in the United States. With a single exception, Dietrich continued to make films only with Sternberg over the next five years: *Dishonored* (1931), *Shanghai Express* (1932), *Blonde Venus* (1932), *The Scarlet Empress* (1934). and *The Devil is a Woman* (1935). Distinguished by a heady visual eroticism centred around their star, the Sternberg-Dietrich films again and again return her to the role of an enigmatic and sensual woman who inspires masochistic behaviour in the men subject to her fatal and provocative charm.

Dietrich's success in Hollywood was immediate. She gained an Academy Award nomination for her portrayal of Amy Jolly in *Morocco;* *Shanghai Express* drew raves. But as the Sternberg-Dietrich films became more insular in their depiction of a fantastic world in which desire is everything and nothing, they also became increasingly problematic at the box-office and with critics, who regarded them as odd if not wilfully perverse. Their failure was blamed on Sternberg, who was let go by the studio.

Although the director was publicized as having a Svengali-like hold over his Teutonic Trilby, Dietrich was capable of scrutinizing and exercising a measure of control over her own image, even to the point of influencing her films' lighting and costuming. Her 'collaborations' with Travis Banton became exemplars of Hollywood fashion design at its best. Thus, Dietrich was able to maintain her glamorous on-screen image, but her Paramount films after Sternberg's departure did not always have those qualities of insolence, sophistication, and sexual ambiguity that Sternberg's films had exploited as being uniquely and mysteriously 'Dietrich'. Although she was amusing as a jewel thief in Frank Borzage's light-hearted romance *Desire* (1936), her career faltered in the late 1930s.

Dietrich's come-back occurred with the unlikely role of 'Frenchy' in George Marshall's comedy Western, *Destry Rides Again* (1939). Bolstered by songs written for her by *Blue Angel* composer Frederick Hollander, she gave a memorably wry performance as a dance hall singer. A short string of successful films (mainly at Universal) followed, with Dietrich often playing a sassy cabaret singer with a heart of gold, as in Tay Garnett's charming Seven Sinners (1940). She was declared box-office poison in 1942 after the release of *Pittsburgh*. As a recently naturalized American citizen, she sold war bonds, then joined a USO tour in 1944–5. Dietrich toured the European front, where she entertained troops with numbers played on a musical saw delicately perched between her gorgeous gams.

After the war, Dietrich often worked with talented directors (Wilder, Hitchcock, Lang, Leisen), but with mixed results. She was most effective in the roles with those qualities of detachment and unsentimentality that Sternberg had often emphasized; as the Nazi-sympathizing songstress in Billy Wilder's *A Foreign Affair* (1948), and in a cameo role as a world weary prostitute in Orson Welles's *Touch of Evil* (1958). Apart from other occasional cameos in the 1960s and 1970s, 'the world's most glamorous grandmother' devoted her time to a touring one woman stage show until the physical toll of drugs, alcohol, and age drove her to retreat to her Paris apartment. There, she would spend the last decade of her life as a bedridden recluse who refused to be photographed.

GAYLYN STUDLAR

Select Filmography

Des blaue Engel The Blue Angel (1930); Morocco (1930); Dishonored (1931); Shanghai Express (1932); Blonde Venus 1932); The Scarlet Empress (1934); The Devil is a Woman (1935); The Garden of Allah (1936); Destry Rides Again (1939); Seven Sinners (1940); Kismet (1944); A Foreign Affair (1948); Stage Fright (1950); Rancho Notorious (1952); Witness for the Prosecution (1958); Touch of Evil (1958); Judgement at Nuremberg (1961)

Bibliography

Riva, Maria (1993), *Marlene Dietrich by her Daughter.*
Spoto, Donald (1992), *Blue Angel: The Life of Marlene Dietrich.*
Sternberg, Josef von (1965), *Fun in a Chinese Laundry.*

insistence on block booking forced exhibitors to show 'sex-smut' regardless of their own or their communities' preferences. They insisted that the only way to secure decency on Main Street was through extensive federal regulation of the industry.

Under attack from several directions, Hays seized on the regulation of film content as an area where the Association might be able to demonstrate its usefulness to both the public and its members. In September 1929 he initiated the revision of the 1927 code, and a committee of producers presented a draft code in November. A quite separate document emanated from Chicago, where Martin Quigley, a prominent Chicago Catholic involved in the Association's work, proposed a much more elaborated Code enunciating the moral principles underlying screen entertainment. He recruited a Jesuit, Father Daniel Lord, to draft it.

The director of the SRC, Colonel Jason Joy, spent January 1930 attempting to compromise the two drafts and their differing ambitions. After much discussion, a producers' committee wrote a 'condensed' version, and Lord and Hays rewrote Lord's draft as a separate document entitled 'Reasons Underlying the Code'. With the consent of both parties, Catholic involvement in the Code remained secret, as did its implementation procedure, the Resolution for Uniform Interpretation, which placed responsibility for making changes in finished films with the companies concerned. It also appointed a 'jury' composed of the heads of production of each of the member companies as final arbiters of whether a film conformed 'to the spirit and the letter of the Code'. This caution in publicly committing the Association to the Code's enforcement had as much to do with recognition of the practical problems of the Code's application as it did with a scepticism about producers' intentions.

The text of the Code provided a list of prohibitions rather than the moral arguments of Lord's original draft. Its 'Particular Applications' elaborated the 'Don'ts and Be Carefuls', and added clauses on liquor, adultery, vulgarity, and obscenity. Lord's contribution was most visible in the three 'General Principles' that preceded the 'Particular Applications':

1. No picture shall be produced which will lower the moral standards of those who see it. Hence the sympathy of the audience shall never be thrown to the side of crime, wrong-doing, evil or sin.
2. Correct standards of life, subject only to the requirements of drama and entertainment, shall be presented.
3. Law, natural or human, shall not be ridiculed, nor shall sympathy be created for its violation.

Although a growing chorus of voices denounced the moral evils of the movies, it would be wrong to conclude that movies became more salacious or vicious between 1930 and 1934. With occasional exceptions, the reverse is the case. The early 1930s was a period of moral conservatism in American culture and elsewhere, and both the SRC and state censors applied increasingly strict standards. The industry's most vociferous critics tended to judge the movies on their advertising, which was far less strictly controlled than their contents, and a small number of visible infringements were sufficient to fuel the flames of their righteousness.

Joy's approach to the improvement of content was gradualist. He thought the 'small, narrow, picayunish fault-finding' of censor boards inhibited his attempts to negotiate strategies of representation that permitted producers 'to paint the unconventional, the unlawful, the immoral side of life in order to bring out in immediate contrast the happiness and benefits derived from whole-some, clean and law-abiding conduct'. He recognized that, if the Code was to remain effective, it had to allow the studios to develop a system of representational conventions 'from which conclusions might be drawn by the sophisticated mind, but which would mean nothing to the unsophisticated and inexperienced'. Particularly in the early years of its operation, much of the work of the Production Code lay in the creation and maintenance of this system of conventions. Like other Hollywood conventions, the Code was one of several substitutes for detailed audience research. Having chosen not to differentiate its product through a ratings system, the production industry had to find ways of appealing to both 'innocent' and 'sophisticated' sensibilities in the same object without transgressing the boundaries of public acceptability. This involved devising systems and codes of representation in which 'innocence' was inscribed into the text while 'sophisticated' viewers were able to 'read into' movies whatever meanings they pleased to find, so long as producers could use the Production Code to deny that they had put them there. As Lea Jacobs (1991) has argued, under the Code 'offensive ideas could survive at the price of an instability of meaning . . . there was constant negotiation about how explicit films could be and by what means (through the image, sound, language) offensive ideas could find representation'.

Censors, however, continued to identify some disturbing developments in movie content. The crime film had been the subject of the municipal censorship as early as 1907, and the genre was regarded as the most threatening to public order. Beginning in late 1930, the brief cycle of gangster films inspired by press coverage of Al Capone revived charges that the movies were encouraging young audiences to view the gangster protagonist as a 'hero-villain', and proved a public relations calamity for the Association. In September 1931 Code procedures were considerably tightened, submission of scripts was made compulsory, and further production of gangster films was prohibited. But every time the Association responded to one kind of complaint, it was replaced by another. As soon as Joy was provided with the means to ensure the overall morality of a movie's narrative, reformers argued that the stories Hollywood told were not the primary source of its influence. The cinema's power to corrupt was now assumed to lie in the seductive pleasure of its spectacle, exemplified in the screen careers of Jean Harlow, Mae West, and the actress Father Lord described as 'the unspeakable Constance Bennett'.

In January 1932 Joseph Breen arrived in Hollywood to oversee its publicity for the Association. His abrasive style constituted a significant shift away from Joy's attempts at consensus. In September Joy left to become a producer at Fox, and his replacement, James Wingate, proved unable to establish a rapport with any of the studio heads, and paid too much attention to details of elimination rather than wider thematic concerns. Joy's resignation coincided with the first publication of extracts from the Payne Fund Studies, a research programme investigating children's attendance at and emotional responses to motion pictures, undertaken by the Motion Picture Research Council (MPRC), which had become the focal point of Protestant and educational concerns about the cultural effects of the movies. A widely circulated sensationalized digest of the Studies, Henry James Forman's *Our Movie Made Children,* made the MPRC's demands for federal regulation a profound threat to the industry. By the end of 1932 nearly forty religious and educational organizations had passed resolutions calling for federal regulation of the industry.

The early months of 1933 comprised the low point of the industry's fortunes. Many studios were facing bankruptcy, and Hays insisted that more than economic action was required to deal with the crisis. Only a more rigid enforcement of the Code, he argued, could maintain public sympathy and defeat the pressure for federal intervention. He persuaded the Board to sign a Reaffirmation of Objectives acknowledging that 'disintegrating influences' threatened 'standards of production, standards of quality, standards of business practice', and pledged them to the maintenance of 'higher business standards'. The Reaffirmation became the implement with which Hays began to reorganize the SRC. The tone of its correspondence changed: as one studio official explained to his producers, 'prior to this time, we were told "it is recommended", but recently letters definitely state, "it is inadmissible", or something equally definite'. Breen relinquished his other work to concentrate full-time on self-regulation, and established his usefulness to the companies by doing what Wingate apparently could not: providing practical solutions to a studio's problem in applying the Code, and thus protecting its investment. From August 1933 he was in effect running the SRC.

Breen was also in almost constant conspiratorial correspondence with Quigley and other prominent Catholics, attempting to involve the Church hierarchy in a demonstration of Catholic cultural assertiveness. By November 1933 they had persuaded the Catholic bishops to establish an Episcopal Committee on Motion Pictures, and in April 1934 the Committee announced it would recruit a legion of Decency, whose members would sign a pledge promising 'to remain away from all motion pictures except those which do not offend decency and Christian Morality'. The Legion was not a spontaneous expression of public feeling. Its campaign was delicately orchestrated to achieve a precise objective: the effective enforcement of the Production Code by the existing machinery. Although its principal weapon appeared to be the economic one of a threatened boycott of films or theatres, its real power lay in its capacity to generate publicity. It was designed to intimidate producers, not to inflict major economic damage. It was, indeed, vital to its success that it separate the question of Code enforcement from issues of industry trade practice like block booking, in order to differentiate the Legion from the MPRC and make it clear that the bishops had 'no purpose or desire to tell the picture people how to run their business'. It was a complete success. In June the MPPDA Board revised the Resolution for Uniform Interpretation. The SRC was renamed the Production Code Administration (PCA), with Breen as its director and an augmented staff. The producers' jury was eliminated, leaving appeal to the MPPDA Board as the only mechanism for questioning Breen's judgement. Each film passed by the PCA would be given a seal, displayed on every print. All member companies agreed not to distribute or release a film without a certificate. A penalty clause imposed a $25,000 fine for violation of the new Resolution.

Given the public attention being paid to the campaign, it was in the industry's best interests to make a show of atonement. Industry publicity emphasized the scale of the 1934 crisis in order to create a dividing line between 'before', when the SRC had been unable to control production, and 'now', when PCA 'self-regulation' had really become effective. As a result of this need for a public act of contrition, the history of the SRC's gradual implementation of the Production Code was concealed behind a more apocalyptic account. The immediate purpose behind this exaggeration was less to flatter the Catholics (although the Legion of Decency remained a powerful influence at the PCA) than to outmanoeuvre those still demanding federal regulation of the industry. But in fact, Breen had largely won the internal battle by March, when most of the studios were showing 'a definite willingness to do the right thing'. Only Warners, always the most recalcitrant of the major companies in their attitude to the Code and the MPPDA, had to be brought into line. With the implementation of the agreement in mid July, conditions tightened further. As in March 1933, a number of films were withheld from release, and drastic reconstruction undertaken: the conversion of Mae West's *It Ain't no Sin* into *Belle of the Nineties* (1934) being the most prominent. A number of films then in circulation were withdrawn before the end of their release cycle: many more were refused certification over the next few years when companies attempted to rerelease them. In another important respect production policy had changed dramatically in early 1934. The wave of Hollywood's adaptation of high-budget literary classics and historical biographies resulted directly from the requirements of the industry's public relations.

The establishment of the PCA did not end discussion over what constituted satisfactory material for films. Writers and producers commonly left material that they knew would be cut in scripts sent to the PCA, often in hopes of using it as a bargaining tool to get something else through, and frequently shots or sequences that the PCA initially objected to survived into the final film. In 1935 disputes over the representation of crime resurfaced with the attempt by several studios to circumvent the prohibition on gangster films in the G-Men cycle, until British censors objected to the trend. On the whole, however, these questions of Code enforcement were relatively minor: the studios had acquiesced to the PCA machinery and, with occasional displays of resistance, acquiesced to its decisions. More importantly, public opinion had generally recovered from its moral panic and accepted the Association's or the Legion's account of the industry's rescue from the abyss in 1934.

Breen's insistence that the PCA was 'regarded by producers, directors, and their staffs, as participants in the processes of production' was perfectly accurate. Beyond the shared assumption that the PCA functioned as an aid, not a hindrance, to production, there were two underlying considerations that governed its working operation. 'Compensating moral values', as understood by Breen, ensured not only that 'No picture shall be produced which will lower the moral standards of those who see it', but also that a calculus of retribution would invariably be deployed to punish the guilty. Plots had to be morally unambiguous in their development, dialogue, and conclusion, so the site of textual ambiguity shifted from narrative to the representation of incident; matters of sex, particularly, were represented in such a way that a pre-existent knowledge was required to gain access to them. As screen-writer Elliott Paul pithily observed, 'A scene should give full play to the vices of the audience, and still have a technical out.'

The difficulties the Association faced over film content in the late 1930s were largely the results of its success. As his dealings with the studios became more assertive after 1934, Breen's correspondence made fewer distinctions between a decision under the Code, advice regarding the likely actions of state or foreign censors, and the implementation of 'industry policy' in response to pressure groups, foreign governments, and corporate interests. Industry policy was, like self-regulation, designed to prevent the movies becoming a subject of controversy or giving offence to powerful interests, but events such as MGM's decision in 1936 not to produce a film version of Sinclair Lewis's *It Can't Happen Here,* and Catholic protest over *Blockade* (1938), set in the Spanish Civil War, led to accusations from liberals within the industry and outside that 'self-regulation . . . has degenerated into political censorship'. However, the PCA case that received most public attention in the late 1930s was as trivial as most publicized instances of moral censorship: the inclusion of the usually prohibited word 'damn' in Clark Gable's last line in *Gone with the Wind* (1939).

INTO AND AFTER THE WAR

Distinctly less trivial were the issues raised by the increasing political tensions in Europe and the world at large. In the United States itself directly political censorship was mostly confined to the banning of some Soviet films by state or local censor boards. Newsreels were generally exempted from state censorship, but they were made with a firm degree of self-regulation, avoiding the coverage of crime as well as political controversy. Meanwhile Nazi Germany and Fascist Italy had instituted severe censorship, aimed not only at regulating the (mainly escapist) content of domestic production but at controlling the content of American and other imports, while Japan and the Soviet Union not only practised internal censorship but had become effectively closed markets. Throughout most of the 1930s Hollywood's reaction to the rise of Fascism was one of economically motivated appeasement, aimed at ensuring that its films would not attract the attention of foreign censors and so lead to the further closure of the market. In 1936, for instance, MGM acquired the screen rights to Robert E. Sherwood's play *Idiot's Delight*, which took place during the outbreak of a new European war brought about by an Italian invasion of France. Recognizing the dangers such a project posed to their European distribution, both the studio and the PCA engaged in protracted negotiations with Italian diplomats in the USA to devise a storyline that contained nothing that would offend the Italian government. The movie's generalized anti-war theme lost the play's specific indictment of Fascist aggression, and the natives of what producer Hunt Stromberg called the 'nondescript' European country in which the movie was set spoke Esperanto, not Italian. Production delays, caused in part by these negotiations, meant that *Idiot's Delight* was not released until early 1939.

By that time, however, the worsening crisis meant that markets were closed anyhow, and the resulting loss of revenue eroded the economic logic behind the industry's earlier policies of appeasement to the Nazi and Fascist regimes. David O. Selznick, among others, argued that the industry should abandon the 'insane and inane and outmoded' Code, but the PCA's censorship of the movies became a political issue primarily as a result of the antitrust suit filed against the major companies by the Department of Justice in July 1938. Implicating the PCA in the majors' restrictive practices, the suit alleged that they used the Code to exercise a practical censorship over the entire industry, restricting the production of pictures treating controversial subjects and hindering the development of innovative approaches to drama or narrative by companies that might use innovation as a way of challenging the majors' monopoly power. In 1939 the PCA's jurisdiction was restricted so that there was a clear distinction between its administration of the Code and its other advisory functions. One effect of this was to acquiesce in the use of politically more controversial content as a way of demonstrating that the 'freedom of the screen' was not hampered by the operations of the PCA. Although PCA officials continued to voice concern over whether such subjects as *Confessions of a Nazi Spy* (1939) constituted appropriate screen entertainment, they were much more circumspect in expressing their opinions.

In Britain, too, liberal criticism of the BBFC in the late 1930s had resulted in some relaxation of its earlier rigidity over politically controversial subjects. During the war government agencies in both Britain and the USA worked in parallel with the industry's self-regulatory bodies rather than replacing them. In Britain, the Ministry of Information (MOI) had a Censorship Division, but it delegated its 'security' film censorship of both feature films and newsreels to an augmented BBFC, which also retained responsibility for 'moral' censorship. The MOI had the power to suppress movies, although it never used it. In the USA, the Office of War Information (OWI) set up a Bureau of Motion Pictures, which had no powers of censorship over Hollywood, but sought to establish a parallel system of script supervision to the PCA's, in order to insert themes promoting the war effort. Under Joe Breen, the PCA remained politically as well as morally conservative, but his dislike of the pro-Soviet propaganda of *Mission to Moscow* was brushed aside by the liberal OWI. The studios co-operated with the propaganda programme so long as it did not put their profits at risk. They were, however, unsympathetic to the OWI's complaint that Hollywood over-represented both frivolity and 'the sordid side of American life'; government reviewers objected to the Preston Sturges comedy *The Palm Beach Story* (1942) as 'a libel on America at war', as strongly as they did to movies in which gangster heroes joined up. The OWI achieved its greatest influence after 1943, when military victories began to open up overseas markets again, and studios needed the approval of the government's separate Office of Censorship to export their product. As in many other wartime industries, government and business found a mutually beneficial way of combining patriotism and profit. The studios' relationship with the OWI also repeated the history of the Production Code: after some initial skirmishes to establish a basis for their dealings, the OWI had found a way of demonstrating that censorship was 'smart showmanship'. According to historians Clayton Koppes and Gregory Black (1987), the OWI's involvement in Hollywood was 'the most comprehensive and sustained government attempt to change the content of a mass medium in American history', since it told the industry not only what material should be omitted but also what should be included.

The censors' rigid standards over sex and violence gave ground during the war, partly because of the imperatives of other agendas: the BBFC refrained almost entirely from making cuts in British, American, or even Soviet propaganda films, even when they transgressed the principles applied before 1939. Some of Hollywood's wartime productions, including *Double Indemnity* (1944), *Duel in the Sun* (1946), and *The Postman Always Rings Twice* (1946), required significant concessions from the PCA's pre-war standards not simply in the details of what they showed, but also in their thematic preoccupations. In other respects, however, the war saw little change. The OWI was unwilling for Hollywood to represent social problems unless it showed a solution for them, and this coincided with PCA standards and studio practice. Studios had, for example, always staged the performances of black musical artists in such a way that their routines could be deleted by local censors in Southern states without disrupting the continuity of the movie.

The war's end, however, brought rapid changes. Germany and Japan were subject to a military censorship imposed by the occupying forces, and, along with Italy, to a heavy influx of American movies, as Hollywood sought opportunities to continue to profit from its patriotism. A Fox executive expressed the widely-held opinion that 'the motion picture must continue as an articulate force in the post-war world so that it can contribute vitally to the development of permanent peace, prosperity, progress and security on a global basis'. Increasingly, producers complained at the thematic restrictions imposed on them by the Production Code. After the PCA withdrew its seal from *The Outlaw* in 1946, Howard Hughes's legal challenge to its authority delayed the liberalization of Hollywood's censorship, but it was clear that even in the reactionary political climate of the early Cold War the ground gained during the war would not be surrendered. As well as the more explicit representations of sexual and psychological variation and psychopathic violence in film noir, movies dealing with racial prejudice challenged the legitimacy of municipal censorship in the Southern states. Local bans on *Pinky* and *Lost Boundaries* (both 1949) were overturned by the Supreme Court, which declared in its ruling on the Paramount anti-trust case in 1948 that it now regarded movies as 'included in the press whose freedom is guaranteed by the First Amendment'. It was not, however, until 1952 that the Court reversed its 1915 ruling on the constitutional status of cinema, in a case in which Rossellini's *The Miracle* (1948) had been banned by the New York censor board on the grounds of its being 'sacrilegious'. Over the next three years the Supreme Court ruled state and municipal censorship unconstitutional on any grounds other than that of 'obscenity'.

In Britain the changing attitude to cinema was embodied in the 1952 Cinematograph Act, which placed greater emphasis on regulation in the interests of children, and coincided with the introduction of the 'X' category to replace the 'H' certificate. The 'X' certificate permitted the exhibition of movies with more sexually daring themes, generally of European origin. State censorship in most of continental Europe had always evidenced more concern with violence than with sex, and this distinction became more pronounced after 1950. In Britain and the USA, the growth of the 'art-house' circuits provided exhibition outlets for these products in a context that challenged the appropriateness of censorship for adults. The liberalization of censorship standards in the 1950s had much to do with the precipitous decline in attendance: as cinema came to be viewed as something other than a form of mass entertainment for an undifferentiated audience, many of the fundamental justifications of its censorship lost their persuasive power.

In the United States, the Supreme Court's decision in *The Miracle* case weakened the authority of the Production Code, but did not destroy it, although in 1953 a Maryland court observed that 'if the Production Code were law, it would be plainly unconstitutional'. The PCA had relied on the sanction of 'political censorship', and the liberalization of standards in both America and Europe eroded that sanction. However, the Court's decision in the Paramount case was actually of greater consequence. The PCA's effective power came from the major companies' agreement that they would not exhibit any movie that did not have a seal; thus PCA approval was vital to a movie's profitability in the American domestic market. The divorcement of exhibition from production and distribution that followed the Paramount decision meant that the PCA could no longer enforce exclusion. In 1950 independent distributor Joseph Burstyn refused to make two minor cuts in *Bicycle Thieves* (1948) to accommodate Breen's PCA, and the movie, which won the Best Foreign Film Oscar that year, was exhibited in first-run theatres without a seal. Three years later, United Artists refused to modify Otto Preminger's comedy *The Moon Is Blue* (1953) as Breen demanded. It became the first major company production to be exhibited without a seal, and was the fifteenth-highest grossing movie of 1953.

The PCA's authority had depended on vertical integration and the majors' oligopoly. Without constitutional sanction, a market censorship as rigid as Breen had imposed was no longer viable. As movie attendance declined in the 1950s, production and exhibition strategies changed so that fewer movies were targeted at an undifferentiated audience. A new genre of 'adult' movies emerged, often adapted from bestsellers and drawing audiences by their sensational treatment of serious social subject-matter that television would not handle. Movies such as *The Man with the Golden Arm* (1955) and *Baby Doll* (1956) led to revisions in the Production Code in 1954 and 1956, after which 'mature' subjects such as prostitution, drug addiction, and miscegenation could be shown if 'treated within the limits of good taste'. Concerns about the cinema's influence on behaviour persisted, however; one source of anxiety being the treatment of juvenile delinquency in movies like *The Wild One* (1953) and *Blackboard Jungle* (1955).

In 1954 Joe Breen retired as director of the PCA. He was replaced by his long -serving deputy, Geoffrey Shurlock, who would oversee the increasing liberalization of Code procedures and practices. Under Breen, the PCA had been among the most powerful influences on Hollywood production for more than twenty years, and although his personal control over the PCA's standards has often been exaggerated, the classical Hollywood of the studio system would have been unrecognizable without the determining market censorship the PCA exercised.

Works Cited

Hunnings, Neville March (1967), *Film Censors and the Law.*
Jacobs, Lea (1991), *The Wages of Sin.*
Koppes, Clayton R., and Black, Gregory D. (1987), *Hollywood Goes to War.*
Leff, Leonard J., and Simmons, Jerold L. (1990), *The Dame in the Kimono.*
Maltby, Richard (1993), 'The Production Code and the Hays Office'.
Moley, Raymond (1945), *The Hays Office.*

Vietnam and the New Militarism

Michael Ryan and Douglas Kellner

Halloween and *Dressed to Kill* appear around 1978–80, at the same time as *The Deer Hunter* and *Apocalypse Now,* two major conservative Vietnam films. All four are distinguished by regressive portrayals of women combined with assertions of male power and right-wing violence. That ideological conjunction, we suggest, is not accidental. It is symptomatic of a turn occurring in American culture at that time, a turn whose trajectory intersects eventually with the rise of the New Right as a force in American politics and with the renewal of militarism during the Reagan eighties. It is also symptomatic of the necessary connection between representations of paranoid projection in the horror genre as a reaction to feminism and representations of revived military might as a result of threats to national self-esteem. The psychological source was similar in each case as was the representational violence that emerged as its solution.

In American culture, film representations of military prowess seem inseparable from national self-esteem. For conservatives especially, greatness as a nation means the ability to exercise military power. In war, the strength and courage of the soldiers who represent male national prestige are tested and proven. In post–World War II cinematic representations of this ritual, proof of manhood was accompanied by a nationalistic idealism that pictured the American fighting man as a heroic liberator of oppressed people and as a defender of freedom. This ideal legend was justified by World War II, when American forces did indeed help defeat right-wing fascist regimes. After the war, however, the defense of political freedom against the right-wing corporatism of the fascist movement was replaced by a defense of free enterprise capitalism against both Soviet communism and national liberation movements throughout the world, from Latin America to Southeast Asia. The legend of the freedom-defending U.S. fighting man soon began to be tarnished by the frequent sacrifice of political freedom and democratic rights that the defense of capitalism entailed. While the overthrow of democratic leftist governments in places like Guatemala and Iran could be tolerated in the Cold War climate of the fifties, in the sixties a new generation, nurtured in a more liberal cultural atmosphere and faced with having to risk their lives in the defense of capitalism overseas, began to question the right of a corporate controlled U.S. government to suppress democracy and socialism throughout the word in the name of "freedom." The equation of "freedom" and "democracy' with capitalism became increasingly strained because antidemocratic military dictatorships were more often than not U.S. allies in policing Third World liberation movements. During the 1960s, the Vietnam War became a focus of popular contestation. American youth refused to fight an unjust war, and by the early seventies, a majority of the people came to oppose the war. In addition, the army began to look increasingly incapable, undisciplined, and demoralized. In 1975, the United States suffered its first military defeat in its history with the liberation of Saigon. The loss created a lesion in the sense of national prestige, and it provoked a heated debate over American foreign policy.

We shall argue that Hollywood military movies of the seventies and eighties need to be read, first, in the context of the national debate over Vietnam, and, secondly, in the context of the "post-Vietnam syndrome," which was characterized by the desire for withdrawal from "foreign involvements" after the debacle in Vietnam and epitomized by the Clark Amendment forbidding intervention in Angola.

In the decade following the end of the war, America's military posture shifted from doubt to assertiveness, as the liberal tide of the mid-seventies receded and a rightist current came to dominate American political life. Films during the period articulate the arguments that led to this change and point the direction American culture was taking regarding the war long before actual political events confirmed the shift. Around the issues of Vietnam and war in general, the failure of liberalism took the form of an inability to transform the widespread antiwar feelings of the time into a permanent institutional change in foreign policy. Once again, in this regard as in economic policy, the liberals were victims of historical circumstances. As Carter and the Democrats staved off new military programs like the B-1 bomber, the Soviets invaded Afghanistan, the Sandinistas overthrew a U.S.-supported dictator in Nicaragua, and Iran's revolution led to the taking of American hostages all in 1979 and 1980. The American empire, which had lasted from 1945 to 1970, was crumbling, and the triumph of conservatism around military policy resulted from the ability of conservatives to take advantage of these circumstances to promote the sort of military buildup they favored. Many films of the period argue the conservative position.

One major factor in the conservative triumph was the social psychology of shame that was a significant motif of American culture after the military defeat in Vietnam. It is for this reason that the returned vet motif is so important in contemporary Hollywood film. Those whose self-identity is in part constructed through the internalization of representations of the nation as a military power no doubt felt a loss of self-esteem as a result of the nation's failure. That sense of loss generated resentment as well as a yearning for compensation. One aspect of the failure of liberalism is the inability of liberals to provide a redemptive and compensatory vision that would replace military representations as a source of self-esteem. Conservatives, on the other hand, managed successfully to equate self-restoration with military renewal.

1. DEBATING VIETNAM

The posture Hollywood initially adopted toward Vietnam is best summed up in the title of Julian Smith's book—*Looking Away.*[1] With the exception of *The Green Berets* (1968), a jingoist war story, no major films dealt directly with the war until the late seventies. Nevertheless, war itself was a topic of great debate in films of the late sixties and early seventies, and many of these touch covertly on the issue of Vietnam. Blacklisted screenwriter Dalton Trumbo's thirties antiwar novel *Johnny Got His Gun* was made into a film in 1971, a time when opposition to the war was peaking, and films like *M*A*S*H* and *Soldier Blue* of the same period indirectly criticized Vietnam era militarism. A similar sort of indirect message from the conservative side was delivered in *Patton* (1970), a promilitarist film scripted by Coppola that supposedly helped inspire Nixon to bomb Cambodia. Indeed, Patton's opening speech, shot against an immense American flag, which exhorted

Americans never to give up the fight, probably had a subliminal topical resonance for many prowar hawks.

The first major 1970s Hollywood film to deal directly with the issue of the war was the independently made feature documentary *Hearts and Minds* (1975), directed by Peter Davis. If *Patton* demonstrated that the conservative militarist pathology is inseparable from male self-aggrandizement, an authoritarian model of social discipline, and the skewing of the personality away from a composite of affectionate and aggressive traits and toward a hypertropism of violence, *Hearts and Minds* by combining clips from war films with scenes of football games, shows how militarism emerges from a culture that promotes aggressivity in young men and furthers a racist attitude toward the world. The film juxtaposes defenders and critics of U.S. policy, and the accompanying documentary footage of the ravages of war positions the prowar speakers as being arrogant and cruel. For example, General Westmoreland's remark that Asians do not value human life is juxtaposed to long and painful scenes of the Vietnamese mourning their dead.

The film is also significant for attempting to establish the historical context and social system out of which the war emerged. Unlike later fictional narrative war films, *Hearts and Minds* adopts a multiple perspective that undermines the power and the blindness of a monocular subjective position. What other films pose as an object (the Vietnamese), this film grants some subjectivity, as when the Vietnamese themselves express their anger and suffering. And it situates the war in a historical context that displaces the conservative concern for violent redemption or the liberal focus on the fate of individual (usually white, male) characters.

It was not until the war was over that fictional films began to appear that dealt directly with or were explicitly critical of the war. The first films to appear concerned returned veterans, frequently portrayed as dangerously alienated or violent (*Black Sunday, Stone Killer*). Later films take a more sympathetic point of view; films like *Cutter's Way, Who'll Stop the Rain?*, and *Some Kind of Hero* portray the vets as confused and wounded victims. Another strain of returned vet films use the motif as a springboard for justifying the kind of violent and racist disposition that initiated the war in the first place (*Rolling Thunder, First Blood, Firefox*). And finally, the vet motif in the eighties (*Uncommon Valor, Missing in Action, Rambo*) becomes a means of affirming the militarism of the new era.[2]

Liberal vet films focused on personal issues at the expense of the historical and global systemic concerns of *Hearts and Minds*. They criticized the war for what it did to good, white American boys, not for what ruin it brought to innocent Vietnamese. The first major liberal vet film—*Coming Home* (1978)—was also the first major Hollywood feature film to deal seriously with the issue of the war from a critical perspective. It skillfully manipulates the personalist and emotive codes of Hollywood to elicit sympathy for a wounded antiwar vet and to generate an empathetic yet critical stance toward a gungho soldier who is driven suicidal by the war experience. The scenes of the military hospital filled with the victims of war lifted a veil of silence, yet at the same time the film reproduces the traditional, Hollywood, sentimentalist vision of postwar experiences (as in, say, *The Best Years of Our Lives*).

Both *Who'll Stop the Rain?* (1978) and *Cutter's Way* (1981) use the figure of the returning vet to engage in social critique. In *Rain* a vet tries to help a buddy's wife who is victimized by drug dealers with whom her husband was involved. He is killed, and his death is cast in such a way as to evoke a sense of victimage. In addition, the fact that the final fight takes place in a carnival atmosphere suggests a critical parallel with the fruitless struggle in Vietnam. Passer's *Cutter's Way* is even bleaker. A bitter disabled vet becomes obsessed with revealing that a wealthy capitalist has murdered a young girl. He associates the man with the class he feels sent him to Vietnam to do its dirty work. Again, the vet dies, while riding a white horse through a lawn party on his way to have justice done. Such liberal vet films are distinguished by the hopeless vision they project, a vision reinforced in *Cutter's Way* by the use of somber color tones and confined spaces that suggest desolation and despair. Yet both direct the violence of the vet against groups or elites who clearly profited from the war at the expense of ordinary working-class soldiers. Conservative vet films turn shame into violent affirmation, but to do so they direct violence against the Vietnamese, in an attempt to win the lost war.

Rolling Thunder (1977) is an example of an extremely reactionary representation of the veteran issue. A veteran returns home to find his wife having an affair (a familiar cultural motif at the time expressed in the popular song "Ruby," concerning a woman who betrays a wounded vet). In this reprise of the post–World War II classic The *Blue Dahlia,* the wife and children are brutally murdered, and the veteran seeks out and kills the perpetrators with the aid of another veteran. Male bonding heals female betrayal, and violence, as usual, cures all ills. The wife's murder could be seen as a symbolic projection of the husband's revenge (his hand is mangled by the attackers, and the two events seem interrelated). And the rest of the violence is directed against non-whites. In this vision, the Vietnam War is not left behind; it is brought home to roost.

The film depicts the psychological basis upon which post-Vietnam Americans are enlisted into the new militarism. The hero is depicted as being shamed ("castrated"), and his reaction is to become violent against non-Americans. The shame associated with sexuality in the film is linked both to military defeat and to being deprived of money (the attack on his family is a burglary attempt). Thus, the denial of self-esteem around economic matters is also in part signaled as a source of resentment.

Returning veteran films range from the critical vision of films like *Coming Home* and *Cutter's Way* to the military revivalist vision of *First Blood, Firefox, and Rambo.* Films directly about the war experience itself are equally mixed, although, as in the returning vet subgenre, none adopts an explicitly oppositional posture toward the war.

Go Tell the Spartans (1978) and *The Boys in Company C* (1978) both criticize the U.S. involvement in Vietnam while forgoing more radical critiques of the military, U.S. foreign policy, or the values that support militarism. *Spartans* shows the army blundering deeper into the war during its early stages, and it stands as an allegory of the futility of the war effort as a whole. A small group of U.S. soldiers in a provincial outpost are ordered to occupy another, even more obscure position. They are overrun, and many are killed in the senseless action. Nevertheless, the critique of the war is executed against the Standard of the "good war," which reproduces a traditional trope of critical Hollywood war films in that it criticizes a specific war while celebrating military values in general. *The Boys in Company C* suffers from a similar drawback. The story follows a platoon of young marines from boot camp through combat in Vietnam. Along the way, they discover that their officers are corrupt and only interested in high body counts. The film points to the futility and misguidedness of the American war effort. It criticizes both the U.S. supported Vietnamese bourgeoisie and the Army high command that treated genocide against Vietnamese as a numbers game and as an excuse for using fancy high-tech weaponry. The common soldiers, in alliance with the Vietnamese people, symbolized by the children, are pitted against these two groups. They and the children are slaughtered in the end. *The Boys in Company C* constitutes one of the few overt statements against the war to come out of Hollywood, yet it resorts to the traditional Hollywood convention of valorizing "good grunt soldiers" over officers, and avoids criticizing the military as such.

Vietnam combat films like *Spartans and Boys* share the same limits as the liberal vet films. Liberals usually avoided the broader implications of the war, its origin in a desire to maintain access to Third World labor, markets, raw materials, etc., and to forestall the rise of noncapitalist sociopolitical systems. The traditional liberal focus on individuals implies a personalistic account that easily permits larger geopolitical issues to be displaced. And the sorts of self-replicating identifications that such an account invites usually evoke sentimentalist reactions to individual suffering rather than outrage at national policies of genocide. What needs to be determined is whether or not such personal evocations can translate into broader systemic lessons.

The rhetoric of liberal films nevertheless marks an advance on that used in conservative films. In simple thematic terms, the liberal films are critical of figures of authority, while conservative films like *Patton* metaphorically elevate such figures to an ideal position. There is a singularity of focus in conservative war films that is lacking in liberal rhetoric. *Boys* concerns a multiplicity of characters, and no one point of view is privileged. The "other" in *Patton,* a German officer assigned to study the general, is there simply to instantiate the implicit narcissistic male (self-)gaze, which takes the empirical form of the German's adulation for the great American hero. *Boys* draws Vietnamese into the narrative and grants them empathy not as admirers of the Americans but as their victims. Finally, *Patton* resorts to overwhelmingly metaphoric rhetorical strategies, while *Boys* is more metonymic in its approach. *Patton* assumes an ideal purity of character, and it even intimates a rather silly sort of universalism in the male militarist spirit. The trope of elevation and subordination fits easily with an authoritarian ideology in this film. In *Boys,* on the other hand, a representational strategy which emphasizes the equality of terms and their material, contiguous interconnections prevails. One soldier reprimands another for endangering all their lives; on the material level at which the soldiers are obliged to operate, metonymic connections are very real.

By the late seventies Vietnam was no longer an explosive issue. Conservatives decried the slow erosion of American international power in the face of Third World liberation movements, and in response to what they perceived as an expansionist USSR, they called for an end to the "post–Vietnam War syndrome." What began was a period of resurgent militarism, and Vietnam films of the time take part in the conservative backlash. They do so in part by rewriting history.

If, from a conservative political point of view, the period of the "post–Vietnam War syndrome" was characterized by national self-doubt, military vacillation, and a failure of will to intervene overseas, then the appropriate counter in the "post-syndrome" period of national revival was a triumph of the will, a purgation of doubt through action, and an interventionist military stance that brooked no restraint of the sort that led to the United State's first military defeat, tarnished national prestige,. and shamed American military manhood. Both *The Deer Hunter* and *Apocalypse Now* contribute to that revival by incorporating Vietnam not as a defeat from which lessons can be learned, but as a springboard for male military heroism.

The Deer Hunter, directed by Michael Cimino, won the Oscar in 1978. The film is more about the accession to leadership of the seer-warrior-individualist hero, Michael Vronsky (Robert DeNiro), than about the war. But this turning away from defeat, loss, and responsibility to an emblem of male strength might itself be symptomatic of a denial of loss through a compensatory self-inflation of the very sort that helped initiate and prolong the war.[3] Nevertheless, the film is multivalent politically. It appealed to working-class viewers who saw in it an accurate representation of the dilemmas of their lives. Radicals praised its implicit critique of certain male myths. And its bleak, ambiguous ending inspired many to read it as an anti-Vietnam-War statement. We respect all of these positions, but we read the film from the perspective of the critique of ideology, and in that light, it seems less progressive.[4]

The story concerns three steeltown buddies—Michael, Steve, and Nick—who are shown united in the first part in a highly ritualized wedding scene that conveys a sense of strong community. The church steeple, a symbol of unreflective faith, spontaneous adherence to hierarchy, and paternalistic authority, rises above the community as its guiding axis. It is returned to repeatedly by the camera, and the gesture underscores the church's centrality as a locus of social authority and an anchor securing community cohesion. All three men go to Vietnam, where they are reunited as prisoners of the Vietcong, who force them to play Russian roulette. Michael outsmarts the VC and saves his buddies. But Nick, apparently unhinged by his experience, remains in Vietnam playing roulette for money. Steve, now confined to a wheelchair in a stateside hospital, refuses to leave and return home. Michael returns to establish a relationship with Linda, Nick's old girlfriend.

He forces Steve to overcome his shame, to be a "man" and leave the hospital. Then, Michael returns to Vietnam at the time of the fall of Saigon to witness Nick kill himself in his last roulette game. The film closes with Nick's funeral and the group of surviving friends singing "God Bless America."

Like so many films of the seventies, *The Deer Hunter* offers as a solution to complex political and social problems the exercise of power by a male individualist who is charged with saving a community through strong leadership. The community is patriarchal; women are present to be fought over, as bossy mothers, and in the role of not altogether faithful, weak, yet at the right moment supportive partners. War breaks the community, and its worst effect is the transformation of men into will-less weaklings (Steve) or addicted obsessives (Nick). It falls to Michael to exercise his natural power of leadership to restore the communal cohesion and order at the end of the film. That restoration requires the sacrifice of Michael's weaker counterpart, Nick, with whose funeral the film ends. The reaffirmation of male military power in the character of Michael is predicated upon the purgation of weakness, vacillation, and the obsessively suicidal behavior in which the country was engaged in Vietnam, all of which seem embodied in Nick. It is important that in the scene immediately following Nick's suicide, the audience sees documentary footage of the U.S. Army's "disgraceful" flight from Saigon. The juxtaposition associates Nick's weakness and self-destructiveness with the military defeat of 1975. The film, then, can be said to work in two dimensions. It concerns the restoration of community through strong patriarchal leadership. And it offers an allegorical solution to the problem Vietnam poses by symbolically purging the source of defeat and proposing a way to renewed national strength and patriotic cohesion.

The call for strong leadership as a solution to historical crises is a political version of the aesthetic transformation in the film of actual history into a moral allegory. Just as the warrior-leader-savior resolves vacillation into a triumph of heroic will, so also the romantic, allegorical form of the film attempts to resolve the contradictions, meaninglessness, and ambiguity of the actual historical war into a meaningful and apparently noncontradictory quest narrative executed in a synthetic style that balances the unity of the individual leader with a formal or aesthetic unity. It is not surprising that a political ideology of the superior individual subject should seem inseparable from an aesthetic of romantic, quasi-mystical exaltation, since both are forms of empowerment. The romantic aesthetic overpowers history and incorporates it into highly subjective fantasy representations. The problem of realistically depicting history, which is linked to the political problem of acknowledging responsibility and loss as a nation, is solved by sublimating history into a stylized, ceremonial fusion of color, sound, and theme that elevates contingent events to a moral allegory of redemption and an ordinary human to secular divinity. It is important that the most stylized and allegorical representations appear while Michael is hunting. The aesthetic transformation of the mountains into a mystical temple (replete with choir) parallels the political and ideological elevation of the member of the gang into the strong, mystical leader, naturally destined to lead the lesser mortals around him. It is also, of course, a means of attaining the sorts of separation we have described as necessary to the more pathological forms of male sexual identity. Heightened mental representations of the sort evident in the mountain scenes are themselves ways of denying connection to the world and to others who might transgress the boundary between self and world which a reactive male sexual identity must establish. It is significant, then, that Michael is most alone in the mountain scenes, most separated from others, and most protected from them by a representational boundary that makes him seem transcendent, unique. Those scenes are also, of course, the most metaphoric.

Yet affirmations of transcendence are necessary only when the actual world is fallen (meaningless, hopeless, unhappy). "My country right or wrong" makes sense or is necessary only if the country can be or is frequently wrong. The quest for transcendence, for turning the everyday into the grandiose, the monumental, and the meaningful, presupposes the absence of the empirical equivalents of these spiritual ideals in the actual world. Indeed, the actual world has to be a positive negation of such things as fulfillment, selfworth, and significance for the quest for other-worldly, transcendent meanings to be activated. The metaphor exists in necessary tension with a more metonymic or worldly and material set of constraints which bring the metaphor into being as a reaction against them.

The transcendent moments of the film can thus be read either as successful enactments of the attainment of a spiritual ideal just short of the clouds that are the floor of heaven, or as the neurotic symptoms of this worldly victimization, attempts to secure a sense of self-worth against a world that denies it nine to five and only allows a few leisure-time pursuits, like the male rituals of drinking and hunting, as metaphoric alternatives. The film depicts both, and our point is that its progressive potential resides in the fact that it cannot avoid this undecidability. The transcendental moments can only appear as such in contrast to a detailed description of a fallen everyday reality. This is why the film is so incredibly dense with ethnographic detail from everyday life, from the long marriage celebration to the scenes inside the industrial workplace. It is important, therefore, that the film opens in the factory, with an establishing shot from under a viaduct at night that makes the factory world seem enclosed and oppressive. The colorful mountain scenes of transcendence gain their meaning from their difference from the darkness of the workplace and the squalor of ethnic neighborhood life. And Michael's individuation is defined as a separating out, a denial of "weakening" social links of the sort that characterize his less strong male cronies.

Thus, the film permits a deconstruction of the premises of its idealization of Michael as the seer-leader. His elevation occurs through the metaphor of the deer hunt, which transforms a literal leisure-time activity into a higher ideal meaning that transcends literality, just as Michael comes to transcend the literal and material social texture, to rise above it. He must do so if he is to give it order, but the metaphor cannot fully rise above the literality that is its vehicle. Part of its literality is that it exists in metonymic or contiguous relation to the opening factory scene of fallen fire, confinement, and darkness where the men seem all alike. Michael's distinction as the superior individual who can read sunspots, like a shaman, or who knows the mystical meaning of a bullet ("This is this"), or who takes down deer with one shot like a true hunter has meaning only in differentiation from the other men, from their sameness in the factory. And the metaphor of transcendental leadership takes on meaning only in distinction from the workaday world; without that contrast, that determining difference, it makes no sense. Yet the film's ideology depends on the assumption that the metaphor subsumes the literal event into an ideal meaning which transcends wordly materiality and meaninglessness (nondistinction) entirely.

The film thus puts on display the interconnections between wage labor oppression and white male working class compensations for that oppression. In this film, a mythic idealization of the individual counters the reduction of all the men to faceless and impersonal functions in the industrial machine at the beginning of the film. An idealized meaning substitutes for the fallen reality of everyday life. The powerful emblem of the church, the extremely ritualized wedding, the mythologized hunt, and the strong bonding between the men should thus be seen as ways of counteracting the banality of life on the bottom of capitalism.

Like many populist films, this one therefore has a double valence. Its depiction of the accreditation of right-wing political leadership points to the way pre-class-conscious working class men can have their resentment against oppression channeled into conservative, even fascist forms in a highly individualistic and patriarchal cultural context that limits the means of attaining communal cohesion to strong male individual leadership. Yet it also points to potentially radical desires to transcend the cruel material conditions to which working class people are reduced (or were being reduced, in the late seventies particularly), conditions that deny a sense of worldly meaning or worth to people, who, as a result, overcompensate for those lacks by turning to either religious or political idealizations.

If both *Deer Hunter* and *Apocalypse Now* indicate the reactionary way of dealing with the Vietnam War, they also testify to something amiss in the country's prevailing conception of itself. The need, demonstrated in these films, to repudiate the war as history and to transfer it into an allegory of militarist manhood is itself symptomatic of a wound, a sense of shame, that seems resistant to the sort of healing these films attempt. And the films merely reproduce the desire to realize a totality of American will in the world that reveals its own problematic anchoring in a web of serial, contiguous nontotalizable relations with other people the more it asserts itself so hyperbolically and hysterically.

By the mid-eighties, the Vietnam syndrome had been at least partially overcome, and conservatives once again felt a pre-Vietnam license to exercise U.S. military power overseas. Yet the country remained convinced by the experience of Vietnam, and it refused to back full-scale interventions that might lead to wars in places like Central America. Our poll suggests that American viewers tended to turn even conservative war films like *The Deer Hunter* into antiwar statements: 69% felt that it portrayed the war as a mistake, and 93% said that it confirmed their opposition to the war. The ending made 27% feel patriotic, while it made 51% feel disheartened. Perhaps the most disturbing result we found was that 74% felt that the representation of the Vietcong in the film was accurate. Even if Americans had learned some lessons regarding foreign wars, they still seemed to need to learn lessons regarding foreigners. And this perhaps accounts for the fact that, although they continued to oppose interventionism on a large scale, they overwhelmingly approved Ronald Reagan's strikes against Grenada and Libya during this period.

2. THE MILITARY REHABILITATED

One consequence of the Vietnam War and the draft that supplied it with men was an undermining of the U.S. Army. By the end of the war, soldiers were "fragging" (deliberately killing) their officers, rather than obeying orders to fight. As a result of this, as well as of the widespread opposition to war that the draft helped inspire, the draft was eliminated, and the army was transformed into an all-volunteer force. That new force was heavily minority, since nonwhite minorities in a retrenching capitalist society dominated by whites had few other career opportunities. Advertisements for the army began to appear on diversionary television shows (sports and MTV especially) that might attract working-class, unemployed, and minority viewers. The restoration of the army became a more pressing concern in the late seventies, when events such as the Soviet invasion of Afghanistan and the taking of U.S. hostages in Iran made it clear that American imperial interests were no longer going to be taken for granted or allowed to go uncontested in the world. Hollywood joined in the effort, and a number of early eighties films "humanize" the army by turning it into a scene for family melodrama, liberal ideals, and humor. The link seemed so overt that one suspected that some Hollywood filmmakers had not heard that culture is supposed to be at least relatively autonomous in relation to political power and the state.[5]

These films are generally liberal in tone; their humanization of the military is laudable in contrast to the more conservative exaggeration of the worst traits of the military—violence, discipline, intolerance, masculinism, etc.—in such films as *Rambo*. Yet these films appear at a time when the country, in the hands of conservatives, was adopting increasingly militarist poses in the world theater and when a "culture of militarism" was developing (in the form of toys, magazines, TV shows, and films). Whatever the intention of these films, their political valence was reinflected in a conservative direction by their historical moment and their social context. Moreover, the liberal vision takes for granted the necessity of an institution like the military. Liberals fail to see the deep structural roots and systemic relations that link the military per se as an institution to the patriarchal socialization patterns that are partly responsible (as we have argued) for war. It is in light of a broader radical critique of the military itself that the liberal position must be judged. Such a critique would see the military as an instrument of class defense, as well as a machine for producing a model of a general social discipline of the sort capitalism (or any work-oriented, inegalitarian society) requires. In addition, the military from this perspective is less a protection than a threat. In the modern world especially, the very existence of the military poses a danger, and it is no longer possible, because of modern weapons, to justify the military as a defense against aggression. Defense and a war of total annihilation are no longer separable concepts.

The format of humanized military films like *Stripes, Private Benjamin,* and *An Officer and a Gentleman* consists of the transformation of an unsuccessful person into a very successful one. Thus, an affirmative personal narrative is laid over an attempt at institutional reconstruction, and, like the ads for the army on television ("Be all that you can be"), the films identify personal achievement with military life. In this way, the films seem to participate in an attempt in the culture to restore the army to its pre-Vietnam credit and, in certain instances, to reintegrate it with a lost patriotic vision of the United States.

Private Benjamin (1980) incorporates feminism into this process. It recounts the transformation of a dependent and ineffectual woman who is at a loss when her husband dies on the night of their wedding into a strong, independent figure. The change is marked by the difference between the first wedding scene, in which she is little more than a sexual servant of her husband, and the last, when she socks her husband-to-be on the jaw because he is a philanderer and stalks off alone. The ideological dimension of the film consists in intimating that the army is what has made her strong. Thus, a very antifeminist institution is made to appear an ally of feminism.

Stripes (1981) and *An Officer and a Gentleman* (1982) both concern the transformation of ne'er-do-wells into successful soldiers and "men." But more important, both are allegories of the metamorphosis of the Vietnam generation, with its anti-bourgeois and antiauthoritarian dropout values, into the fighting machines of the eighties, who believe in patriotism, nationalism, and militarism. In *Stripes* an underemployed goof-off whose girlfriend has left him is transformed by the army into a good soldier who becomes a leader of his squad as well as a sexual success.

The most popular humanized military film, *An Officer and a Gentleman* is neo-forties in outlook and tone; advertisements made it seem like a story out of the past, but that attempt to step back into the generic form and style of an older, more innocent male military ethos was very much a statement about the present. The film recounts the transformation of Zack (Richard Gere) from an undisciplined, motorcycle-riding, down-and-out tough guy into an officer and a gentleman." Brutality saves, the film says, as the hammer shapes steel. Foley, Zack's black drill instructor (Lou Gossett), brutalizes him until he renounces his selfishness and becomes a team player. Zack stops treating women badly and does the honorable thing by carrying off his working-class girlfriend (Debra Winger) at the end. And he sacrifices his chance to set a new obstacle course record by returning to help a female classmate. The film elicits audience sympathy (even applause) at points like this. It plays on human, even liberal sentiments (integrationist and token feminist), but it does so in order to reinforce the military institution. Zack's military training seems to make him a better man, a "gentleman." We would argue that the film should be understood, then, as an allegory of a transformation being promoted by the Right in contemporary U.S. society. Zack represents a generation of youth who grew up disaffected with traditional institutions like the military. Through Zack, we see that generation overcome its alienation and accept such values as military honor and team play. The price is submission to discipline, authority, and brutality, but the prize is self-respect and love.

The love story is sweet and reassuring; its retreat from modernity to the sort of "torrid romance" of early Hollywood films invests libidinal energies into militarism—soldiers get the "girls," the film suggests. In a film where men must learn to be "men," it is fitting that women's goal should be portrayed as "getting a man." The love story, in fact, depicts the real state of affairs of many working class women in a society that fails to satisfy real human needs and that makes women's survival often depend on men. Such romance has a double edge. It permits a hothouse closure to be established which reinforces the film's masculinist-militarist ideology. But romance also testifies to structural differences between male power and female dependency that could never be fully sublated to an ideological closure and are underscored, even as their reality is denied in a film like this. They remain outside such closure always, for they are the very things that make ideology necessary in the first place.

Films like *Officer* were some of the most successful ideological narratives of the era. Yet for that very reason, they are some of the most interesting for understanding the rhetorical procedures of ideology as well as the social system of militarism. They are open to deconstruction precisely because they seem such perfect exercises in ideology. Strong personal needs for romance or family are transferred metaphorically or by analogy onto the military. And by virtue of metaphoric substitution, the military stands in as the answer for the personal desires. Yet this exercise in metaphoric closure also signals literal connections between the realms which are joined metaphorically. The films do not merely compare male-dominated romance or the patriarchal family to the military; they inadvertently dramatize the real material or metonymic relations between these realms of socialization.

For example, in *The Great Santini* (1982), a narrative of intergenerational strife between a gung-ho old-style military man and his son is mapped over a justification of the military. The narrative proceeds as a movement toward a moment of recognition when the children finally see that the father was a good man despite his excesses. He becomes a locus of sympathy when he dies sacrificing himself so that a town will not be destroyed by his crashing jet. The son, who seemed to reject his father's values, dons his flight jacket, assumes his father's position at the driver's wheel of the family car, and begins to act like him. The gesture is indicative of the patriarchal character of the military. It is passed from fathers to sons, bypassing women, who serve in this film as breeders. If the family is not just a legitimating model by metaphoric analogy for the military, but also a literal seed-bed of militarist values, then this division of labor is not accidental. The socialization patterns of the two seemingly separate domains form a continuum.

Liberal films like *Taps* (1981) and *The Lords of Discipline* (1983) criticize military excess in the name of a humanized military, one in which militarism must be tempered by restraint and respect for life. Indeed, *Taps* thematizes this very position. Cadets at a military academy, in order to defend the existence of the academy, engage in an armed revolt, which results in the deaths of several of them. The most fervent apostle of military honor, an aging general, also dies, and his disciple, the young cadet who leads the revolt, learns that militarism must give way to good judgment. Yet the military itself is affirmed.

Films like this display the crucial ingredients of the failure of liberalism to develop a program for significantly transforming American society. Liberalism operates from within patriarchal presuppositions, which, like the similar procapitalist presuppositions liberals hold, limit the ability of liberals to see beyond the walls of the ideological prison in which they operate. Militarist patriarchs are okay, these films seem to say, though we'd be better off with nicer ones. But in a world in which one trigger-happy fool can send everyone to happy vaporland, even nice militarist patriarchs must be seen as pathological. It is such a shift of vision, whereby the most everyday assumptions of patriarchy and capitalism, especially the assumption that strong, rambunctious men are needed to lead and defend us, are relinquished forever, that lies beyond the capacity of liberals. Indeed, liberals should probably be defined as people incapable of such structural conceptualizations.

Liberals do not see the military as a social problem that must be eliminated, in part because they accept the patriarchal logic of the Cold War—that the only way to keep peace with an antagonist is through the threat of aggression or annihilation. Yet this position is itself a product of a patriarch socialization to competition and power. In other words, if you only look a the world with sunglasses, you'll never see anything but a dark world. In order to perceive the military itself as an unnecessary and potentially dangerous institution, liberals would have to step outside their own socialization, exit from the structure they inhabit, question the very words that come automatically to their lips.

A more radical position would argue that the outlawing of armies and weapons is not a utopian dream; it is a precondition of the modern world' survival. Beyond patriarchal and capitalist socialization to competition aggression, and domination reside alternative socialization possibilities, and alternate ideals of cooperation, demilitarization, and peaceful communal existence. But that would require a different set of structuring assumptions, as well as a different set of social institutions. If the problem of the military is wedded to the social institutions that justify it metaphorically, then it is not likely to change until they are changed. Indeed, one could say that something of that potentially emergent reality is signaled by even the ideology of some of the humanized military films. For by comparing the military with the family, they indicate the possibility of a breakdown of the boundaries that separate the two realms. The family is a patriarchal form, and for this reason, it can successfully legitimate the military. But it is also a communal form. The very "humanity" that it lends the military also threatens the military. The price of analogy is comparison. And in comparison to the family, the military can only ultimately appear as being inhumane. For if the family breeds children, the military murders them. *Taps* and *Lords* at least point this out. They just don't follow the point to its logical conclusion. And they couldn't, because of the very patriarchal assumptions which underwrite the military, assumptions which also limit any critique of the military by immediately branding accurate critiques as unreal, utopian, or, worse, not manly enough.

3. THE NEW MILITARISM

Liberals succeeded in stemming the growth of the military in the mid to late seventies, but they were incapable of turning the loss in Vietnam into a permanent structural reform of U.S. militarism. This was so in part because of historical events that made a renewed defense of the American empire necessary. That empire consisted of a network of client states overseas, in places like the Philippines and Iran, that were tied into the imperial economic and military system by treaty and corporate investment. These states helped assure that leftist or anticapitalist governments would not come to power in areas American corporations deemed necessary to their interests. Usually they brutally repressed liberation movements, in places like Indonesia and Chile, for example, and they protected the flow of raw materials and the supply of cheap labor for American firms. Military buildups within the United States were thus closely related to the status of the imperial client states, and they both have an economic dimension. In the late seventies and early eighties several client states fell to liberation movements (Nicaragua, Iran, the Philippines), others (South Korea, South Africa, El Salvador) were troubled by incipient liberation movements or unrest, and other U.S.-supported military regimes (Argentina, Brazil, Peru, Chile) were subject either to internal disturbances or to overthrow by democratic forces repulsed by the exercise of state terror in the name of defending capitalism. At the same time, several previously "secure" colonial nations became socialist—Angola, Ethiopia, Mozambique—as a result of revolutions. The empire was trembling, and the Iran hostage crisis of 1979–80 heated up jingoist sentiment enough in the nation to give the new conservative power bloc the support it required to begin carrying out a momentous military buildup decked out in militarist and anticommunist rhetoric.

Yet public sentiment was not entirely homogeneous on the subject of militarism. Polls indicated that in general people opposed foreign interventionism. For this reason, perhaps, there was a cultural offensive to enlist support for the conservative ideals of an aggressive, combative defense of imperial interests. If the public didn't need to be whipped up, there would not have been so much whipping going on in the early to mid-eighties, especially in films.

The revival of militarism was not spontaneous, however. Conservative groups like the Committee on the Present Danger campaigned throughout the seventies for greater "defense" spending and for a firmer foreign policy.

The new militarism is not an effect of the Reagan era; rather, Reagan himself is in part an effect of the culture of militarism born in the late seventies, with some help from Democrats like Jimmy Carter. *The Final Countdown* (1979) is an example of a film that prefigures the conservative military buildup of the early eighties. It concerns an aircraft carrier that travels through a time warp to emerge on the day before Pearl Harbor. The captain has to decide whether to intervene and change the course of history. The purpose of this historical displacement is to suggest that the United States needs a powerful military in order to prevent another Pearl Harbor. Indeed, in a number of new militarist films, the Vietnamese, the Russians, or the "enemy" are decked out in uniforms that markedly resemble Japanese and German World War II battle gear. This evocation of the notion of the past "just war" in the contemporary context recalls the American Right's persistent equating of communism with German Nazism, a movement which was in fact conservative and rightist in character as well as being devoted to the eradication of communism.

Militarism in the United States is inseparable from anticommunism. Although anticommunism has been a staple of post–World War II culture, after the late sixties, during the period of détente, it faded somewhat from American consciousness and from Hollywood film. But in the late seventies and early eighties it was revived and promoted in conjunction with the new militarism. It ranged from military revival allegories like *Firefox* to dance musicals like *White Night*. The new anticommunism worked either by projecting its own aggressive animus onto the "enemy," thus justifying itself as a "defense" against a hypothetically offensive Red Terror, or by dehumanizing the ideological adversaries of the United States through the use of racial and social stereotypes in such a way as to excuse the use of violence against them. For example, *Megaforce* (1982) was a Pentagon-supported advertisement both for military hardware and for elite military manpower. It concerns an elite group of fighters known as "Megaforce" (who look and taste like the Pentagon's Rapid Deployment Force). They use some of the most sophisticated military technology available to fight Castro-like, south-of-the-border bandits and their communist allies, who overthrow governments like dominoes, not for social ideals, but out of greed for money. The film presents social revolutionaries as venal criminals. And this criminalization and dehumanization of foreign people struggling for liberation from capitalism and feudalism seems to be essential to the promotion of weapons designed for their liquidation.

Perhaps the most audacious anticommunist film of the era was John Milius's *Red Dawn* (1984), about a hypothetical Soviet invasion of the United States. A group of youngsters hide out in the mountains and become a successful guerrilla unit. In the end, they are all killed. Along with the usual right-wing themes (the Soviets are subhuman concentration camp guards, Latin American revolutionaries are merely their agents, the United States is the last bastion of justice and freedom), the film is distinguished by certain ideological motifs that hark back to fascist and national socialist ideologies of the twenties and thirties. At one point, an intellectual liberal and a jock conservative fight over how to proceed in the group. The liberal's call for democracy loses out to the conservative's assertion of his right to command the others. The authoritarian leadership principle is linked to the assumption that those with greater force or power should prevail—not those with the best principles or rational arguments. Such force derives its authority from nature, from what the Nazis called "blood and soil." The blood motif in the film appears as the ritual drinking of a deer's blood as proof of one's warrior manhood; it refers to the Nazi fetishizing of powerful animals, and it elaborates the conservative idea that human life is primitivist, a struggle for survival in a civil society that is no different from nature. The soil motif appears at those moments when Milius's camera meditates on nature, positioning it as a still, immense, unmoving presence. The existential loneliness of the individualist warrior leader is associated with expansive fields and high mountains, fetishes of power and strength.[6]

Thus, the film displays the close relationship between contemporary American right-wing ideology and Nazism. Indeed, one curious dimension of the film's argument is that what it poses against communism, depicted as totalitarian domination, is a social model of authoritarian leadership. The authoritarian camp in the mountains is not much different from the totalitarian "camp" in the town. At this point in history, conservatives like Jeane Kirkpatrick argued for a distinction between totalitarianism (authoritarianism for the sake of communism) and authoritarianism (totalitarianism for the sake of capitalism). The film shows why such a distinction might have been necessary to avoid confusion.

While films like *Red Dawn* were not particularly successful at the box office, they are shown repeatedly, for months on end, on cable television. In fact, this phenomenon points to the breakdown of the distinction between film and television as well as to the eventual erosion of the importance of box-office figures in the determination of the potential effects of films. Since blockbusters must be kept off the market in order to maintain their scarcity and value, lesser films arguably acquire a greater ability to influence audiences by virtue of saturation showing on TV.

In the late seventies and early eighties, the "world communist conspiracy" becomes associated with "terrorism," the use of non-state-sanctioned violence to gain political ends. Conservative fantasists like Claire Sterling made careers out of tracing all violent opposition to U. S. interests back to an "international terrorist network" emanating from Moscow. Numerous Hollywood films transcode this discourse, from Stallone's *Nighthawks* (1981) to *The Final Option* (1983), which suggests the peace movement is communist-inspired, and Chuck Norris's *Invasion U.S.A.* (1985), in which terrorists invade the United States. Norris and Stallone were also involved in promoting fantasies of veterans who return to Vietnam to free American POWs—*Missing in Action* (*I and II*) and *Rambo*.

In *Rambo* (1985), a veteran, who is depicted mythically as a super-killer, is enlisted to rescue missing POWs in Vietnam. He succeeds through heroic effort and a display of primitive violence that kills off numerous Russians and Vietnamese. The film satisfies several contemporary conservative prejudices. Asian communists are portrayed as subhuman. The film rewrites history in a way that excuses American atrocities against the Vietnamese. And it portrays Americans, not the Vietnamese, as the ones fighting for liberation. The overall significance of the film seems to be to try to make certain that the Vietnam War would be won in Nicaragua. It is less about an event than an attitude. The theme of betrayal that characterized the conservative attitude toward the liberal critics of the war (Reagan's remark that the army did not lose the war but was prevented from winning it)—and that is also reminiscent of post–World War I German attitudes that aided the rise of Nazism—appears in the way Rambo is misled by a Washington bureaucrat who wants him to fail in his mission so that the book can be closed on Vietnam. Yet we suggest that a film of this sort needs to be read as a symptom of victimization. A paragon of inarticulate meatheadedness, the figure of Rambo is also indicative of the way many American working-class youths are undereducated and offered the military as the only way of affirming themselves. Denied self-esteem through creative work for their own self-enhancement, they seek surrogate worth in metaphoric substitutes like militarism and nationalism. Rambo's neurotic resentment is less his own fault than that of those who run the social system, assuring an unequal distribution of cultural and intellectual capital.

We read the new militarist phenomenon as being both a psychological problem of patriarchal society and a problem of a threatened and defensive capitalism. Reagan's "hard line on defense," his stubborn hewing to a stern, punitive, and intolerant attitude toward the world, is symptomatic of patriarchal pathology, as much a matter of socialization as of social organization. Rambo is important, because it displays the roots of that pathology. The male need to feel singular, to separate out from dependence on initial caretakers, is metaphorized in Rambo's mythic isolation. Because the social world is necessarily interdependent, such isolation is necessarily aggressive. Aggression separates, whereas affection binds and makes one dependent. The isolated male is therefore without affectionate ties. Freedom of action is his norm; it requires the repudiation of anyone who threatens his space or his sense of singular importance, from the communists to the federal bureaucrats—both enemies in the film. War is, as we have argued, in part a matter of representation, images that people identify with and internalize which mobilize action. Loss in war can in consequence be experienced as self-diminution, damage done to internal representations that have become inseparable from the self. Given the prevailing socialization patterns, such loss draws out male dependence and vulnerability, male "femininization." It is the rejection of this possibility, of its intolerable shame, that results in the sorts of hypertropic representations of violence in *Rambo*.

Yet within this problem lurk the rudiments of a solution. For the need for a confirmation of manhood signals a broader need for a feeling of self-worth of a sort that can only be provided by others. It depends on others' affection, just as all singularizing metaphors depend on contextualizing metonyms. To a certain extent, Rambo's violence is simply an expression of such a need. Such a radical compensation for lost self-esteem is in some respects a demand for a return of the other's recognition. If we call such needs "socialist" it is because the ideals of socialism are communal support, mutual help, and shared dependence. Even the male militarist's pathos articulates needs for such social structures. Even as he rejects dependence as shame, he affirms its necessity as the need for self-worth. And such unrecognized dependencies and unrealized desires cannot be recognized or realized in a patriarchal and capitalist social context. Indeed, this film is a testament to that reality.

One major consequence of this argument is that it is not only male sexualization that is at stake in militarism. Women, as they are socialized to be passive, to need strong men in order to survive, are complicit in the socialization process of men for war. This was made particularly clear to us at a viewing of *Rambo*. Women in the theater were especially loud in their demands for blood and vengeance. We were reminded of the housewives of Santiago de Chile who beat their pots at night to help bring down the leftist government. The sort of male self-display evident in *Rambo* requires an adulatory other in conservative women whose applause validates male violence. Thus, a reconstruction of male psychology is inseparable from a broader reconstruction of the patriarchal socialization system that produces both sexes.

The new militarism did not go uncontested. Films like *War Games, Wrong Is Right, The Dogs of War, Blue Thunder, Full Metal Jacket,* and *Platoon* opposed certain forms of militarism in the eighties. And several films like *Testament* and *Countdown to Looking Glass* during the same period criticized nuclear war policy. This cultural mobilization, in conjunction with public protests, had an effect. Reagan moved from statements regarding the feasibility of limited nuclear wars in the early years of his tenure to a defensive and somewhat disingenuous call for the avoidance of all nuclear war in his later years. Comedies also contributed to the continuing liberal critique, especially such Chevy Chase vehicles as *Deal of the Century,* a satire of the arms industry, and *Spies Like Us,* a satire of Reagan's "Star Wars" program (the "Strategic Defense Initiative") and of the militarist-Americanist mentality in general. In *Spies,* two trickster figures (played by Chase and Dan Ackroyd) overturn the military's plan to initiate a nuclear attack by the Soviet Union in order to use a new space defense system. The system fails, and one character remarks: "Such a short time to destroy a world." In the film's carnivalesque vision, military authority figures are little worthy of respect, and the irrationality of conservative nostrums ("To guarantee the American way of life, I'm willing to take that risk" [of nuclear destruction]) is underscored. What is noteworthy in this and other antimilitarist films is the attempt to depict alternative social attitudes (toward gays or sexuality, for example) that are necessary correlates of a post-repressive, post-militarist social construction. What the comedies underscore is the importance of irony and humor to such a process, since so many of the militarist films are distinguished by high levels of self-seriousness and an inability to engage in the plunge into indeterminacy that the carnivalesque inversion of hierarchy entails.

What all of this points to is that if militarism is a public projection of private or personal human relations and attitudes, then its reconstruction is something more than a matter of foreign policy. Liberal antimilitarist films like *War Games, 2010, Testament,* or *Platoon* frequently contain images of nonauthoritarian, nonexploitative, equal relations between people. Many conservative films offer just the opposite sorts of relations, and the positive relations are frequently oiled with sentimentalism, a form of alienated positive affect that often accompanies an equally alienated aggressivity that takes authoritarian and militarist forms. What this suggests is that one necessary route to a world free from militarism is a reconstruction of the alienated and skewed affective structures feeding the distrust and enmity that operate behind militarism. Militarism is a collective neurosis, not just a foreign policy alternative. The micrological or interpersonal dimension of human existence, therefore, is not apolitical, nor is it entirely distinct from the macrological dimension of political interaction. A different nonantagonistic structure of international relations, one purged of genocidal impulses, would be predicated in part on a different psychology and a different social construction of interpersonal affection and aggression.

The Return of the Hollywood Studio System

Thomas Schatz

Like death and taxes, the Hollywood studios seem to be forever with us. Paramount and Warner Bros. and the other entertainment behemoths who ruled Hollywood in its golden age of the 1930s and '40s now utterly dominate the so-called New Hollywood as well. These are scarcely the studios of old, however, given the structure and scope of the contemporary media marketplace and the changing form and function of the movies themselves. During Hollywood's classical era, the studios were geared to produce a singular commodity, the feature film, and to control a single culture industry. The New Hollywood studios, conversely, operate with an increasingly diversified, globalized "entertainment industry," and represent only one component of the vast media conglomerates which own them—media giants like Viacom, Sony, News Corp., and Time Warner. And while the driving force in the global entertainment industry is the motion picture, here, too, there are crucial differences from the classical era.

Over the past two decades—an unprecedented period of sustained financial success for the film industry—the studios have been geared to produce not simply films but "franchises," blockbuster-scale hits which can be systematically reproduced in a range of media forms. The ideal movie today is not only a box-office smash but a two-hour promotion for a multimedia product line, designed with the structure of both the parent company and the diversified media marketplace in mind. From

Jaws to *Jurassic Park,* the New Hollywood has been driven (and shaped) by multipurpose entertainment machines which breed movie sequels and TV series, music videos and sound track albums, video games and theme park rides, graphic novels and comic books, and an endless array of licensed tie-ins and brand-name consumer products.

By way of brief example, consider *Jurassic Park,* the 1993 "summer blockbuster," which typifies the New Hollywood media franchise. The movie itself was a high-cost, effects-laden thriller and, of course, a monstrous hit. Created by Steven Spielberg and released by MCA-Universal, *Jurassic Park* cost $56 million to produce, with another $20 million spent on marketing (prints and advertising). It grossed a record $50.2 million in its opening weekend, reached $100 million in only nine days, and eventually grossed over $350 million in its domestic (United States and Canada) theatrical release. Its overseas box-office performance was even stronger, and together with its huge success on video cassette, pay-cable, and other ancillary markets, pushed the film's total revenues to well over a billion dollars.[1]

Jurassic Park, as an actual movie (in whatever delivery mode), represents only one facet of the franchise. According to an MCA merchandising executive, the film generated "the most comprehensive licensing program ever, both in terms of the volume of licenses and the huge number of promotional partners." The number of licensed product lines was approaching one thousand in the first year of release, and revenues from product tie-ins were expected to exceed the film's domestic box office. Among the more significant merchandising ventures in the United States was the Sega video-game version. MCA licensed the title and story line for *Jurassic Park* (adapted from Michael Crichton 's best-seller) to a number of game manufacturers, and the most successful was the Sega version. Released in the United States on the same day as the movie, the Sega game also raced to record revenues, due largely to the fact that the player had the option of being a rampaging dinosaur rather than a fleeing human.[2]

Another record-setting reiteration was "Jurassic Park—The Ride," which opened in the summer of 1996 at Universal Studios Hollywood (the "studio tour" which has been redesigned as a theme park). The ride boosted attendance some 40 percent over the previous year, and it was touted as the primary reason for a general upswing in southern California tourism. On July 5, 1996, Universal set a one-day attendance record of forty-three thousand, which, at $30 per ticket, totals $1.3 million. Park-goers also can enjoy rides "based on" other films such as *King Kong, Back to the Future,* and *ET,* with the latter the most popular until the *Jurassic Park* spin-off. Spielberg designed the *ET*-inspired ride (as well as the *Jurassic Park* ride) at a cost of $110 million, some three times the cost of the original film. It debuted in 1991, a full decade after the release of the film, but in the midst of the theme-park frenzy which has steadily escalated since the mid-1980s.[3] Spielberg currently is working on the summer 1997 sequel to *Jurassic Park,* with the film and theme-park ride being designed and engineered simultaneously.[4]

As even these few examples indicate, "*Jurassic Park*, the franchise" comprises a profitable product line and a cultural commodity whose form directly reflects the structure of the media industry at large. It indicates, too, that the industry can scarcely be treated in terms of movies and video games and theme-park rides as separate entities or isolated media texts. Rather, they are related aspects or "iterations" of entertainment supertexts, multimedia narrative forms which can be expanded and exploited almost ad infinitum, given the size and diversity of today's globalized, diversified entertainment industry.

The essential UR-text within these media franchises is the Hollywood-produced blockbuster film and, thus, the key holding for today's media conglomerates is a film studio. Indeed, for Time Warner, and Disney, and the other media conglomerates, the studio's output tends to set the agenda for the entire company—which is scarcely surprising, given the enormous payoff of a successful franchise. And as the global entertainment industry has reached a certain equilibrium over the past decade, the production and calculated reformulation of these blockbuster films into multimedia franchises has become more systematic. In the process, the Hollywood "studio system" has been reformulated as well—albeit along very different lines from the system of old.

THE STUDIO SYSTEM IN THE "OLD" HOLLYWOOD

The New Hollywood studio system is both an outgrowth of and a distinct departure from the system which emerged during the classical era. From the 1920s through the 1940s, the "studio system" referred to the factory-based mode of film production, and also, crucially, to the "vertical integration" of production with film distribution and exhibition. The Big Five "integrated major" studios—MGM, Warner Bros., 20th Century-Fox, Paramount, and RKO—ruled the industry not only because they produced top films, but because they collectively (and collusively) controlled the movie marketplace as well. The Big Five distributed their own films and ran their own theater chains. And while they owned only about one-sixth of the nation's movie theaters in the 1930s and '40s, this included most of the all-important "first-run" theaters—i.e., the downtown theater palaces that screened only top features, seated thousands of patrons, and generated well over half the total industry revenues.[5]

The major studios could not produce enough films to satisfy audience demand in an era when up to one hundred million persons per week went to the movies. Thus their output was supplemented by Universal, Columbia, and United Artists (UA), the "major minor" studios—major because they turned out A-class movies with top contract talent and had their own distribution arms; minor because they did not own their own theaters. The 1930s also saw the emergence of number of "minor" or "poverty row" studios like Monogram and Republic, which produced low-budget B-movies. These studios were outside the Hollywood power structure and only incidental to the studio system, since they did not produce A-class features and did not distribute their own films.

Vertical integration took hold during the 1920s and became standard operating procedure during the Depression and World War II, two national crises which led the government to sanction (or at least tolerate) the studios' monopolistic control of the film industry. This ensured the revenue flow and financial leverage for the studios to maintain their factory operations; it also enabled them to maintain a contract system, which kept crucial filmmaking talent at all levels, from top stars to stagehands, directly tied to the company.

In terms of movie product, the mainstay of the studio system was the A-class feature film, invariably a formulaic "star vehicle" with solid production values and a virtually guaranteed market. The studios turned out occasional big-budget "prestige" pictures, and they also cranked out a steady supply of low-cost formula quickies; in fact B-movies comprised up to half the total output of major studios like Fox and Warners in the 1930s. But the key commodity in classical Hollywood was the routine star-genre formulation—an MGM costume romance with Greta Garbo, a Warners' gangster saga with James Cagney or Edward G. Robinson, a Fox swashbuckler with Tyrone Power, and so on. Each studio's stable of contract stars were product lines unto themselves and, thus, the basis for each company's distinctive "house style." These trademark star-genre formulas gave each studio a means of stabilizing marketing and sales, of bringing efficiency and economy to top feature production, and of distinguishing the company's output from its competitors'.

Studio management in that vertically integrated system was a classic top-down affair, with the power emanating from the sales (i.e., distribution and exhibition) "end" of the business, centered in the home office in New York. Power passed from the top executives in New York to the "front office" of the studio on the West Coast. And while the New York office controlled the direction of capital (sales, marketing, budgeting, etc.), the studio executives, a continent away, oversaw production and thus controlled actual filmmaking. Indeed, it was not the so-called moguls or corporate CEO's in New York but these studio executives—men like Irving Thalberg, Darryl Zanuck, and David Selznick—who were the chief architects of Hollywood's golden age.

The Hollywood studio system flourished during World War II but then collapsed rather abruptly due to various factors, and three in particular. First and foremost was the Supreme Court's 1948 Paramount decree, an antitrust ruling which effectively disintegrated the studio system by forcing the studios to sell their theater chains. Second, was the emergence of television, which quickly transformed the American media landscape. The third factor involved wholesale changes in American lifestyles after the war—most notably via suburban migration and the so-called baby boom. With millions of returning servicemen marrying and starting families in the suburbs, "watching TV" soon replaced "going to the movies" as the nation's dominant form of habituated, mass-mediated narrative entertainment.

Although the Hollywood studios saw their audience fade and their revenues plummet in the 1950s, they managed to survive by radically changing the way they operated. In the process, they changed the very nature and structure of the movie industry. The studios recognized that without their theater chains, they lacked the cash flow to sustain their factory system and their contract talent. Thus they turned from production and exhibition to financing and distribution. The strategy here was to lease their studio facilities to the growing ranks of independent producers, and to provide a portion of a film's financing in return for the distribution rights. The studios also began cultivating a blockbuster mentality, realizing that releasing fewer, "bigger" films (many of them in wide-screen and Technicolor) was not only more practical and profitable in the 1950s movie marketplace, but also was an effective means of competing with TV.[6]

By the mid-1950s, this strategy clearly was paying off, with films like *The Ten Commandments* and *Around the World in 80 Days* redefining the profit potential and event status of Hollywood movies. At that point the studio powers decided to throw in with the television industry by selling or leasing their old films to TV syndicators, and also by producing "telefilm" series. Warners was the most aggressive in its television pursuits, and by 1961 was supplying over one-third of ABC's prime-time schedule. By then Hollywood was turning out far more hours of TV programming than feature films, having reactivated their B-movie production process to feed TV's voracious appetite for programming. In 1960, the networks started running feature films in prime time, and soon movies were on every evening of the week. Thus what once were studio "vaults" of virtually useless old movies were now "libraries" whose value increased with each passing year.[7]

Despite their growing rapport with the TV industry, however, the studios were seriously foundering in the late 1960s due to several key factors. One was the continued erosion of movie attendance, which had fallen to barely twenty million moviegoers per week (down from nearly one hundred million in the mid-1940s). Another factor was the nature and composition of that audience, i.e., the politically hip, disaffected youth who clearly preferred films like *Bonnie and Clyde* (1967), *Easy Rider* (1969), and *M*A*S*H* (1970) to the blockbusters that the studios were trying to sell. A third factor was a succession of big-budget flops, most of which were lavish musicals designed to replicate the huge success of *The Sound of Music* (1966). A fourth factor was the unprecedented surge in film imports which, by the late 1960s, represented almost two-thirds of the total U.S. releases.

The deepening movie industry recession left the studios ripe for takeover in the late 1960s, and in fact many were bought by large conglomerates—Warners by Kinney Corporation, Paramount by Gulf and Western, UA by Transamerica, and MGM by financier Kirk Kerkorian. At that point, the studios were valued more for their film libraries and TV series productions than for their filmmaking operations, and many observers felt that the studios—and the movie industry at large—were on the brink of complete collapse.

INTO THE NEW HOLLYWOOD

Reports of Hollywood's death were greatly exaggerated, however, and in the early 1970s, the industry began to rebound with films like *The Godfather, American Graffiti, The Sting,* and *The Exorcist.* The real breakthrough came in 1975, spurred by a single film, *Jaws,* which both revived and redefined Hollywood's blockbuster tradition. *Jaws* was "pre-sold" via Peter Benchley's best-selling novel and "packaged" by a talent agency, ICM, which represented Benchley as well as the top talent involved in the movie, including director Steven Spielberg, who was among a new generation of film-makers (Francis Ford Coppola, George Lucas, et al.) who appealed not only to the hip, cine-literate, film-school generation, but to mainstream moviegoers as well. The film itself was a deft melding of genres—horrific revenge-of-nature film, supernatural thriller, slasher film, disaster film, buddy film, action-adventure thriller. And most fundamentally, *Jaws* was a chase film whose story was utterly conducive to Spielberg's visual technique, John Williams' pulsating score, and the wizardry of special effects experts.[8]

Jaws was targeted for a summer release (due mainly to the subject matter) in an era when most important films came out during the Christmas holidays. The producers mounted an unprecedented marketing campaign built around a massive network TV-ad blitz in the weeks before *Jaws'* nationwide release in over four hundred theaters. This "saturation" marketing campaign, although risky, proved eminently successful, creating the prototype for the "summer blockbuster." *Jaws* attracted thirty-eight million moviegoers in its first month of release enroute to a record box-office performance—the first movie ever to gross over $200 million and to return over $100 million in rentals to its distributor, Universal. The film also generated myriad commercial tie-ins, from toys and video games to sequels and soundtrack albums. Thus *Jaws* represented a movie franchise and product line very different from the star-genre formulas of the Old Hollywood; it was a veritable genre unto itself whose story could be reiterated in any number of media forms.

Opportunities for reiteration were about to increase due to enormous changes in media technology—changes crucial to the emergence of the New Hollywood which just happened to coincide with *Jaws'* release. The most important of these involved the emergence of the pay-cable and home video industries. In August 1975, an unknown cable outfit, HBO, became a nationwide cable movie channel via the launch of SATCOM I (the first geostationary commercial satellite). And, in October 1975, Sony introduced its Betamax video cassette recorder (VCR), thus launching the home-video industry. Other important developments in the mid-to-late 1970s included the explosive growth of the mall-based multiplex theater and the concurrent emergence of a new generation of moviegoer—younger and more conservative than the "youth market" of only a few years earlier, with a penchant for repeated viewings of their favorite films. Equally important was the rapid rise of two talent agencies created in the mid-70s, ICM and CAA, which specialized in packaging New Hollywood media franchises and which, along with the venerable William Morris Agency, grew even more powerful than the movie studios. The late 1970s also saw an upswing in defensive market tactics, notably an increase in sequels, series, reissues, and remakes.[9]

During the late 1970s, Hollywood's economic recovery was well under-way, fueled by its revitalized blockbuster mentality. Total domestic grosses, which had reached $2 billion for the first time in 1975, surged 40 percent in only three years, with hits like *Rocky* (1976), *Star Wars, Close Encounters, Saturday Night Fever* (1977), *Grease* and *Superman* (1978) all doing record business.[10] While *Star Wars* was the top hit of the period, doing $127 million in rentals in 1977, and another $38 million as a reissue in 1978, *Saturday Night Fever* was a breakthrough as well, signaling the erosion of various industry barriers and the multimedia potential of movie hits, with its TV sitcom star (John Travolta), best-selling Bee Gees sound track, and "music movie" dynamic which helped spur both the "disco craze" of the late 1970s and the music video industry of the early 1980s.

In terms of both narrative structure and marketing, however, *Star Wars* was the ultimate New Hollywood commodity—a high-speed, hip-ironic, male action-adventure yarn whose central characters are essentially plot functions, with the plot itself eminently adaptable to ancillary media forms. The Lucas-designed "space epic" surpassed *Jaws* as Hollywood's all-time box-office hit, while securing the future for adolescent, by-the-numbers, male-action films. Indeed, from *Jaws* to *Star Wars* and onward into the 1980s, Hollywood's dominant products would become increasingly plot driven, increasingly visceral, kinetic, and fast-paced, increasingly "fantastic" and reliant on special effects, and increasingly targeted at younger audiences.

In an effort to broaden their appeal, however, these films also were strate-gically "open" to other formal and narrative possibilities. An important aspect of films like *Star Wars, Raiders of the Lost Ark, E.T.,* and their myriad successors, was the radical amalgamation of genre conventions and the elab-orate play of cinematic references. *Star Wars,* as J. Hoberman writes, "pio-neered the genre pastiche," and indeed the film's hell-bent narrative does career from one genre-coded episode to another—from western to war film to vine-swinging adventure. This was reinforced by its nostalgic quality and evocations of old movie serials and TV series—references undoubtedly lost on younger viewers but relished by their cine-literate elders.[11]

Spielberg and Lucas were charter members of what Hoberman termed "Hollywood's delayed New Wave" whose "cult blockbusters" had elevated "the most vital and disreputable genres of their youth . . . to cosmic heights." The two joined forces on *Raiders of the Lost Ark* (1981), establishing the billion-dollar Indiana Jones franchise. Whether working together or on their own projects, Lucas and Spielberg rewrote the box-office record books in the late 1970s and 1980s. With the release of their third Indiana Jones collaboration in 1989, the two could claim eight of the ten biggest hits in movie history, all of them surpassing $100 million in rentals. The auteur-entrepreneurs were, without question, the prime movers behind what *Variety's* A.D. Murphy termed "the modern era of super-blockbuster films."[12]

The blockbuster films (and media franchises) of the late 1970s and the 1980s spurred not only the economic recovery of the movie industry but the emergence of the global, diversified entertainment industry as well. While Hollywood's domestic box-office revenues climbed at a steady pace (from $3 billion to over $5 billion in the course of the 1980s), its "ancillary" or "secondary" markets simply exploded. The principal growth areas throughout the 1980s were in home video and pay-cable, with the overseas markets (both theatrical and video) taking off later in the decade. During the 1990s, all of these markets have continued to grow at record levels, with the secondary markets steadily overwhelming Hollywood's once-sacrosanct domestic theatrical market. In the early 1980s, the domestic box office generated well over 50 percent of the studios' movie-related income; it now accounts for less than 15 percent By 1995, foreign theatrical revenues surpassed Hollywood's domestic theatrical income, while the domestic home-video market generated over twice the revenues of the U.S. theatrical market.[13]

Thus the so-called ancillary markets, some of which were nonexistent in the early 1980s, now generate far more revenues for the studios than the domestic box office. But because all of these secondary markets are driven primarily by the Hollywood-produced blockbuster, the domestic theatrical market remains Hollywood's prime venue and primary focus. It is a movie's U.S. theatrical release—and, crucially, the accompanying marketing campaign—which serves as the "launch site" for its franchise development, establishing its value in all other media markets.[14]

MEDIA CONGLOMERATION IN THE NEW HOLLYWOOD

As it became evident that the Hollywood-produced blockbuster was the key commodity in an expanding global media marketplace, the status and value of the movie studios steadily grew. The result was a merger-and-acquisitions wave which began during the 1980s, with the movie studio as the central component in a new generation of media conglomerates. Beyond ownership of a major film studio, the basic requirements of these new media giants were deep pockets and "tight diversification." A media company today needs the financial muscle to have a reasonable chance to produce a blockbuster hit, and also the marketing muscle to make the most of a hit when it occurs. Equally important, especially in expanding a bit film into a full-scale franchise, is tight diversification or "synergy"—i.e., bringing the studio into direct play with other media production entities and distribution outlets: TV series and video producers; broadcast networks and cable systems; music and recording companies; book, magazine, and newspaper publishers; video game and toy companies; theme parks and resorts; and electronics hardware manufacturers.[15]

Thus, the media conglomerates in the New Hollywood differ considerably from the studios of old and also from their more recent predecessors. In the Old Hollywood, the studios were all variations on the same corporate model; the parent company was primarily a theater chain, with its distribution system and movie factory as essential components. The parent companies of the 1960s and '70s, conversely, had little or nothing in common with one another or with their movie studios. Gulf & Western, Kinney Services, Transamerica, et al., had deep enough pockets, but they were too top-heavy and widely diversified to effectively exploit their media holdings. During the 1980s, those companies either sold off their media interests or "downsized" to achieve tighter diversification. Gulf & Western, for instance, siphoned off all but its media holdings in the course of the decade and, in 1989, changed its corporate name to Paramount Communications. Kinney created a media subsidiary in Warner Communications, which also downsized during the early 1980s, then steadily expanded until its epochal 1989 merger with Time Inc. Twentieth Century-Fox was bought (in 1985) by News Corp., thus becoming part of Rupert Murdoch's global media empire.

Other studios underwent less successful merger-acquisition alliances in the 1980s. UA collapsed in 1980 after a series of big-budget flops (most notably *Heaven's Gate*), and in 1981 merged with MGM. The once-glorious

Metro-Goldwyn-Mayer was foundering itself at the time; in fact, it had ceased distribution altogether for much of the 1970s. In 1986, MGM sold off its film library to TBS (Turner Broadcasting System), and in 1989, was purchased—and essentially saved from bankruptcy—by the French company, Pathe Communications. Meanwhile Columbia Pictures, in the wake of its failed efforts to create an alliance with CBS and HBO in the early 1980s, was acquired by Coca-Cola in 1982 (the same year Columbia created its TriStar Pictures subsidiary). Coke and Columbia simply did not "fit," however, and in 1989, the studio was purchased, along with the highly successful CBS Records, by the Japanese media giant, Sony. The "hardware-software" alliance between Sony and Columbia, which was duplicated in 1990 when Matsushita acquired Universal-MCA, took synergy into another direction altogether.

The numerous media mergers and acquisitions in 1989 marked not only the end of the decade but a watershed of sorts for the Hollywood film industry. While the 1980s brought sustained economic recovery to the industry, it was also a period of considerable "churn" and uncertainty. Synergy was continually debated and redefined, affected by new technologies and new delivery systems, by an expanding and increasingly diversified media marketplace, by media deregulation, and by myriad other factors. But the principal of tight diversification steadily took hold, fueled by the output of blockbuster-scale hits and the cultivation of media franchises, and culminating in the veritable tidal wave of mergers and acquisitions in 1989—the biggest year ever for media-related deals. A total of 414 media deals were struck in 1989, worth over $42 billion, the most notable of which were the Time Warner merger ($14 billion) and Sony's buyout of Columbia and CBS Records ($5.4 billion).[16]

The wave subsided but then surged again in the mid-1990s, with 1995 setting yet another record with 644 media mergers totaling an astounding $70.8 billion. This included Viacom's buyout of Paramount in 1994 and Blockbuster Video in 1995 (for a total of $15.8 billion). Other 1995 transactions included Disney's purchase of Cap Cities/ABC ($19 billion), Time Warner's buyout of Turner Broadcasting ($7.3 billion), and Seagram's purchase of MCA/Universal ($5.7 billion). Also of note in 1995 was the Westinghouse buyout of CBS ($12.6 billion), as well as the creation of the DreamWorks SKG "studio" by Steven Spielberg, Jeffrey Katzenberg, and David Geffen.[17]

The merger wave undoubtedly will continue—an alliance between Westinghouse and a film studio seems all but inevitable, for instance—and the logic of tight diversification will continue to be refined in response to new technologies, new entertainment forms, changing consumer behavior, and an expanding global marketplace. But whatever their power and reach, the new media conglomerates can scarcely predict, let alone control, the vagaries of consumer behavior and the uncertainties of the media marketplace. And whatever the advantages of their size, in terms of economies of scale and maximization of profit on successful media ventures, these companies invariably face daunting problems coordinating their far-flung operations, integrating their disparate management cultures into a cohesive business strategy, and dealing with the shifting relations of power within and between their various units.

Despite the uncertainties and confusion, however, these new media conglomerates are enjoying record revenues and increasing hegemony over an expanding media marketplace. Indeed, just as the Big Five major film studios and the three TV networks once controlled their respective media industries, these conglomerates are now establishing their oligopoly power within the global entertainment arena. Disney, Time Warner, Viacom, News Corp., Sony, and Seagram's are among the most powerful media and entertainment companies in the world, and their success clearly is the result of tight diversification centering on the output of their film studios.[18] Indeed, the status of the film studio for these media giants is emphatically underscored by the current obsession with "branding"—i.e., the relentless marketing of the studio's name, its corporate logo, and its trademark stars and media figures. And increasingly, the studio's filmed entertainment division tends to set the agenda for the entire corporation, including the parent conglomerate.

With the studios' collective return to power, and especially since the 1989 merger wave, the Hollywood studio system itself has undergone a steady, seemingly inexorable, rebirth. Simply stated, the 1990s has witnessed the regeneration of the studio system, albeit reconfigured to the economic and industrial contours of the New Hollywood. Rather than a return to the system of old, in other words, this rebirth has involved a seismic paradigm shift.

Disney, Warners, and the New Hollywood Studio System

The most successful and powerful of the studios over the past decade and the defining entities in the revitalized studio system have been Disney and

Warner Bros. The two have utterly dominated the motion picture industry, finishing first and second at the box office every year since 1991 while sharing 35 to 40 percent of the market. Meanwhile their parent companies (The Walt Disney Company and Time Warner, Inc.) have become the two leading global media powers in terms of revenues and volume of business.[19] In fact, the recent Disney merger with Cap Cities/ABC and the Time Warner merger with Turner (both of which were initiated in 1995, withstood various legal challenges, and were approved by the FCC in 1996) put the two in a class by themselves among media conglomerates.

The emergence of Warner Bros. and Disney as a veritable media duopoly has been propelled by the strategic expansion of their parent companies over the past decade. In both cases, this "upsizing" has been keyed, on the one hand, to the film studio and its signature franchises, and on the other, to the rapid changes in the global entertainment industry. The two parent companies are models of tight diversification as well, in terms of both vertical and horizontal integration. Warner and Disney have integrated vertically by complementing film production with distribution-exhibition "pipelines" to consumers. And they have integrated horizontally by developing an array of entertainment subsidiaries, from music to print media to theme parks, to augment their studio output and, when appropriate, to better exploit their franchise operations.

Interestingly enough, the recent Disney-ABC and Time Warner-Turner mergers have brought the two companies into fairly close alignment structurally, even though the earlier expansion process for each company has been quite different. Disney, until 1995, expanded primarily from within, either by upsizing an established division (adding theme parks in Tokyo and Paris, for instance, or expanding film production via Touchstone and Hollywood Pictures), or else by developing a new venture on its own (most notably its chain of retail stores). The 1993 purchase of Miramax for the relatively modest sum of $65 million indicated Disney's willingness to go the merger acquisition route, but no one in the industry was expecting the mammoth ABC deal.[20] The $19 billion purchase of Cap Cities/ABC was a necessary move, however, because it gave Disney key components it simply could not cultivate from within. Chief among these were broadcast and cable outlets, including the ABC network with its 225 affiliates and eight "O&O's" (owned-and-operated stations), a nationwide radio network (with twenty-one stations), as well as the ESPN, A&E, and Lifetime cable networks. ABC also had developed video and cable interests overseas, with coproduction deals and programming alliances in England, Germany, France, Japan, and elsewhere.[21]

While the primary benefits of the merger involved vertical integration, it also enhanced Disney's horizontal expansion, especially in terms of Cap Cities' magazine and newspaper publishing divisions. Thus the makeup of the newly merged Disney-ABC empire, as indicated by the proportionate revenues its divisions, was as follows.[22]

broadcasting, cable	32%
filmed entertainment	29
theme parks, resorts	21
consumer products	11
publishing	7

Whereas Disney grew mainly from within until its epochal ABC merger, Warners' development throughout the 1980s and '90s simply extended a long history of mergers and acquisitions. Warner Communications had entered the 1980s, in fact, in the throes of an ill-fated, high-stakes alliance with the video game and home computer giant, Atari. Warner soon abandoned these pursuits, while it enjoyed more effective acquisitions with Geffen Records and with Lorimar, the telefilm producer. At the point of its 1989 merger with Time, Warner was on a remarkable roll. The studio was number one in film rentals, thanks largely to *Batman,* and had been among the top three for seven straight years. The Warner-Lorimar telefilm arm had eighteen series on prime-time TV. Warner Bros. International and Warner Home Video were enjoying steady growth, and the Warner Music Group boasted the world's largest and most profitable music recording, publishing, and distribution setup.[23]

The Time Warner alliance created a remarkably well-balanced media conglomerate, with the proportionate revenues of its main divisions as follows:

magazines	24%
filmed entertainment	17
cable television	15.5
music recording, publishing	15
programming (HBO)	15
books	13.5

But while it was envisioned as an ideal merging of publishing and entertainment, the greatest benefits came via the vertical integration of Warners' media production and Time's video and cable interests—i.e., HBO and Cinemax, a stake in TBS, and the ATC cable system with its 4.4 million subscribers.[24]

Time Warner steadily expanded during the 1990s, most notably via its half-stake in the Six Flags theme parks and its buyout of Turner's TBS. The 1995 TBS deal was crucial on several counts: First, the cable and broadcast networks (CNN, TNT, superstation TBS, et al.) gave Time Warner a guaranteed outlet for its media products. Second, the addition of several "smaller" film studios (Castle Rock, New Line, Fine Line) would augment Warner Bros.' mainstream films with more specialized fare. Third, TBS' massive film and TV series holdings gave Time Warner the largest library in existence—including movie holdings of over 3,500 titles. And fourth, the Time Warner news division now enjoyed both cable and print components. The TBS deal also gave Time Warner several Atlanta-based pro sports franchises, although the value of these holdings to Time Warner remains to be seen.[25]

After the merger, Time Warner began operating with three primary divisions: entertainment, news, and telecommunications. The longtime studio management team of Robert Daly and Terry Semel ruled the entertainment division and functioned as seconds-in-command to CEO and Chairman Gerald Levin. They enjoyed more authority, in fact, than even Ted Turner, who as vice-chairman and majority stockholder (with 11 percent of the voting stock) was the closest thing to an "owner" and "mogul" at Time Warner, and who had a history of hands-on management at TBS.[26]

The Daly-Semel situation at Time Warner points up two crucial aspects of the resurgent studio system, both of which were evident at Disney as well. The first was the centrality of the movie studio and filmed entertainment division to the overall operation and market strategy of the company; the second was the importance of stable management to the studio's success. At both Time Warner and Disney, filmed entertainment has far out-paced the other divisions in terms of growth and performance, becoming the shaping force in the company's development. At Warner, revenues from filmed entertainment (including both movies and telefilm) grew from $1.2 billion in 1985 to $5 billion in 1995; after the merger with Time, film revenues grew from roughly one-sixth to over one-third of the company's total income by 1996.[27] The growth of Disney's filmed entertainment division was even more pronounced. In 1986, studio revenues were $512 million, only 20 percent of Disney's total. In the fiscal year prior to the 1995 Cap Cities merger, film studio revenues were $4.7 billion, nearly one-half of Disney's $10.06 billion total.[28]

This growth in filmed entertainment was orchestrated at both companies by a stable, capable management team—by Daly and Semel under CEO Steven Ross at Warners, and by Michael Eisner and Jeffrey Katzenberg under Frank Wells at Disney. Moreover, these studio executives were able to operate with little interference from a hands-on owner-mogul (like Rupert Murdoch of News Corp. or Sumner Redstone of Viacom). *Variety* editor Peter Bart, an astute analyst and former studio executive, has noted the "Napoleonic" complex displayed by the new breed of media mogul—a key factor in the heavy turnover of studio management executives at Fox, Paramount, and elsewhere.[29]

Daly and Semel, who have run Warner Bros. since the late 1970s, remain firmly ensconced at the studio despite the shakeups after Ross's death (and the ascent of Gerald Levin) in 1994, and the Turner deal in 1995. The role of Turner himself as vice-chairman of Time Warner remains uncertain, although he seems willing to maintain a hands-off rapport with the film studio and the entertainment division. The situation at Disney, meanwhile, is far more uncertain and, in fact, has been quite volatile since Wells' sudden, unexpected death (in a helicopter crash) in 1994. Eisner took over Wells' role as CEO but then balked at promoting Katzenberg—who promptly left to create Dreamworks SKG with Steven Spielberg and David Geffen. Meanwhile, Eisner hired Michael Ovitz, cofounder and CEO of Creative Artists Agency (CAA), as his second-in-command, and promoted Joe Roth to studio chief. Ovitz's move from CAA to Disney sent yet another signal of the changing power structure in Hollywood, as the control of film production shifted from the stars and talent agencies back to the studios. But Ovitz lasted only a year at Disney, leaving in late 1996 due to conflicts with Eisner, who began showing symptoms of a Napoleonic complex of his own atop the Disney-ABC empire.[30]

FRANCHISE FEVER: "THE WHOLE MACHINE OF THE COMPANY"

Regardless of who manages the major film studios, he or she necessarily will pursue the now-dominant franchise mentality—particularly at Disney and Warner Bros., whose enormous success in the 1990s has come via the blockbuster-scale film and the resultant media franchise. The trademark Disney franchise, of course, is the animated feature—although this was decidedly not the case when "Team Disney" (Wells, Eisenberg, Katzenberg, et al.) took over in the mid-1980s. At the time, Disney had not had an animated hit in decades, and the only one in active production was *The Black Cauldron,* its most expensive and ambitious cartoon feature since *Sleeping Beauty* in 1959. While the studio turned out a number of successful live-action films in 1986, notably *Down and Out in Beverly Hills, Ruthless People,* and *The Color of Money,* the prime objective of Team Disney, and particularly Jeffrey Katzenberg, was to reestablish the animated feature as Disney's signature product.[31]

Over the next few years, the animation unit was steadily expanded from 150 to over 700 employees and by 1988, there were clear indications that Katzenberg was turning things around: *Who Framed Roger Rabbit?,* a breakthrough amalgam of animation and live action; *The Fox and the Hound,* the first fully-animated feature under the new regime; and the successful reissue of *Bambi,* originally released in 1942.[32] Disney's first animated hit was *The Little Mermaid* in 1989, and from that point on Disney has enjoyed one blockbuster after another with both its new films and its reissues: *The Jungle Book* (reissue, 1990), *Beauty and the Beast* (1991), *Aladdin* (1992), *Snow White and the Seven Dwarfs* (reissue, 1993), *The Lion King* (1994), *Pocahontas* (1995), *Toy Story* (1995), and *The Hunchback of Notre Dame* (1996).

Without question, these animated features spurred the Disney surge. As *Variety* reported in 1993: "While filmed entertainment accounts for approximately 35 percent of Disney's total operating income, Chairman Michael Eisner readily acknowledges that the animation division drives the entire company—providing rides for theme parks, products for the merchandising division, even inspiration for the logo for Disney's new hockey team, the Mighty Ducks."[33] Disney closed out 1996 with yet another variation on its animation franchise strategy with a live-action version of its 1961 animated feature, *101 Dalmations*—a huge box-office hit which pushed the total number of Dalmation-related product lines to a staggering seventeen thousand.[34]

Warner Bros., meanwhile, specialized in the lone-hero, action-adventure formula—most notably Clint Eastwood and Mel Gibson vehicles, whose long association with the studio renders them the New Hollywood equivalent to the "contract stars" of old.[35] Both have been associated with familiar Warners series—Eastwood with the Dirty Harry films and Westerns, Gibson with the Lethal Weapon films—and have become veritable franchises unto themselves. These have been vital to Warner's success, but its signature franchise of the 1990s has been its *Batman* series. As Corey Brown noted in a recent *Premiere* profile: "Warners is the studio that *Batman* built. Not only did the $250 million grosser create the billion-dollar *Batman* industry, it inspired Semel and Daly to create the worldwide chain of Warner retail stores, as well as give a boost to the long-dormant animation division." In that article, Semel is quoted as saying, "The first picture that blew us out was *Batman*. . . . It was the first time we utilized the whole machine of the company. The marketing, the tie-ins, the merchandising, the international."[36]

The success of Time Warner's *Batman* franchise is virtually incalculable, given the range of related products generated since the 1989 series regeneration. Besides its performance as a film—$250 million domestic box office, $160 million overseas, $180 million in video cassette sales, etc.—*Batman* was "a milestone in entertainment licensing and merchandising," according to *Variety,* generating a reported half-billion dollars in worldwide merchandising. The sequel, *Batman Returns* (1992), was a solid box-office hit ($163 million domestic; $120 million foreign), but a severe disappointment in terms of merchandising. Its dismal commercial afterlife was attributed to several factors: the darkness of the story (and Tim Burton's direction), Michael Keaton's grimly heroic Batman, and the manic intensity of the film's antagonists (especially Danny Devito's "Penguin"). Warners decided to "lighten up" the next series installment, *Batman Forever* (1995), replacing Burton with director Joel Schumacher and Keaton with Val Kilmer, and centering the story—and the advertising campaign—on rising comic star Jim Carrey as the Riddler, a more upbeat, engaging nemesis.[37]

The *Batman* series redesign was an obvious success. *Batman Forever* grossed $185 million in the U.S. and another $150 million overseas, and was a merchandising bonanza. According to Dan Romanelli, head of Warners' consumer products division, *Batman Forever* has generated over one billion dollars in licensing and tie-ins. The *New York Times* reported in 1996 that Batman merchandise had earned over $4 billion.[38] This did not include the *Batman*-related theme-park rides, which represent yet another kind of tie-in. In May 1992, Six Flags (half-owned by Time Warner) introduced "Batman—The Ride" to coincide with the release of *Batman Returns,* and it introduced "Joker's Revenge" in the summer of 1996 to coincide with *Batman Forever.*[39]

The success of *Batman* in home video well indicates the importance of the movie library" in the age of the VCR. Here, too, Warner and Disney have dominated the field—albeit with markedly different strategies. While *Batman* set an industry standard as a "sell-through" (versus rental) videotape with just over ten million units sold, it was actually an exception for Warners, which has preferred rental over sell-through—thus maintaining the value of its own library rather than the "home libraries" of consumers. Disney pioneered the sell-through strategy, retailing its animated franchise hits on cassette via its Buena Vista Home Video arm, with both reissues and new titles breaking one sales record after another. In 1993, for instance, *Aladdin* sold 10.6 million copies in only its first three days, enroute to a record total of 24 million; and in 1994 the reissued *Snow White and the Seven Dwarfs* surpassed that total, generating over $300 million in borne-video revenues.[40]

Time Warner has continued to concentrate on its own library, with the TBS merger adding over 3,500 feature film titles to Warner Bros. holdings of some 1100 titles.[41] Among the films in its library, of course, are Warner Bros. vintage Looney Tunes shorts with Bugs Bunny, Daffy Duck, et al. These have enjoyed spectacular and surprising success in syndication, and their shelf life may render them the most valuable of Time Warner's franchises. According to Consumer Products Chief Romanelli, total revenues of merchandise related to Warner Bros.' Looney Tunes figures reached an astounding $3.5 billion in 1996.[42]

This underscores yet again the importance of merchandising and product licensing, which may be the single most significant current (and future) development in the New Hollywood. In 1994, worldwide retail sales of all licensed products surpassed $100 billion for the first time ever; roughly 70 percent of that business was done in the U.S. In 1995, sales of entertainment-related merchandise was an estimated $28 billion. Besides producing these enormous revenues, merchandising and product licensing benefit the media conglomerates in other important ways as well. They forge brand-name identity and awareness, with thousands of licensed products "branding" not only a particular film or franchise but the studio itself. Tie-ins can spur more rapid and efficient expansion into foreign markets, and also can lead to joint ventures with other high-visibility corporations, from fastfood giants to video game and toy manufacturers. Here, the financial as well as promotional benefits can be substantial. Burger King's record deal with Disney for *Toy Story* in 1995, for instance, was worth an estimated $45 million in ads and other promotions.[43]

Disney has long been the industry leader in the licensing and merchandising arena, and that success encouraged Eisner to develop another aspect the consumer products division—namely, the Disney-owned chain of retail stores. This move is scarcely surprising, considering both the economic and synergy-related benefits of the studios selling their own entertainment-related products. Disney initiated this effort in 1987, opening a retail store in Glendale, California. The store was an instant success, and by 1990, Disney had added over fifty retail outlets, thus openly competing with its licensees for what *Business Week* described as a $2 billion U.S. market for "Disney knickknacks."[44] Disney has continued to globally expand its retail chain at a remarkable rate—including one hundred new U.S. outlets in 1995 and a 30,000-square-foot flagship store in New York City in 1996.[45]

Warner Bros. has been the most aggressive among the other studios in following Disney's lead, and it, too, has enjoyed huge success in the retail arena. After creating a consumer products division in 1987, Warners launched its own retail chain in 1991. The total number of Warner Bros. stores surpassed 150 in 1996; and its New York flagship store (on Fifth Avenue) also underwent massive expansion to nine floors and 75,000 square feet. That expansion was demanded by the tremendous volume of business—an average of some twenty thousand shoppers per day—and by other factors as well, particularly the TBS deal which brought Hanna-Barbera Productions and its animated stars (Huckleberry Hound, The Flintstones, et al.) into the Time Warner fold. By now, the other media powers are quickly following suit. Viacom-Paramount is planning its own flagship store in Chicago, for example, and even the television networks have announced similar ventures.[46]

The importance of the studios' retail chains and consumer products divisions can scarcely be overstated. The ultimate objective here is to blur or erase altogether the distinction between shopping and entertainment—to create, in *Variety's* terms, "theme-park-style gift shops." Scarcely "shops" in any conventional sense, these entertainment-related facilities will contain movie theaters of various kinds (including IMAX), interactive arcades, simulated theme-park rides, virtual reality playscapes, and, of course, retail stores.[47] Disney and Warner are both at a tremendous advantage here, due not only to their substantial lead over the competition but also to the sheer number (and obvious durability) of their franchises—especially the presold, animation-based stories and figures which tend to have the widest demographic appeal.

Whatever their franchise inventory, however, Disney and Warner Bros., and the other studios must continually renew their product lines via new blockbuster-scale hits—an ever more costly venture as the "risk-reward" quotient steadily increases. Thus, the studios are producing more (and more expensive) films every year, and spending more to market those films as well. In 1990, the average cost of 169 major studio productions was $28.8 million, with another $11.6 million spent on marketing (prints and advertising). In 1995, the average cost on 212 productions was $36.4 million, plus $17.7 for marketing, pushing the total cost per feature over $50 million for the first time ever. The most significant increase was in "ad buys," which totaled $1.94 billion for all releases in 1995—up 107 percent over 1990.[48]

Disney far out-paced the other studios in ad buys, spending $432.6 million on film-related ads in 1995—over 60 percent more than its nearest competitors, Sony and Warner (both at about $265 million).[49] Disney was widely criticized for this seeming extravagance, but studio head Joe Roth dismissed such criticism as "narrow thinking" in an interview with *Variety's* Peter Bart. "You can't think of advertising in terms of domestic theatrical films alone," said Roth. "A major studio spends to stimulate all of the revenue streams, from merchandising to video to theme parks. . . . To not see the strategy of release dates and ways to create event advertising as weapons sometimes equal to the movie idea is missing the point."[50]

CONCLUSION

Roth's view seems reasonable enough, given the structure and economic imperatives of the New Hollywood. It also serves as a reply of sorts to the now-legendary "Katzenberg memo" issued by Roth's predecessor. In January 1991, in an internal memorandum to Eisner, Wells, and other top Disney executives, Jeffrey Katzenberg lamented the "tidal wave of runaway costs and mindless competition" and "the 'blockbuster mentality' that has gripped our industry." Successful films, he said, are "primarily based on two elements—*a good story, well executed.*" And the bottom line was conceptual, not commercial: "We must not be distracted from one fundamental concept: the idea is king."[51] This was a far cry, indeed, from Roth's notion of marketing strategies "as weapons sometimes equal to the movie idea."

Katzenberg's memo was motivated by the cost overruns and relatively weak box office of *Dick Tracy*, the 1990 Disney film that cost $46 million to produce and an astounding $55 million to market and release.[52] It was motivated, too, by the huge success of Disney's *Pretty Woman*, which along with *Home Alone* and *Ghost*, dominated the box office in 1990, outgrossing (and far outearning) such calculated blockbusters as *Total Recall, Die Hard, The Hunt for Red October, Back to the Future III, Another 48 Hours,* and *Days of*

Thunder. Bolstered by this apparent reversal of box-office fortunes and perhaps a dose of New Year's resolve, Katzenberg advocated a return to films like *Pretty Woman,* "the kind of modest, story-driven movie we tended to make in our salad days."[53]

The success of those more "modest" 1990 films turned out to be an aberration, however. The movie marketplace since then has been ruled by high-cost blockbusters and blatant franchise fare, with Disney's animated features like *Aladdin* and *The Lion King* (both number one box office films in their respective release years) managing to strike a balance between the crassly commercial and the well-crafted classical product. Katzenberg may have seen these as endorsing the views in his 1991 memo but, in fact, the kind of tight, well-crafted story he espoused is no longer viable in an industry whose films are designed to spawn product lines and theme-park rides. Katzenberg's final animation project before leaving Disney is a case in point. *The Hunchback of Notre Dame* (1996) transformed Victor Hugo's dark tale into an upbeat, user-friendly musical, and its horrific hero into an endearing and eminently marketable cartoon figure.

As the blockbuster mentality and franchise fever steadily intensify, distinctions between film culture and consumer culture are steadily being eradicated. That is precisely the objective of the studios and their parent companies, of course, and is endemic to a culture industry which always has subordinated craft to commerce. Indeed, the imminent convergence of movie theater, theme park, and retail store is the New Hollywood equivalent of the studio-owned movie palace of old—i.e., the site at which "the whole machine of the company," in all its integrated glory, can be most efficiently and profitably exploited.

This presupposes the ongoing appeal of movies themselves, and, in fact, the Hollywood-produced motion picture does continue to attract audiences—in ever increasing numbers, in fact, when the international marketplace is taken into account. Moreover, Hollywood's worldwide market provides yet another rationale for by-the-numbers chase films and tales of adolescent fancy, which tend to sell so well overseas. And in the view of Hollywood's consummate auteur-entrepreneur, Steven Spielberg, the blockbuster is less a matter of dumbing down the classical narrative than of endowing it with the simplicity and essence of myth. Commenting on the global success of *Jurassic Park,* Spielberg has said: "Once upon a time it was a small gathering of people around a fire listening to the storyteller with his tales of magic and fantasy. And now it's the whole world. . . . That's what has thrilled me most about the 'Jurassic Park' phenomenon. It's not 'domination' by American cinema. It's just the magic of storytelling, and it unites the world."[54]

In terms of both storytelling and myth-making, Speilberg's point is well taken. *Jurassic Park* may be lacking in terms of character and plot development and in thematic complexity, but it is a wondrously well-crafted movie—a visceral theme-park ride (in fact, a preview of the ride itself) and a dazzling display of digital effects. It is scarcely on a par with *Jaws*, the New Hollywood's UR-Blockbuster; but as template for the 1990s global franchise, *Jurassic Park* is a masterwork. Equally important is its elemental treatment of nature and technology, an opposition which operates not only on the levels of style and story but in the generation of the images themselves. Thus the notion that Hollywood's traditional myth-making function now operates on a global scale, particularly in the blockbuster and franchise fare with its exponential growth rate overseas. Perhaps the clearest signal of the "end of history" and triumph of capitalism in the post-Cold War era is the steady diffusion of Hollywood-produced entertainment and the seemingly inexorable Disney-fixation of global culture.

Whether the media conglomerates can continue to expand their far-flung operations and maintain their synergies on a worldwide scale, however, is open to question. "To survive in the '90s," writes Peter Bart, "a company must mobilize a vast array of global brands to command both content and distribution. Indeed, such an enterprise must be more than a company—it must be a virtual nationstate."[55] Bart fears that the conflicting agendas of their various sectors and their sheer size will "immobilize" these companies, which is a serious concern regarding markets like China and India. But the media conglomerates are aggressively pursuing these markets just the same, given the size and thus the financial rewards at stake.

As the media empires continue to extend their global reach, they also are considering ways to tighten diversification and thus to function more economically and efficiently. At present, the governing wisdom is that the media conglomerates could streamline operations and reduce debt by siphoning off their print and publishing divisions. Seagram's, Universal-MCA's parent company, recently followed this course by selling Putnam Berkley, its publishing subdivision. Commenting on the sale, Seagram's Vice Chairman Bob Matschullat explained that "we didn't see substantial synergies" between MCA and Putnam. But other companies have enjoyed tremendous success with their film-publishing tie-ins—Viacom's Simon & Schuster with an entire division devoted to Star Trek, for instance, and News Corps recent success with novels based on Fox-TV's *X-Files* series.[56]

Interestingly enough, the most successful movie-related publishing franchise is Bantam Books' *Star Wars* series, developed in an alliance not with Fox (which produced and released the films) but with Lucasfilm Licensing. In one of the savviest moves in media history, George Lucas waived a half-million-dollar bonus on *Star Wars* in 1977 in exchange for the merchandising and sequel rights to the film. While costing Fox untold billions of dollars, this deal provided Lucas with the seed money to create his own media empire (Lucasfilm Limited, Industrial Light and Magic, et al.), and to develop the franchise without the resources or the constraints of a parent company. It also underscored the importance of "top talent" in the creation and cultivation of both hit movies and media franchise.[57]

Controlling top talent—particularly directors, stars, writers, composers, and producers—has been a key objective of the rejuvenated studios in recent years, in an effort to revive the "contract system" which was so essential to the Old Hollywood studio system. This has been less than successful, however, in an era when film stars, directors, and other media celebrities can become veritable franchises unto themselves, while their agents and attorneys arrange strategic alliances (rather than binding contracts) with the studios. The success of Lucasfilms' new *Star Wars* trilogy, slated for release in 1998–2000, and the fate of Spielberg's new Dreamworks setup should provide a good indication of whether top talent can maintain their relative autonomy and financial leverage in the current climate of concentrated media power and renewed oligopoly.

This concentration of power raises other concerns as well—concerns which far outweigh the status of artists who have long since accepted the commercial exigencies of the contemporary entertainment industry. Hollywood's top talent have done the bidding of the blockbuster-driven, franchise-fevered studios all too well, and consequently the filmed entertainment divisions are dictating and defining not only the agendas of the media conglomerates but the very nature and shape of media expression. Well beyond the convergence of moviegoing and shopping, we are witnessing the confluence of entertainment, information, and advertising at a rapid and alarming rate.

In an era when information is power but is also packaged as "consumer entertainment," the concentration of media control in the hands of a conglomerate cartel grows increasingly worrisome, due less to any fears of the political clout of the new media moguls and their communication empires, than to their blithe disregard for the political—i.e., for the free and open flow of information so crucial to social and economic justice. In a global media culture unified by rituals of entertainment and patterns of consumption, those who cannot afford to consume are likely to be factored out of the cultural and political equation. And those social and political issues which cannot be rendered in sufficiently "entertaining" terms are likely to be either ignored or relegated to the far reaches of the 500-channel universe.

The likelihood of any international regulation of these media giants or of the global entertainment marketplace at large seems highly remote, especially in light of the difficulties in dealing with international copyright and intellectual property issues. In the United States, both the FCC and Congress have indicated a willingness to deregulate the media industry (most recently in the revised Communications Act), thus enabling Viacom, Disney, Time Warner, et al., to compete in the high-stakes global media marketplace with precious few constraints. While this bodes well for these companies and for bedazzled media consumers, the outlook regarding the aesthetics of cinema or the enlightenment of the audience is rather dismal. Indeed, the continued growth and ever expanding power of these media giants will test, perhaps more than anything else, whether these communications empires and the moguls who control them have any real sense of moral, political, and cultural responsibility to the global community which their companies are both creating and exploiting.

ENDNOTES

1. *Variety,* June 28, 1993, 5; *Variety* Sept 21, 1993, 7–8; *Variety* Oct 18, 1993, 1; *Variety,* Oct 17-23, 1994. By late 1994, according to *Variety, Jurassic Park* had grossed $356.5 million in the domestic (U.S. and Canada) theatrical market, and $555.8 million in theaters overseas. Here and throughout this essay, I refer to "*rentals*" (or "rental receipts") and also to "gross revenues" (or "box-office revenues"). This is a crucial distinction, since the gross revenues indicate the amount of money actually spent at the box office, whereas rental receipts refer, as *Variety* puts it, to "actual amounts received by the distributor"—i.e., the moneys returned by theaters to the company (usually a "studio") that released the movie. Unless otherwise indicated, both the rentals and gross revenues involve only the "domestic" market—i.e., theatrical release in the U.S. and Canada. All of the references to box-office performance and rental receipts in this articles are taken from *Variety,* most of them from its most recent (May

9–15, 1994; 40–52) survey of All-Time Film Rental Champs," which includes all motion pictures returning at least $4 million in rentals. Because this survey is continually updated, the totals include re-issues and thus may be considerably higher than the rentals from initial release. In these cases I try use figures from earlier *Variety* surveys for purposes of accuracy.

2. "Special Report" on the merchandising of *Jurassic Park, Variety,* Dec 27, 1993, 57+.

3. Aaron Latham, "At Universal, It's Only a Movie," *The New York Times,* Sept 29, 1996, 14+ (Sunday Arts & Leisure).

4. *Variety,* Apr 29–May 5, 1996, 1+.

5. Recent studies of "classical" Hollywood and the "studio system" include *The Classical Hollywood Cinema: Film Style and Mode of Production to 1960,* David Bordwell, Janet Staiger, and Kristin Thompson (New York: Columbia University Press, 1985); Douglas Gomery, *The Hollywood Studio System* (New York: St. Martin, 1986); and Thomas Schatz, *The Genius of the System: Hollywood Filmmaking in the Studio Era,* (New York: Pantheon, 1988).

6. For a thorough treatment of Hollywood's postwar transformation through the 1980s, see *Hollywood in the Age of Television,* Tino Balio, ed. (Boston: Unwin Hyman, 1990). See also Christopher Anderson, *Hollywood TV* (Austin: University of Texas Press, 1994).

7. Tino Balio, "Introduction to Part II," and William Lafferty, "Feature Films on Prime-Time Television" in Balio, ed. *Hollywood in the Age of Television.*

8. Thomas Schatz, "The New Hollywood," in *Film Theory Goes to the Movies,* Jim Collins, et al., eds. (New York: Routledge, 1993), 8–36.

9. On home video and pay-cable, sec Michelle Hilmes, "Breaking the Broadcast Bottleneck," and Bruce A. Austin, "Home Video: The Second-Run 'Theater' of the 1990s," in Balio, ed. *Hollywood in the Age of Television.* On sequels and reissues, see Joseph R. Dominick, "Film Economics and Film Content: 1964–1983," in *Current Research in Film* (Norwood, N.J.: Ablex, 1987), 144. From 1964–68, sequels and reissues combined accounted for just under five percent of all Hollywood releases. From 1974–78, they comprised 17.5 percent. *Jaws,* for instance, was successfully reissued in 1976, and in 1978 the first of several sequels, *Jaws 2,* was released, returning $49.3 million in rentals and clearly establishing the *Jaws* "franchise."

10. From *The Sound of Music i*n 1965 through 1976, only seven pictures (including *Jaws*) had returned $50 million in rentals; in 1977–78 alone, nine films surpassed that mark.

11. J. Hoberman, "Ten Years That Shook the World," *American Film* (June 1985), 42.

12. Hoberman, op cit., and A. D. Murphy, "Twenty Years of Weekly Film Ticket Sales in U.S. Theaters," *Variety,* March 15–21, 1989, 26.

Theater of Mass Destruction

Stephen Prince

Flying airplanes into buildings on a holy warrant from God is behavior that hungers for apocalypse. Indeed, many terrorists throughout history have shared a desire for apocalypse. The Irish terrorist O'Donovan Rossa, for example, dreamed of destroying a city and launched a "dynamite campaign" in the 1880s that aimed to reduce London to ashes.[1] Dynamite alone couldn't accomplish his epic goal, but more than a century later, expanding technologies of violence promised to give terrorists the means at last of fulfilling grand ambitions. The destruction of the World Trade Center promised terrible things to come—the potential scope and scale of future incidents was now off the charts.

In pursuing visions of epic destruction, filmmakers got there first, well before al Qaeda did. During the decade-and-a-half that preceded September 11, numerous films gave us stories in which terrorists launch grandiose plans for destruction, and many of these movies—*Nighthawks, Speed, Broken Arrow, Die Hard 2, Blown Away*—picture voluptuous spectacles of fiery death. Others—*Die Hard, Executive Decision, True Lies, The Peacemaker, The Siege*—seem to anticipate in often eerie ways the events of September 11. In still others—*Independence Day, Godzilla, The Day After Tomorrow*—filmmakers blew up, burned down, and knocked over beloved public landmarks, including the Empire State Building, the World Trade Center, and the Statue of Liberty. As if it were an obsessive-compulsive disorder, moviemakers repeatedly reduced Manhattan to smoldering ruins. By the time the attacks did occur, they seemed disturbingly entangled with the movie fantasies that Hollywood had spun so regularly. Exclamations that the destruction of the Twin Towers seemed like something out of a movie were common. This helped to give the event what Claire Kahane called "an uncanny ambiguity."[2]

To understand where American film went after September 11, we need to see where it was before al Qaeda's attack, and this chapter surveys terrorism-themed films produced during the 1980s and 1990s, in a period when heightened awareness about terrorism overseas was coupled with an odd complacency about the probability of an attack on American soil. Terrorism seemed for many like something that happened elsewhere and not in the United States. This complacency helps to account for why Hollywood was so slow in making movies on the subject. Before getting to these films, a quick historical overview will show how wrong the idea itself was. One of the things commonly said after September 11 was that now everything had changed because the events of that day showed that America was not immune from terrorism. In fact, for a long time the U.S. had attracted theoreticians and advocates of terrorism and also suffered from terrorist violence. The assassination of President McKinley in 1901 was a local accompaniment of the wave of political violence—bombings and killings of public figures—that swept Europe in the late nineteenth century and that marked the onset in the West of terrorism as a political weapon. McKinley's killer was an anarchist inspired by the murder of King Leopold I of Italy.

European anarchists immigrated to America and found in the ongoing labor struggles a receptive climate for their advocacy of political violence. In the early 1880s, in the pages of his journal Freiheit, Johann Most published articles providing advice for terrorists and instruction manuals on how to prepare dynamite. "Rescue mankind through blood, iron, poison, and dynamite," he proclaimed.[3] Freiheit also published Karl Heinzen's terrorist manifesto, "Murder," in which he explains the imperative for carrying out acts of massive political violence and declares that, "The greatest benefactor of mankind will be he who makes it possible for a few men to wipe out thousands."[4]

Luigi Galleani was the most influential Italian anarchist operating in the United States at the beginning of the new century.[5] Convinced that capitalism was an oppressive system and needed to be destroyed, he preached the necessity of violent war against the government and its political institutions.

A very gifted orator, his rhetoric inspired thousands of followers. Like Most, he published a bomb-making manual, and beginning in 1914 his followers launched an ambitious and extensive bombing campaign directed against financiers, politicians, judges, police officers, and such institutions as banks, courthouses, and churches. This campaign, which aimed to smash the institutions of capitalist power, bears striking similarities to the current threat posed by al Qaeda. Galleani's followers were secretive, living and operating underground, possessed of a messianic fervor and devoted to the cause of "propaganda by the deed" (i.e., political persuasion achieved through violence), implacably opposed to the capitalist West, and were mobile and capable of striking throughout the country. Their actions, in turn, elicited a government crackdown on civil liberties in an effort to smash the movement. Following Galleani's arrest in 1917, his followers mobilized for war against police, judges, politicians, and financiers. Bomb plots were carried out in numerous cities from New York to San Francisco.

Enraged by the government's efforts to deport their members, in April 1919 the Galleanists launched a new plot, sending nearly three dozen bombs through the mail to prominent financiers, mayors, government and city officials, and a Supreme Court justice. Most of these mail bombs were identified before they were delivered, so casualties were few. One month later Galleanists detonated eight bombs simultaneously in Boston, New York, Paterson, Philadelphia, Pittsburgh, Cleveland, and Washington, a feat that demonstrated their powers of organization. (Similarly, al Qaeda's simultaneous 1998 bombings of U.S. embassies in Kenya and Tanzania were intended to demonstrate its tactical skills.) One of these bombs mostly destroyed the house of Attorney General A. Mitchell Palmer when the bomber inadvertently blew himself up while placing the charge. Enraged, Palmer launched a crackdown marked by the arrest and deportation of aliens that became known as the Palmer Raids, targeting anarchists, socialists, and communists.

The most spectacular attack attributed to Galleanists was the September 16, 1920, bombing of Wall Street, which many in government believed was retribution for the arrest and prosecution of Sacco and Vanzetti, known Galleanists. The perpetrators were never identified, though a resourceful Galleanist named Mario ("Mike") Buda is believed to have driven the wagon. Shortly after noon, as workers poured into the intersection of Wall and Broad Street on lunch break, Buda parked a horse-drawn wagon in front of the J. P. Morgan bank. The wagon carried 100 pounds of dynamite packed with iron slugs and wired to a timer. The iron was meant to shred and pulverize bystanders in the street, which it did. Forty people were killed, and the bank was damaged. As on 9/11, this attack targeted the symbols of American financial power, and as on 9/11 soldiers formed a protective ring around the financial district because further attacks were feared. Most importantly, this bombing was the kind of modern terrorism that we recognize. As Beverly Gage has written, "The blast on Wall Street . . . seemed to be purely symbolic, designed to kill as many innocent people as possible in an assault on American power."[6] In a lament whose terms are familiar to us today, the *St. Louis Post-Dispatch* wrote, "There was no objective except general terrorism. The bomb was not directed against any particular person or property. It was directed against a public, anyone who happened to be near or any property in the neighborhood."[7] Such wholesale targeting of civilians was unusual for the anarchists. As Walter Laqueur has pointed out, they typically targeted official figures—generals, police chiefs, politicians—and aimed to avoid killing women and children, unlike al Qaeda jihadists.[8] Galleani was deported in 1919 and by the time of his death in 1931 anarchist terrorism had been crushed in the United States.

In the modern period terrorists have been a familiar feature of American life. The eclipse of the global youth movement of the 1960s spawned several left-wing terrorist groups that plagued Western democracies. Italy saw the Red Brigades and Germany the Baader-Meinhof group and Red Army Faction. Their counterpart in the U.S. was the Weathermen, which went on a very prolific bombing campaign during the 1970s. Also known as the Weather Underground Organization, this group bombed police departments in Berkeley, San Francisco, and New York, a National Guard headquarters in Washington D.C., courthouses in Washington D.C., New York, and California, prison facilities in New York and California, the corporate offices of Gulf Oil, the Kennecott Corporation, and the Anaconda Corporation, the U.S. State Department, the U.S. Capitol, and the Pentagon.

This is an impressive list of targets, and yet the campaign has been largely forgotten today, perhaps because it was mainly directed at property rather than people. Also active in this period was the Black Liberation Army, which specialized in bombings and in gunning for police officers. FALN, an acronym designating the group of guerrillas fighting for the independence of Puerto Rico, set off numerous bombs in Manhattan in 1975, and the following year it bombed the New York office of Mobil Oil and threatened to bomb the World Trade Center. It continued its bombing campaign through the end of the decade. The Unabomber employed mail bombs to wage a

Luddite vendetta against engineering and computer science professors, geneticists, and an array of other victims. The campaign lasted from 1978 to 1995. In the 1990s the Army of God launched a campaign of bombings directed at abortion clinics and shootings of abortion providers.

Clearly, then, neither Oklahoma City nor the events of September 11 marked the beginning of terrorism in the United States. The spillover of anarchist philosophy from Europe to America in the 19th century brought with it numerous advocates of political violence, and the 1970s had seen a wave of bombings. But Oklahoma City and September 11 did bring something relatively new, which was the wholesale targeting of people, something not witnessed in the U.S. since the 1920 Wall Street bombing. The Weathermen aimed to end the Vietnam War. The Black Liberation Army and the FALN saw themselves conducting a war for racial or national liberation, which was a predominant political framework in the period, in which the targets for violence were selectively chosen and in which the objective did not include killing people en mass. As Martin Miller has emphasized, the "limited terrorism" of earlier periods has been replaced by the "terrorism without boundaries of our time."[9] As Walter Laqueur has stressed, the old terrorism "was, by and large, discriminate, selecting its victims carefully." By contrast, "contemporary terrorism has increasingly become indiscriminate in the choice of its victims. Its aim is no longer to conduct propaganda but to effect maximum destruction."[10]

This shift was one of the most sinister things that September 11 represented. It compelled U.S. political culture and public life to assimilate the probability of future acts of mass murder. But if this eventuality seemed to become more real after September 11, in the realm of popular culture it already existed. Since the 1980s, movies about terrorism had been offering audiences the promise of mass destruction as a means of providing entertainment. But before the 1980s this was rare—until then few American films focused on terrorism. Indeed, in comparison with literature, where terrorism is a subject that has interested a great many writers, it occupied a small niche in American cinema until recent years. Surveying terrorism as a theme in the two mediums, Walter Laqueur concluded that film producers and directors seemed to feel it was of little audience interest.[11] Laqueur was writing in the mid-1980s, just before the big surge in film production on this subject. Nevertheless, the disparity between the wealth of literature that he analyzes and the relatively paltry number of films is striking. From the world's greatest authors—Dostoyevsky (*The Possessed*), Joseph Conrad

(*The Secret Agent*), André Malraux (*The Human Condition*), Jean-Paul Sartre (*Dirty Hands*)—to the countless writers of popular fiction (Thomas Harris, Frederick Forsythe, Alistair MacLean), the topic has retained an enduring interest.

HOLLYWOOD'S INITIAL FLIRTATIONS WITH THE TOPIC

Hollywood had remained uninterested in terrorism, except for the odd production such as John Ford's *The Informer* (1935), based on a novel by Liam O'Flaherty, who had fought with the IRA. A number of films dealt with subjects that, with a nudge here or there, could have encompassed a terrorist theme. In *Suddenly* (1954), Frank Sinatra leads a determined group of men planning to ambush and assassinate the President of the United States. Elia Kazan's *Panic in the Streets* (1950) is a crime film about the threat of bubonic plague being spread in a city, except in this case it isn't deliberate. The killer on the loose doesn't know that he carries the disease. In *The Manchurian Candidate* (1962), agents of a foreign power (Red China) plot to assassinate a Presidential candidate using a "sleeper," a sniper whose subconscious mind has been programmed to carry out the plot, but the portrait carries no terrorist inflection. Nor do the portraits of crazed, lone snipers in *Targets* (1968) and *Two Minute Warning* (1976), even though in the latter film the killer sets up his gear in a football stadium during a big league game.

The Satan Bug (1965), directed by John Sturges from a novel by Alistair MacLean, got much closer to the mark in its story about the theft of a secret, government-manufactured super-toxin and the threat it poses if unleashed in American cities. In *Rollercoaster* (1977), a bomber extorts money from amusement parks by threatening to blow up their roller coasters. And in *Juggernaut* (1974), a bomber places seven explosive devices aboard a luxury ocean liner and threatens to detonate them unless he's paid a huge sum. Although this is an extortion plot more than a politically motivated act of terrorism, the template that it offered of a mad bomber or extortionist threatening massive violence proved to be very durable and influenced numerous films in the 1980s and 1990s.

In *The FBI Story* (1959) a killer blows up a passenger airliner carrying his mother because he wants her insurance money. It's an act of mass murder but not terrorism. Threats of violence against airplanes could be found in *Skyjacked* (1972) and in the popular hit, *Airport* (1970), wherein a madman played by Van Heflin detonates a bomb on board a Boeing 707. Were this movie made today, it would be inflected more strongly as a terrorist narrative, but in 1970 terrorism wasn't on Hollywood's radar. *Airport, Juggernaut, Rollercoaster,* and others were part of a genre in the period known as "disaster movies." The disaster film emphasized extraordinary physical calamity befalling a cross-section of characters, often played by aging Hollywood stars (Ava Gardner, Fred Astaire, Jennifer Jones) then in the twilight of their careers. In many instances, the disasters were natural calamities rather than ones that today look like terrorism. *Earthquake* depicts the destruction of Los Angeles. A tidal wave upends an ocean liner in *The Poseidon Adventure.* An out-of-control train carries plague in *The Cassandra Crossing.* A midair collision cripples a 747 in *Airport 1975.* A fire rages through a high-rise in *The Towering Inferno.*

The disaster movie was a prominent genre in the 1970s, and while it might be inflected to include bomb threats against public targets, these were not emphasized with the kind of self-consciousness that would be routine today. One simply doesn't find a terrorist focus very often in American cinema before the 1980s. In addition to some of the disaster movies, Hollywood's spy films occasionally seemed to broach the subject of terrorism, but always in an outlandish fashion. Some of the James Bond movies, for example, such as *You Only Live Twice* (1967), feature megalomaniac villains bent on either world domination or world destruction, and they aim to achieve their goals by threatening massive violence. And spy movies inspired by Bond's popularity, such as *Our Man Flint* (1966), which features a cabal of eco-terrorists bent on world domination, did the same. On occasion, Hollywood's international coproductions took up the subject of terrorism. *Hennessy* (1975), for example, produced by American International Pictures, starred Rod Steiger as an IRA bomber who journeys to London intending to blowup Parliament. In the climax, he wears a suicide vest laced with explosives, much like a modern jihadist might do.

Ironically, one of Hollywood's best-known directors—Alfred Hitchcock—provided the most indelible, powerful, and literal image of terrorist violence in early cinema, and yet this was before he joined the American film industry. In *Sabotage* (1936), made during his British period, young Steve (Desmond Tester), son of the film's heroine (Sylvia Sidney), unwittingly carries a bomb to Piccadilly Circus. Verloc (Oscar Holmolka), the anarchist agent who gave him the bomb, insists that the package must be delivered before 1:30 that afternoon, but, alas, poor Steve is delayed by a passing parade which he pauses to watch and is also corralled by a street peddler selling toothpaste and hair tonic. When Steve does get free of the peddler and the parade, he boards a double-decker bus, which becomes bogged down in heavy traffic. And time grows late, too late. At 1:45, the bomb explodes, killing Steve and the other passengers on the bus.

Hitchcock later said that he felt it was a mistake to have killed the boy because audiences hated that turn of events. He told interviewer François Truffaut that "when the bomb exploded and he was killed, the public was resentful."[12] All the delays in the sequence—the peddler, the parade, the heavy traffic—enabled Hitchcock to generate considerable tension and anxiety, and he felt, having done this, having worked viewers up, that it was too cruel for the bomb actually to explode on screen. But this very cruelty is the essence of terrorism when it targets innocent people instead of property, as in the 1920 Wall Street bombing. It is Hitchcock's evocation of this quality, against his own inclinations, that makes this such a signal sequence—it points toward our world today. The shock of the sequence is sharpened by Hitchcock's emphasis on the humanity of those on the bus who are about to die. (This evocation is very similar to what Gillo Pontecorvo shows in *The Battle of Algiers* when he turns his camera on the faces of people who are about to be killed by bombs placed in a bar and a discotheque.) The conductor, at first, won't let Steve on because he's carrying flammable canisters of film which are forbidden from public transport. But when he sees that one of the films is "Bartholomew the Strangler," evidently a personal favorite, he relents, cracking a joke that as long as Steve isn't Bartholomew, he can come aboard. Steve sits next to an elderly lady holding a puppy, and he interacts with the dog, playing with it and petting it. Another woman sits across from Steve with a book on her lap. All these people, whose humanity Hitchcock has carefully evoked, will die, and this turn of events is not typical of Hitchcock's moral universe. Despite his frequent depiction of murderers, spies, and sabotage, Hitchcock's moral sensibility is worlds away from the indiscriminate violence of modern terrorism. Violence in Hitchcock's films usually occurs on a smaller scale. He enjoyed, on occasion, terrifying his audience, but terrorism itself was not a type of violence that he comfortably explored. He much preferred the pathology of elegant killers like Uncle Charlie (in *Shadow of a Doubt* [1943]) to the cold and depersonalized calculus of the political terrorist.

Sabotage was based on Joseph Conrad's novel, *The Secret Agent,* in which Conrad views the political world and its agents of anarchist subversion, in the words of Irving Howe, "from a great and chilling distance."[13] Whereas

Hitchcock shows the bombing in a straightforward, linear fashion, Conrad embeds its portrait in different chapters across the novel, and he goes much farther in portraying the physical toll the violence exacts. The body lies in a morgue, "a heap of rags, scorched and bloodstained, half concealing what might have been an accumulation of raw material for a cannibal feast." The investigating officer says the victim was "blown to small bits: limbs, gravel, clothing, bones, splintersóall mixed up together. I tell you they had to fetch a shovel to gather him up with." Hitchcock doesn't show these details; he couldn't, in this period of cinema, even if he had wanted to. And this reticence about the effects of bombs on the human body would continue to inform the visual design of terrorist films into the 1980s and 1990s and beyond.

Sabotage isn't about terrorist acts carried out on American soil. But with the bus bombing in Piccadilly Circus, Hitchcock had vividly delineated a type of violence that Hollywood filmmakers of subsequent generations would study more closely. As we have seen, they initially broached it in terms of the disaster film, and in 1977 that genre morphed in a way that gave us the first prominent disaster spectacle that was also explicitly and emphatically about terrorism. Jack G. Shaheen has described *Black Sunday* (1977) as "the first feature film to display Palestinian terrorists on American soil."[14] Directed by John Frankenheimer from a novel by Thomas Harris (in his pre-Hannibal Lecter days), the film portrays a group of Black September terrorists that hatches a plot to detonate the Goodyear Blimp over the Orange Bowl, hurling thousands of steel rifle darts into the crowd in the stands. To accomplish this, Black September member Dahlia Iyad (Marthe Keller) seduces and manipulates a disaffected Vietnam veteran, Michael Lander (Bruce Dern), into prepping the blimp with the bomb and darts and piloting it into the stadium.

Dern made a career specialty of playing psychos, and his volatile character here is in line with a widespread tendency in seventies cinema to scapegoat Vietnam veterans as crazed and villainous characters. Dahlia works for Mohammad Fasil (Bekim Fehmiu), who, in the narrative, is said to have masterminded the assault on the Israeli athletes at the 1972 Munich Olympics. This was one of the period's most notorious real-life acts of terror, which led to the death of all the kidnapped Israelis when German authorities launched an ill-considered and bungled rescue attempt. The origins and affiliations of Black September remain murky; some scholars view the group as a vehicle for parent organizations (the PLO's Fatah, for example) to carry out terrorist acts which would be too risky to pursue openly.[15] The

Munich events, along with the group's acts of sabotage in West Germany and the Netherlands, its hijacking of a Belgian airliner, and its attack on the Saudi embassy in Khartoum in 1973 gave Black September sufficient cachet for popular culture to invoke its name as a means of motivating the action in *Black Sunday*. Two U.S. officials were killed in the Khartoum attack, but Black September had never launched any actions inside the United States. Nevertheless, the film proposes that Black September is engineering the attack at the Orange Bowl as a means of revenge on the United States for its support of Israel. Dahlia tapes a message to be used after the attack in which she says, "The American people have remained deaf to all the cries of the Palestinian nation." Therefore, she concludes, Americans now will be made to suffer "as we have suffered."

Dahlia and Fasil are portrayed as stone killers, in contrast to the Israeli agent who is hunting them, David Kabakov (Robert Shaw). Kabakov has gained a reputation as a ferocious assassin who targets Israel's enemies, but now he has grown tired of killing and has come to feel that the world is no better now than when he started. "Doubt has entered in," he tells his assistant, Robert Moshevsky. In the film's opening act, a raid on Fasil's Beirut headquarters, Kabakov had cornered Dahlia but spared her life. When she subsequently murders Moshevsky, Kabakov realizes that his moral qualms need to be put aside. The film thus pits a group of cold killers plotting mass murder against a hero who has a conscience and is troubled by violence. The film briefly raises a more complex moral perspective on Kabakov when an FBI agent (Fritz Weaver) lectures him about not pursuing his assassin's game inside the U.S. "Whatever you think of our methods, you'll play by our rules or leave," he tells Kabakov. But this critique of Kabakov's extra-legal methods is quickly abandoned. It is trumped by the spectacular nature of the violence that Dahlia and Lander are planning. The large scale of the attack situates the film inside the era's cycle of disaster movies, and at the same time, because the attack is premeditated political violence that targets ordinary people for slaughter, it takes the action from disaster to terrorism proper.

The climax has Kabakov in a helicopter, chasing the blimp, now commandeered by Lander and Dahlia. This time he doesn't hesitate—Kabakov machine-guns Dahlia, and he uses the helicopter to tow the blimp offshore where the explosion occurs without loss of life. On one level, the climax seems very far-fetched, like something out of a James Bond film, with Kabakov performing outlandish heroics as he tries to seize control of the blimp, and with the terrorists' rather surreal conception of the blimp as an attack weapon. But what in 1977 seemed like outlandish fantasy has been overtaken by events. Today one can't watch the climax without feeling uneasy. What seemed improbable then no longer is. *Black Sunday's* climax is no more garish and startling than the effort on 9/11 to hijack four airplanes and crash them into U.S. landmarks. But *Black Sunday* was a fantasy—it offered its audience a reassuring message about heroic action preventing mass murder, unlike what happened on 9/11. The palliative effect of this kind of reassuring narrative closure became a persistent feature of Hollywood's films about terrorism, which, as a group, seek to reassure their audiences that government authorities are taking all necessary measures to protect them.

However, unlike many subsequent films, *Black Sunday* proposes a blowback theory of terrorist violence. "Blowback" is a CIA term designating the unintended consequences of foreign policy. The idea pictures "chickens coming home to roost." Although the film's Dahlia and Fasil are caricatures, the story motivates their action as a response to U.S. policy in the Middle East. Dahlia explains that she is acting because of U.S. anti-Palestinian policies. Chalmers Johnson, a policy analyst who has written extensively about blowback, notes

> The United States has obviously not proved immune to terrorist attacks—witness the 1993 bombing of the World Trade Center in New York, the blowing up of the Murrah federal office building in Oklahoma City in 1995, and the assaults on New York and Washington of September 2001. In one way or another—one of the Murrah terrorists was a Gulf War veteran—these incidents all suggest blowback from U.S. government activities in foreign countries.[16]

Osama bin Laden always has explained his motives in these terms. In a 2004 videotape, he pointed to U.S. support for Israel's 1982 invasion of Lebanon as a chief example. "They started bombing, killing, and wounding many, while others fled in terror. I still remember those distressing scenes: blood, torn limbs, women and children massacred. All over the place, houses were being destroyed and tower blocks were collapsing, crushing their residents . . . As I looked at those destroyed towers in Lebanon, it occurred to me to punish the oppressor in kind by destroying towers in America, so that it would have a taste of its own medicine."[17]

In a 2002 letter addressed to the people of America, he set out to answer the question, "Why are we fighting and opposing you?" Among the reasons he enumerated were these: "You attacked us in Palestine. . . .You attacked us in Somalia; you supported the Russian atrocities against us in Chechnya, the Indian oppression against us in Kashmir, and the Jewish aggression against us in Lebanon." He wrote, "Your forces occupy our countries, you spread your military bases throughout them; you corrupt our lands."[18] All this made it necessary to "punish the oppressor in kind."

Black Sunday's invocation of blowback in explaining the motives of Dahlia and Fasil gives the film a contemporary resonance. But in this respect the film is relatively singular among Hollywood movies about terrorism. Hollywood's productions rarely give blowback due consideration as a motivation underlying terrorist actions because American political culture as a whole does not invite this kind of inquiry. It often is seen as being unpatriotic or as not a responsible line of inquiry. But acknowledging that blowback can occur does not necessarily mean validating an adversary's cause or motives. Understanding those motives provides a way of knowing one's enemy, and knowing one's enemy provides a good strategy for understanding how to defeat that enemy or neutralize his appeal. Hollywood terrorists tend to have minimal motives for acting or stereotypical ones—bin Laden, by contrast, has clearly articulated his reasons for waging jihad. He is a wily, intelligent, dedicated, and deadly adversary of the United States. Hollywood's terrorists, in contrast, have tended toward caricature, especially when the Middle East is involved, and they are rarely given motivations that have much political specificity.

At the same time, *Black Sunday's* portrait of the Palestinian terrorists points to a major difference between the terrorism of this earlier period and our own. Neither Dahlia nor Fasil is an Islamist, a religious fundamentalist. Their politics are those of national liberation, and, in this, they mirror the secular, Marxist-Leninist orientation of the PLO's two main groups in that era, Fatah and the Popular Front for the Liberation of Palestine (PFLP). This focus also informs the depiction of Palestinian terrorism in *The Little Drummer Girl* (1984), whose story involves the efforts of an Israeli intelligence unit to use an American actress, Charlie (Diane Keaton), to infiltrate a terror cell led by Kalil (Sarni Frey). The climax involves Kalil's attempt to bomb an Israeli advocate for peace, but it isn't the kind of suicide bombing that targets civilians and that is now so closely identified with Islamist terror. And Kalil is not portrayed as a fanatic but as a quiet, reflective guerilla commander who has a sense of irony and humor. While the film sides primarily with the Israelis, it does show a measured regard for the Palestinians, and it evokes the grievances on each side. This gave the film a degree of controversy in its day.

Islamist terror has its roots in the 1930s and Egypt's Muslim Brotherhood, an organization formed in 1928 in opposition to the British military occupation of Egypt, but by the 1970s it was a growing force in several of the region's repressive states (Egypt as well as Saudi Arabia and Pakistan). It began to focus its animus on America in the wake of the Soviet defeat in Afghanistan, and in 1996 and again in 1998 Osama bin Laden declared jihad on the United States because of its military presence in Saudi Arabia, which is home to Mecca and Medina, the two holiest cities in Islam.[19] He considered the U.S. military presence an affront to Islam. Before Islamist terror ripened into its present international scope, however, it was not religion but anticolonialism and armed struggle for national liberation that furnished the motivation for terror groups. Italy's Red Brigades, Germany's Red Army Faction, Peru's Shining Path, Fatah and the PFLP saw themselves as fighting for national liberation or against Western imperialism, and in this regard, the success of Algeria's National Liberation Front (FLN) in its use of terror against French colonialism was an inspiration. This sense of a shared struggle encouraged cooperation among some of these groups. In 1972, for example, the Japanese Red Army launched an attack on Israel's Lod Airport on behalf of the PFLP. In 1976 the PFLP hijacked an Air France plane to Entebbe, Uganda, and demanded the release of several of Germany's imprisoned Red Army Faction members. The following year, the PFLP hijacked a Lufthansa flight and demanded that Germany release the captured members of the Red Army Faction who the year before had kidnapped the German industrialist Hanns-Martin Schleyer. Thus in this period there emerged a kind of "international brigade," composed of German, Japanese, Arab, and Latin American commandos (one of the hijackers in a 1970 PFLP plot was Nicaraguan).[20]

This internationalizing of a cadre of violent political radicals provides the context for the portrait of the terrorist Wulfgar (Rutger Hauer) in *Nighthawks* (1981), which was marketed as an action vehicle for Sylvester Stallone. Wulfgar is a lone contractor who works for several groups. He is probably modeled on Ilich Ramirez Sánchez, aka "Carlos the Jackal," who gained prominence following his 1975 attack on OPEC headquarters in Vienna. Wulfgar is German, and he has an Irish contact in London, a Moroccan assistant, and a Middle Eastern employer, a profile that evokes a combination of the IRA, the Red Army Faction, and the PLO/PFLP. As the film begins, he bombs a London department store and telephones a newspaper to announce that "the Wulfgar command has just struck a blow against

British colonialism." Thus our character is firmly positioned within the international brigade of secular, left-wing terrorists that had dominated world attention throughout the 1970s.

Intent on spreading mayhem, Wulfgar travels to New York City, pursued by an Interpol agent, Peter Hartman (Nigel Davenport). Hartman says, with unfortunate prescience relative to 9/11, that Wulfgar has come to Manhattan because if you want worldwide coverage of a terrorist incident, this is where you stage it. The bulk of the film is a cat-and-mouse game between Wulfgar and the Manhattan cop tracking him. The cop, Deke DaSilva (Sylvester Stallone), is recruited by Hartman to join an elite squad—Anti-Terrorism Attack Command (ATAC)—formed as an alliance between Interpol, U.S. federal and state authorities, and the NYPD with the purpose of hitting back hard at terrorists. DaSilva is troubled by the tactics Hartman is advocating, and the conflict between these two characters enables the film to pose questions about the response of democracies to terrorist attack.

Hartman believes that, until now, the police have not been ruthless enough in responding to terrorism, and he intends to teach methods that will enable the ATAC recruits to "meet your terrorist adversary on equal terms." He tells the ATAC squad that human rights, civil liberties, and a proportional use of force have all hindered police efforts to fight terrorists. DaSilva objects that Hartman is training them to be nothing but assassins, and Hartman explodes, "Oh, for Christ's sake, man, to combat violence you need greater violence. To defeat a violent people you have to be trained to react in a given situation with ruthless, cold-blooded violence as well."

Hartman personifies the deep-level threat posed by terrorism to democratic states, namely, the erosion of civil liberties by political authority, a process justified by leaders as a necessary way of coping with violence against the state. The 1970s had provided several object lessons in this regard, and these motivate the film's delineation of Hartman. Responding to the Red Army Faction, West Germany greatly expanded its internal security apparatus as the political Right gained strength. Released from prison after sixteen years, a former Red Army Faction member bitterly remarked that the RAF's tactics had seemed only to succeed at strengthening the authoritarianism of the state and at being used by right-wing politicians to pursue their agenda. "West German terrorism had . . . this unbelievable effect because it allowed itself from the very beginning to be used by interested parties. We thought with our political actions to overcome the exploitation and domination and, in reality, were only used to make the conditions that we wanted to change uglier yet."[21] Left-wing violence in Argentina during the 1970s produced a more extreme response from the government, which abducted and "disappeared" upwards of 9,000 Argentines after the 1976 military coup, in comparison to 700 victims of violence by leftist guerrillas.[22]

The authoritarian responses by the state in West Germany and, in more extreme form, in Argentina loom behind the strategic debates over antiterrorist policy in *Nighthawks*. Furthermore, in a post-9/11 world that has seen the administration of President George W. Bush greatly expand warrantless surveillance of the American public by the CIA, the FBI, and even the Pentagon,[23] and declare that the President has supreme powers to imprison anyone without warrant, trial, or judicial review, the debate within the film has proven to foreshadow the dialogue that is now ongoing within America. Despite this relevance for today, *Nighthawks* in its period was mainly intended as a cop action film; as a result, the debate between DaSilva and Hartman does not go very far. In the storyline, the two men eventually become friends, and subsequent scenes fail to extend the issues. Certainly *Nighthawks* is no *Battle of Algiers* (1966), Gillo Pontecorvo's classic depiction of the Algerian FLN's fight against the French and the French counterstrategy carried out by the OAS, including the military occupation of Algiers and the torture of Muslims by the Tenth Paratroop Division. Nevertheless, in its halting way, *Nighthawks* envisions that a time will come when the United States will be tempted to revise its own Constitutional system in the interest of formulating an appropriately ruthless response to terrorist violence. This gives the film its chief claim on our attention today. Wulfgar, of course, is subdued and defeated by DaSilva, who guns him down in a manner that invokes the assassination policy that he had earlier objected to. And this denouement enables *Nighthawks* to provide the same kind of therapeutic reassurance to the audience that *Black Sunday* had provided. It offers a vision of the nation's security forces rising to the occasion and stopping a deadly terrorist. As we will see, until 9/11 this was a basic formula of Hollywood's terrorist thrillers. If *Nighthawks* has a troubled conscience, it lies in its awareness of how fragile democracy is—but its conception of terrorism in terms of the lone operator, Wulfgar, ultimately means that the threat isn't too severe and therefore the state's own corruption isn't truly imminent.

HOLLYWOOD MARKETS TERRORISM AS ACTION-ADVENTURE

With its terrorist focus, *Nighthawks* was a bit of an outlier in 1981. The subject was not yet a familiar trope for American cinema, but this changed in just a few years. By the mid-1980s, a cinematic focus on terrorism began to take shape across a large cycle of films, many of them cheapie exploitation pictures. Chuck Norris was an action star in the period, and in *Invasion USA* (1985), which he cowrote, a hodge-podge band of terrorists—Latin, Asian, Black, Arabic—invade America at Christmas and begin blowing up shopping malls, churches, and families at home celebrating the holidays. A renegade Soviet officer leads the team, and only Chuck Norris as America's hero can save the day. The cartoonish nature of the film set a tone that other pictures emulated. In *Terminal Entry* (1986), Muslim assassination squads plot to kill U.S. politicians and military figures. In *Wanted: Dead or Alive* (1987), Arab terrorists go on a killing spree in the United States and threaten to release poison gas. Rutger Hauer, now a hero and reformed from his *Nighthawks* villainy, aims to stop them. *Terror Squad* (1987) gives us Libyans threatening Indiana, and in *Terror in Beverly Hills* (1991) the title tells all. While these films pictured a terrorist threat on U.S. soil, other films had U.S. forces project their muscle overseas to attack and defeat terror threats in the Middle East. These pictures included *The Delta Force* (1986), *Death Before Dishonor* (1987), *Iron Eagle II* (1988), and *Navy Seals* (1990).

Why was there a sudden upsurge in terror-themed films? A likely answer is that by the mid-1980s, American targets of political violence from groups in the Middle East seemed more common than a decade earlier. Throughout the 1970s, the PFLP put airline hijacking on the map as a favored terrorist stratagem, but the targeted nations were typically Israel and on a few occasions Germany in order to free captive Red Army Faction members. Abu Nidal struck in Germany and Belgium, and Fatah in France. One of the most sustained terrorist campaigns in the period didn't involve the Middle East at all. The IRA waged a very aggressive bombing campaign against England, frequently striking in London (at tube stations, Hyde Park, Regents Park, the Houses of Parliament, Westminster Palace, and other locales). In the United States, the Unabomber struck periodically since 1978, but these incidents were not as theatrical and attention-grabbing as an airline hijacking or airport bombing. And they were not the work of a foreign power.

Things began changing in 1983. A suicide truck bomber hit the U.S. Marine Barracks in Beirut, killing more than 200 Marines. Also in Beirut that year, the U.S. Embassy was bombed, killing more than 60. The group responsible remains unknown, although Hezbollah, a radical Islamist group known to employ suicide attacks, seems the likeliest candidate. In 1985, two members of Hezbollah hijacked TWA Flight 847 and beat and killed a U.S. Navy diver on board. Also that year, Palestinian terrorists hijacked the *Achille Lauro* cruise ship and singled out a Jewish man from New York, Leon Klinghoffer, and executed him despite the fact that he was confined to a wheelchair. In 1986, Libyan agents bombed a discotheque in Berlin where U.S. soldiers were known to congregate, and in 1988 Libya again struck against the U.S. by bombing Pan Am Flight 103 over Lockerbie, Scotland, killing 270 people. This was also a fateful year in that the Soviet Union began to withdraw its forces from Afghanistan, and the following year the Islamist mujahideen, who had been financed by the CIA, Saudi Arabia, and Pakistan, took control of the country. Believing that their jihad had vanquished one superpower, they began to refocus Islamist rage on the United States, the world's remaining superpower, because of its military presence in Islamic lands.

This string of attacks on the U.S. from the Middle East seemed to crystallize the topic of terrorism for Hollywood. Jack G. Shaheen has suggested that there was a political motive behind many of the anti-Palestinian films of that period. A number of these (e.g., *The Delta Force, Invasion USA, Bloodsport* [1988]) were made in Israel and by Cannon Films, owned by Israeli producers Menahem Golan and Yoram Globus.[24] But the effusion of terrorism into American film in this period is broader and more extensive than the anti-Palestinian films alone. In the second half of the 1980s, terrorism crossed over from exploitation pictures of the Golan-Globus variety and became an item in numerous big-budget, high-profile Hollywood movies. Many of these blockbusters did not deal with Middle Eastern terrorism at all. Recent events established a kind of cognitive priming for the culture, establishing "terrorism" as a label and a prism through which to view not just modern political violence but crime itself. Thus, some films, like *True Lies* (1994) or *Executive Decision* (1995), might portray Arab terrorists while many others avoided the Middle East entirely and used terrorism as a convenient generic prop for mounting high-octane action thrillers that had plenty of explosions. *Die Hard,* for example, which was one of the highest-grossing films of 1988 and launched the film career of Bruce Willis, is actually a heist film in which the bad guys are attempting to steal millions of dollars in negotiable bearer bonds from a high-rise office building. But everybody the movie behaves as if they are in a film about terrorists.

A gang of high-tech thieves led by Hans Gruber (Alan Rickman) takes over the Nakatomi Building and holds the company's employees hostage along with their chief executive, Joseph Takagi (James Shigeta). Gruber interrogates Takagi and tries to intimidate him into divulging the access code to the company's vault where the bonds are stored. Gruber tells Takagi the truth, saying that he wants the bearer bonds. Takagi is astonished. "You want money?" he exclaims. "What kind of terrorists are you?" Gruber replies, "Who said we were terrorists?"

Indeed, the gang has made no political demands or speeches of any kind. And yet many of the film's characters reflexively apply the concept of terrorism in order to explain what is happening. It's a default cognitive response, which makes sense in terms of the string of high-profile bombings and killings of U.S. targets in the Middle East that had begun a few years previously. Thus, during one of his early skirmishes with the gang, our cop hero, John McClane (Bruce Willis), gets the drop on one of Gruber's men and kills him. Until now McClane has been running about shoeless. So now he takes the dead man's shoes and remarks, "Nine million terrorists in the world, I gotta kill one with feet smaller than my sister." It never occurs to McClane that the gang might be something other than terrorists. When word of the building takeover leaks to the news media, a local reporter (William Atherton) does an on-camera report in which he editorializes about what he believes is happening. "This is Richard Thornburgh live from Century City. Tonight Los Angeles has joined the sad and worldwide fraternity of cities whose only membership requirement is to suffer the anguish of international terrorism." Much later in the film, when McClane's wife, Holly (Bonnie Bedelia), sees Gruber with the bearer bonds, she remarks with some disappointment that he is nothing but a common thief. She would, it seems, have preferred a terrorist. "I'm an exceptional thief," Gruber sniffs. For his part, he is willing to play to the general perception. In a bluff, he tells the police that his demands are freedom for his "revolutionary brothers" held prisoner in Northern Ireland, Canada, and Sri Lanka. In an aside to one of his men, Gruber says he has no idea who those people might be.

The disjunction between what is actually going on in the movie, and the interpretations placed on events by characters, is fascinating and suggests that by the late 1980s "terrorism" had emerged as a potent political label and a conceptual template for understanding and perceiving acts of violence in the world. *Die Hard* shows that the label doesn't need actually to connect with the phenomena it is invoked to describe—the invocation itself is sufficient to orient characters to their environment and to provide a sense of the meaning of events. As employed in the film, "terrorism" is not an empirical term because none of the violence is politically motivated or is intended to terrorize a public larger than the hostages Gruber holds and who are his principal targets. It is a rhetorical term that creates its own kind of theater and makes the characters feel that they are caught up in events that are more significant than they actually are. Being held hostage by an international terrorist is more exciting than being held by a common thief, and the police that surround the building expend more energy on a perceived terrorist than they may have otherwise. *Die Hard,* then, is a film that points to an ongoing investment by characters in finding terrorism wherever they look and to the emotional gratifications that this search for theater-in-real-life provides them. The film, though, doesn't do much with this disjunction between rhetoric and actuality, beyond noting it, and for the film's popular audience, it was the explosions that provided much of the emotional gratification.

HOMEGROWN ENEMIES PROLIFERATE

Die Hard grossed nearly $140 million worldwide on a production budget of $28 million. Terrorism, even of the pseudo variety found in this film, could be a major box office attraction because it provided a vehicle for action, violence, and explosions. *Die Hard* and its sequels (1990, 1995, 2007) were successful blockbusters that offered audiences the high-octane violence that action films in the period were establishing as their norm. *Die Hard's* commercial success meant that there would be the inevitable sequels. The third film, *Die Hard: With a Vengeance,* is, like the first picture, a heist film in which Hans's brother, Simon (Jeremy Irons), plots to rob the Federal Reserve Bank in New York. Its terrorist element lies in the bombing threats that Simon phones in to the police to disguise his true plans. The second film, *Die Hard 2: Die Harder,* introduces a plot device that numerous terrorist films of the period utilized—this time around, the chief bad guy terrorist is one of "us." There were two categories of homegrown enemies in the pre-9/11 films. One category, examined in this section, was composed of renegade figures from the security services—police officers, military officers, covert operations specialists—that had turned against Americans or their government.

Discussing the many action films that feature a homegrown enemy, Eric Lichtenfeld writes, "This is an ideal Hollywood villain for a post-Cold War America, in which the climate of political correctness made foreign villains seem anachronistic at best and downright racist at worst."[25] In *Die Hard 2,* a U.S. Army Colonel named Stuart (William Sadler) leads a band of mercenaries who take control of Washington D.C.'s Dulles airport and commandeer a runway so that a fugitive Latin American general, Ramon Esperanza (Franco Nero), can land and, with the mercenaries' help, escape extradition by U.S. drug authorities. Esperanza is a notorious, high-level drug-dealer, and while it is never very clear why Stuart and his men are determined to help Esperanza, their threats to blow up airplanes and destroy innocent lives carry more of the blowback implication that we saw operating in *Black Sunday,* namely that unsavory aspects of U.S. foreign policy have the potential to cause trouble at home. The Esperanza-Stuart relationship seems to have been modeled on the Manuel Noriega-CIA relationship, which eventually soured, producing an invasion of Panama by the U.S. amid accusations that Noriega was running drugs. There are also echoes in the film's premise of the durable but unsubstantiated charges that the CIA used drug shipments in the 1980s to help fund the Nicaraguan "Contras" in their effort to overthrow the elected government of Nicaragua. In that era, the United States used Honduras as a military base to support the Contras and intimidate the Nicaraguan government. In the film, the first mercenary that hero John McClane kills is revealed to have been an American adviser in Honduras.

So the film connects Stuart's terrorism to the U.S. military role in Latin America, although this connection is definitely a subsidiary aspect of the story. The main business involves Stuart's threats to exercise extraordinary violence against airplane passengers, and, in a sequence that possibly took its cue from Hitchcock in *Sabotage,* Stuart's men sabotage the electronic ground-level information that the airport sends to planes coming in, causing them to think the ground is 200 feet lower than it actually is. One flight inbound from London carries 230 people on board. It's low on fuel and needs to land, and, as Hitchcock did with the bus passengers in *Sabotage,* director Benny Harlin portrays the people on the plane who are about to die, humanizing them, and then brutally extinguishes their lives as the pilots unwittingly fly the aircraft into the ground. The explosion that results is one of the film's key moments, one of its "money shots," the kind of expensive image of something big blowing up that audiences had come to see.

In *Chill Factor* (1999), an embittered Army officer aims to steal a deadly chemical weapon and sell it to the highest international bidder. In *Broken Arrow* (1996) a rogue officer in the Air Force steals two nuclear missiles and intends to extort $250 million from the government in exchange for not detonating the bombs. Major Deak Deakins (John Travolta) is a stealth bomber pilot who is embittered because he's been passed over for promotion, so, rather like Colonel Stuart, he recruits a band of military commandos to assist with his extortion plans and help him transport the bombs to their destination. In *Die Hard 2,* once Stuart has taken over the airport, an Army Special Forces unit arrives to try and stop him, but the members of this unit turn out to be in league with him, thereby broadening the web of the conspiracy. In *Broken Arrow,* by contrast, Deakins' treachery is offset and counterbalanced by the heroic actions of his copilot, Captain Riley Hale (Christian Slater), who risks his life to find the bombs and stop Deakins. If, then, *Die Hard 2* suggests that terrorism can begin at home, *Broken Arrow* is more ambivalent about the extent to which the institutions of government or the military may help to inculcate a terrorist response. By contrast, *Under Siege* (1992) is far less ambivalent. Its villain, William Stranix (Tommy Lee Jones), is a rogue CIA officer who has become psychotic and uses his agency-trained skills at violence to hijack a battleship and seize its nuclear-tipped cruise missiles, which he hopes to sell on the black market. He is assisted by the battleship's executive officer, Commander Krill (Gary Busey).

As *Die Hard 2, Broken Arrow,* and *Under Siege* suggest, fears that rogue or disaffected elements in the American military or intelligence community might turn to terrorism furnished a durable template for thriller narratives in this period. But the template offered a crude conception of terrorism— the villains here are mentally unbalanced or criminal or are angry because the government isn't treating them or their friends well. In contrast, Timothy McVeigh, who is the clearest real-life analogue of the homegrown military movie terrorists, destroyed the Alfred P. Murrah Federal Building in Oklahoma City in what he considered to be a political action. Whereas movies like *Broken Arrow* and *Under Siege* give us villains who are raving, out-of-control narcissists, McVeigh explained his actions in composed and clear terms, without the kind of ranting that movie villains display. He said that he attacked the government (personified for him in the Murrah building) because of its violent assaults on the Branch Davidian headquarters at Waco, Texas, and on Randy Weaver and his family at Ruby Ridge in Idaho (both events were seen by McVeigh as examples of excessive federal government power and its abuse of liberty). During the FBI raid on the Weaver property in 1992, federal agents and a sniper wounded Weaver and killed his son and his wife. At Waco in 1993, the Treasury Department's Bureau of Alcohol, Tobacco, and Firearms (ATF) raided the Davidian ranch, precipitating a gunfight in which six Davidians and four ATF agents died. The FBI then laid siege to the ranch for fifty-one days, playing blaring music and amplified animal screams as part of a psychological warfare strategy. The FBI fired tear gas into the building, and a devastating fire broke out. Seventy-six Davidians died, twenty-one of them children. McVeigh had gone to Waco to witness the siege.

He had been a decorated soldier in the Gulf War, honored with the Bronze Star, an award for bravery and meritorious service. But he was disturbed by the violence directed against Iraqis in the war, and his experiences there helped to turn him against the American government. Waco and Ruby Ridge solidified this alienation. In a letter to writer Gore Vidal, he explained why he blew up the Murrah building, where the ATF and FBI had regional offices. "Foremost, the bombing was a retaliatory strike: a counter-attack, for the cumulative raids (and subsequent violence and damage) that federal agents had participated in over the preceding years (includingbut not limited to Waco)."[26] He continued, "I decided to send a message to a government that was becoming increasingly hostile, by bombing a government building and the government employees within that building who represent that government. Bombing the Murrah Federal Building was morally and strategically equivalent to the U.S. hitting a government building in Serbia, Iraq, or other nations." He concluded, "From this perspective what occurred in Oklahoma City was no different than what Americans rain on the heads of others all the time."

McVeigh's example informs *The Rock* (1996), a big-budget Don Simpson-Jerry Bruckheimer action extravaganza. Angry because the U.S. government abandoned his special operations group in the Gulf War, Marine Corp. Brigadier General Frank Hummel (Ed Harris), gathers a group of mercenaries and steals fifteen VX poison gas rockets. Hummel's group positions these rockets on Alcatraz Island, aims them at San Francisco, and threatens to release the gas on the city unless its demands are met. Like McVeigh, the Gulf War has turned Hummel against his government. The film begins with imagery of Hummel reverently donning his uniform and visiting his wife's grave. He kisses the headstone, lays his medal atop it, tells her that he misses her, and asks, for what he is about to do, that she not think less of him. The opening presents Hummel as an honorable and decent officer who takes extreme action only as a last resort and after deep reflection. These are also the terms by which McVeigh viewed himself and his actions.

Once they have setup the missiles at Alcatraz, Hummel gives his men a pep talk, telling them that, for what they are about to do, they will be branded as traitors, just as George Washington and Thomas Jefferson were branded as traitors by the British government when, in fact, they were acting as the greatest of patriots. McVeigh, too, felt that he was expressing a higher form of patriotism by attacking a government that, in his view, had become tyrannical and oppressive. In McVeigh's and Hummel's logic, the U.S. government is an unjust regime which true patriots are duty bound to resist. But whereas McVeigh believed that he was counterattacking the government using its own methods, Hummel's plan is an extortion scheme. He tells the men that his group, Marine Force Recon, carried out illegal operations throughout the world, about which the government maintained a policy of official denial. Eighty-three of his men were killed in China, Laos, Iraq, and other places. The families of these men were denied benefits and told lies about how the men died. Hummel says he's choked on these lies all of his career and now they must stop, and his action with the VX missiles is designed to expose the government's duplicity. One of his demands will be for money to pay reparations to the families.

The Rock has worked so hard to endorse Hummel's sense of moral outrage that it seems not to notice his unsavory background. What sort of illegal operations did Hummel and his group carry out? The movie doesn't say, but it seems reasonable to assume that these included assassinations, sabotage, bombings, and other acts of violence against regimes that the U.S. was not at war with. To people on the receiving end, these might be viewed as acts of terrorism. What Hummel wants, therefore, is not for the government to renounce these acts of violent subversion but to carry them out openly, although being honest about such policies would instantly make the United States into a renegade and rogue nation. Hummel's policy would brand the U.S. as a nation openly sponsoring terrorism and turn it into an international outlaw. But the film seems unaware of this eventuality.

The Rock offers some counterarguments to Hummel's position. One of the heroes, John Mason (Sean Connery), tells Hummel, "I don't quite see how you cherish the memory of the dead by killing another million, and this is not combat. It's an act of lunacy." A Navy Seal commander (Michael

Biehn), sent to retake Alcatraz, tells Hummel that his duty is to defend the country against enemies external and internal, but then he admits that he agrees with Hummel's political position. Counterarguments are not given much weight in the film, and in the climax Hummel reveals that it was all a bluff, that he never intended to fire the missiles, as if that excuses his previous actions. Inevitably, the story's conflicts are resolved with numerous fireballs, gunfights, and explosions.

Marketing terrorism for entertainment, as all the films examined in this chapter do, seems to entail that audiences and filmmakers share a tacit acceptance, within the realm of imaginary fiction, that death on a massive scale is necessary, even if it is not overtly and openly desirable according to the moral terms proposed by the narratives. Its necessity is not moral but rather is a matter of narrative need and aesthetic appeal. The narrative basis lies in the manner in which massive death and destruction furnish the premise and motor of the story, and its aesthetic basis lies in the manner in which filmmakers treat violent slaughter in a voluptuous and sensual way. The attention lavished on explosions and fireballs, for example, is close and loving. In the imaginary realm, then, most of these films propose that terrorism is a desirable act; within the realm of fiction, terrorist violence provides the transaction between filmmaker and audience with its reason for being. It may be startling to contemplate this fact, and certainly the stories in the films overtly disavow any affiliation with terrorist violence and often portray terrorists as nasty villains. And viewers who enjoy the big bangs are not thereby assenting to real-world violence. Nevertheless, these films need their terrorists as a way of motivating the explosions that provide the appeals of visual spectacle.

This goes some way toward accounting for the moral confusion that sometimes creeps into these movies, the way in which characters such as Frank Hummel are portrayed as hero and villain or in which a Deke Deakins in *Broken Arrow,* whom Travolta plays with boyish charm and enthusiasm, is proffered as a companionable guide to mayhem. They do objectionable things, but the movies often find these characters to be charismatic and appealing. A case in point is the freelance arms merchant, Gabriel Shear, whom Travolta plays with rakish charm in *Swordfish,* a film that was released in June 2001, just before the al Qaeda airplane attacks. Shear is another of the "one of us" villains. He's a kind of special operations commando in league with Senator James Reisman (Sam Shepard), who is chairman of a joint subcommittee on crime. Together, they plan for Shear to rob a bank that contains billions in stored DEA money, and the film begins in medias res, with Shear at the bank holding hostages while police and FBI agents encircle the building. Shear has rigged the hostages with C4 explosive and packets of ball bearings. When one of the hostages explodes, the ball bearings devastate the surrounding property and, of course, shred the hostage and a few police officers. Shear's ruthless and deadly nature is thus established.

But the film wants to have things two ways, giving us Shear as a cold-blooded terrorist and as a hero defending America. When Shear reveals his reasons for stealing the money, it turns out that he plans to launch a war on overseas terrorists, and the money will fund it. He belongs to an ultra-secret, elite group called Black Cell, which, according to the film, J. Edgar Hoover founded in the 1950s to protect American freedoms at all costs. "That's my job," Shear tells Stanley Jobson (Hugh Jackman), a computer hacker Shear is coercing to help in the bank job. Americans take their freedoms for granted, Shear says, and have no idea what it really takes to protect those freedoms. As in *The Rock*, the charismatic terrorist whom the film offers as a figure to admire honors a conception of freedom that would make the U.S. a rogue, outlaw nation. Shear tells Stanley that America is at war with terrorist states. "Someone must bring their war to them. They bomb a church, we bomb ten. They hijack a plane, we take out an airport. They execute American tourists; we tactically nuke an entire city. Our job is to make terrorism so horrific that it becomes unthinkable to attack Americans." Shear admits to being a murderer but one with ethics and rules. His ethic is rooted in a concept of the greatest good—people will have to die so that American citizens may continue with their lives unmolested.

Shear's willingness to kill innocent people leads Stanley to say that he's no different from the terrorists he's after. It's a valid point but one that the film insists on fudging. The story concludes by endorsing Shear's mission. He gets away with the DEA money, eludes the FBI, and embarks on his program of vengeance against overseas terrorists. At the end we see Shear and his girlfriend in Monte Carlo. Shear pilots a boat out to sea as a jaunty musical theme kicks in, and a newscaster in voice-over on the soundtrack announces that a notorious Middle Eastern terrorist suspected of bombing the U.S. embassy in Istanbul was killed in an explosion aboard a yacht in the Mediterranean, the third such killing of a terrorist in as many weeks. The film ends here, switching gears to make Shear a hero, and giving us a glimpse of Shear on his mission, portrayed as an exciting and glamorous adventure.

Of course, it helps that he isn't blowing up a church or nuking an entire city as he had threatened to do. Who could object in the imaginary world of a movie to the targeted assassination of a terrorist, especially when his crime resonates with real headlines? The fictional bombing of the Istanbul embassy evokes one of al Qaeda's opening acts of aggression against the United States, the August 1998 bombings of the U.S. embassies in Nairobi (Kenya) and Dar es Salaam (Tanzania). The bombings killed nearly 300 people and wounded more than 5,000. In this respect, Shear provides an imaginary solution to real events, representing a wish-fulfilling response to circumstances that in the real world proved more complicated and intractable. In 1996, for example, the CIA's Counterterrorist Center established a special office whose purpose was to track Osama bin Laden's activities, and the following year the CIA began formulating plans to abduct bin Laden and bring him to trial for funding terrorist activities from his base in Afghanistan. These efforts accelerated following the 1998 embassy bombings. But, according to Steve Coll, in his history of the CIA in Afghanistan, taking the next step, toward an official policy of trying to kill bin Laden, proved to be very difficult for the CIA because of the Presidential ban on assassinations signed by Gerald Ford and renewed by President Reagan. Coll describes a lengthy series of debates in 1997 and 1998 by agency officials and White House lawyers over the legality of undertaking a program to hit bin Laden amid fear that such a program could tarnish the CIA. "They spent long hours on subtle legal issues that arose in America's lethal covert action programs: When is a targeted killing not an assassination? When is it permissible to shoot a suspect overseas in the course of an attempted arrest?"[27] Moreover, in 1998 the Lewinsky scandal had weakened Clinton's Presidency and undermined his abilities to launch covert actions that might be both risky and controversial. As Coll points out, Clinton could have authorized the CIA to use deadly force against bin Laden. "The assassination ban did not apply to attacks carried out in preemptive self-defense where it seemed likely that the target was planning to strike the United States."[28] But Clinton did not take this step. Instead, he signed a series of top-secret Memorandums of Notification (MON) that seemed to lean in all directions, authorizing the CIA to arrest bin Laden, to shoot down his helicopter, and to kill him. As Coll writes, "The exact language Clinton sent to [CIA headquarters] in his bin Laden-related MONS zigzagged on the issue of lethal force."[29] CIA head George Tenet, as well, canceled several operations at the last moment. As Tim Weiner writes in his history of the CIA, "Commanders in the

Pentagon and civilian leaders in the White House continually backed down from the political gamble of a military mission against bin Laden."[30] This hesitation angered some members of the CIA's bin Laden unit, who felt that there had been several good opportunities to kill him.

In contrast, then, to the gratifications offered by a fantasy figure like Gabriel Shear, who, in pursuit of terrorists, acts above the law with impunity and ruthlessness, the actual events surrounding U.S. efforts to go after Osama bin Laden were far more halting, hesitant, conflicted, and ambivalent. While some CIA field agents lobbied for bin Laden's assassination, President Clinton instead opted to fire cruise missiles into Afghanistan at locations that intelligence suggested bin Laden might be found. But he wasn't there, and the outcome on 9/11 of these failed policies was evident.

This gap between the fantasy solutions proposed by *Swordfish* and the complexities and hesitancies that characterized actions in the real world is a striking one. At a time when the United States was tripping over its own feet in an effort to get bin Laden, the film proffers the charismatic and ruthless Shear as the answer for dealing with terrorist enemies. Moreover, the terms of the movie's fantasy suggest a collective yearning to dispense with the legal rules of nation-to-nation conduct in the interests of dispensing vigilante justice. Like *Nighthawks,* the film also suggests that America's democratic foundation might be a very fragile thing and that the government might move quickly to sacrifice it, although in some ways the movie seems to view this as a good thing. But these reflections are neither deep nor substantive. Until 9/11, most films in Hollywood's cycle of terrorism-as-entertainment go out of their way to avoid evoking real-world complexities or to overly complicate their storylines with irony or completing moral perspectives. In fact, some of the most reliable story props ensured the least irony. "Mad bomber" characters, for example, provided effective hooks for action and an abstract way of motivating it that might avoid real-world complexities. Why is he planting bombs? Because he's crazy. In the stripped-down, straight-ahead plotting of an action-adventure movie, no further motivation is needed, but this level of abstraction also shows how disconnected from the actual world many of these movies had become.

Mad bomber stories, which go back at least to Richard Lester's *Juggernaut,* proved to be a trusty standby in the period. The Wesley Snipes action film, *Passenger 57* (1992), pits Snipes as hero John Cutter against a psychotic aristocrat with a penchant for blowing up airplanes. Charles Rane (Bruce Payne) thrives on chaos and violence and has already bombed four airplanes when he and his men hijack a plane carrying Cutter to the West Coast. Cutter fights back aboard the aircraft and eventually defeats Rane. The film's terrorist-as-psycho premise makes for efficient action storytelling because motivations never need be explored. Rane has no political demands and is a figure of simple, stark anarchy. The terrorist-as-psycho also makes an appearance in the form of the mad bomber played by Dennis Hopper in *Speed* (1994). Howard Payne (Hopper) is an embittered, retired ex-bomb-squad officer who bombs buildings and busses as a means of extorting money. The film makes a flip gesture toward the political world of terrorism only to mock it. Aboard a bomb-rigged bus, Annie Porter (Sandra Bullock) asks the film's hero, Jack Traven (Keanu Reeves), "Why is all this happening? I mean, what'd we do? Bomb the guy's country or something?" Traven replies, "No, it's just a guy who wants money."

Another mad bomber creates havoc in *Blown Away* (1994) but, again, not for political reasons. Ryan Gaerity, a psychopathic IRA member, escapes from a prison in Northern Ireland and comes to Boston where he learns that another ex-IRA member, James Dove (Jeff Bridges), now works for the Boston Bomb Squad. Gaerity hates Dove for purely personal reasons that date to their days in the IRA, and he launches a bombing campaign designed to kill everyone in Dove's squad. As Gaerity tells him, "I've come here to create a new country for you called chaos and a new government called anarchy." Chaos and anarchy substitute in the film for anything approaching a political motivation. The IRA also figures in *The Devil's Own* (1997). On the run from the police, IRA member Rory Devane (Brad Pitt) hides out in America, living with a solid New York family headed by cop Tom O'Meara (Harrison Ford). In contrast to the mad bomber plot of *Blown Away*, however, *The Devil's Own* spends little screen time depicting terrorist acts, focusing instead on the friendship that develops between Devane and O'Meara. The film is a psychological drama, not an action thriller like the other pictures in this film cycle.

Another prominent terrorist-themed film of the period was *Air Force One* (1997), a preposterous fantasy about a group of Russian terrorists who seize the President's plane in order to blackmail the U.S. and Soviet governments into releasing a right-wing, nationalist Russian general from prison. Harrison Ford, as the President, goes mano a mano with the terrorists and, of course, wins the day. In the film's prologue, President Marshall (Ford) is in Moscow, where he announces that the U.S. will no longer tolerate state-sponsored terrorism. About states that support terror, he declares that it's their turn to be afraid and says that the new policy of the U.S. will be to strike militarily at any government that supports or sponsors terrorism. Immediately, in the storyline, Saddam Hussein moves two Republican Guard brigades to Iraq's northern border. This plot device demonstrates that, following Desert Storm, Saddam and Iraq were still handy villains for Hollywood storytelling, but, more importantly, the prologue and Marshall's announcement reflect the prevailing view of U.S. terrorist policy in that period, which regarded threats as mainly coming from other states, such as Iran or Libya, which funded such groups as Hezbollah and organized bomb plots such as the one that brought down Pan Am Flight 103. In 1996, when this film was made, the international Islamist threat, which was stateless and globally dispersed, and had gained strength during the previous decade in Afghanistan, largely was off the government's radar. In this regard, the perspective on terrorism in *Air Force One* has an archaic quality about it, at least in terms of where the most potent threat was now originating. Once the hijacking gets under way, the film becomes increasingly far-fetched and disconnected from any actual world in which terrorism might really occur. *Air Force One,* then, opens with a prologue that situates the action within the perceived threat coordinates of the period only to rather quickly abandon these in the interests of far-out action-adventure.

CASUALTIES OF THE POST-9/11 LANDSCAPE

The events of 9/11 made the prevailing fantasy world of movie terrorism look unacceptably irresponsible and disconnected, at least for a little while. Two prominent films—*Collateral Damage* and *The Sum of All Fears*—in production before September 11 and released after the attacks, seemed instantly anachronistic and irrelevant because 9/11 had obliterated Hollywood's terrorist-thriller conventions. Released on February 4, 2002, *Collateral Damage* was an Arnold Schwarzenegger action thriller. Arnold plays a fireman, Gordy Brewer, whose wife and son are blown up in a bombing of Colombia's embassy in Los Angeles. They are having a snack at a sidewalk café next door when the notorious and elusive Colombian terrorist El Lobo (Cliff Curtis) arrives disguised as an L.A. cop and detonates the bomb. The film's director, Andrew Davis, stated that the bombing was filmed before 9/11 and that his main point of visual reference was Pontecorvo's *The Battle of Algiers,* which contains several bombing scenes in which Pontecorvo's camera surveys the damage to people and property.[31]

Pontecorvo's film, however, is much more vivid in dramatizing the dazed, stunned, and pained reactions of the survivors, and he also spent more screen time humanizing those who were about to die. Davis gives the camera to Gordy's wife and son before the blast, but the other victims remain anonymous, helping to make the violence relatively sanitized. Pontecorvo showed bodies being extracted from the rubble and burned survivors staggering out of it, but there are almost no bodies visible in the aftermath of the explosion in *Collateral Damage*. Following the explosion, the narrative jumps forward to the FBI investigators on scene, and all the bodies have been removed save for a few that are tastefully draped with sheets. There are no screams of pain and confusion, howls of rage or despair, except briefly from Gordy as he witnesses the bombing from across the street. The sequence is emotionally flat, expressionless, save for the special-effects pyrotechnics on hand in the fireballs that erupt from the buildings. The scene, in other words, largely erases the human cost of the explosion, except as a means for motivating the film's revenge plot, which has Gordy improbably traveling to Colombia to hunt and execute El Lobo.

The scene's lack of human feeling provides a reliable measure of how terrorism was functioning in the world of action-adventure. It served to motivate the hero's righteous vengeance and carried little emotional valence beyond that function. Thus we accept that Gordy's wife and kid need to die—if they don't, we don't have a story, and we won't get to see Arnold in action. In the world of action-adventure, people are expendable because they are plot devices, a characteristic of the form that shows yet another point of affinity with the acts of terrorism that are being depicted. Upon the film's release, the bombing scene was criticized as being in bad taste; the slaughter on September 11 had made it so. But it wasn't merely the film's sanitizing of bomb violence and its reduction of human tragedy to a plot device that made *Collateral Damage* so out-of-synch with the period in which it was released. It was the way the film so completely falsified the political world of contemporary terrorism.

The film's portrait is anachronistic. It looks backward in time, as if it were still part of the Cold War landscape, specifically, the United States' covert war during the 1980s against indigenous guerrilla movements in Latin and South America which the U.S. perceived as Soviet proxies.[32] The guerrilla groups, active in Nicaragua, El Salvador, Guatemala, and Colombia, were manifestations of the global rise of anticolonial liberation movements in the post-World War II period. A coalition of groups in Colombia challenged its government and military—the Revolutionary Armed Forces of Colombia, the 19th of April Movement, the National Liberation Army, and the Popular Liberation Army. As in El Salvador and Guatemala, the challenge by leftist guerrillas elicited a program of state-supported terrorism from the ruling authorities in the form of violence by paramilitary groups and death squads.[33] Despite the egregious human rights record of these countries, the United States provided massive military assistance to the Colombian government, as it did for El Salvador and Guatemala.

The fanciful spin given to these events by *Collateral Damage* is the invention of the rogue terrorist El Lobo, who has decided to strike back at the U.S. for what he sees as interference in Colombia. "As long as America continues its aggression in Colombia, we will bring the war home to you, and you will not feel safe in your own beds. Colombia is not your country. Get out now." This rhetoric and tactic of launching wholesale violence against Americans in their own country had no basis in the left wing guerrilla struggles of the period, but it did characterize Osama bin Laden's declaration of war against Americans, which he launched from Afghanistan in 1998. In his manifesto for the International Islamic Front for Jihad Against Jews and Crusaders, he declared, "The judgment to kill and fight Americans and their allies, whether civilians or military, is an obligation for every Muslim who is able to do so in any country."[34] Thus, El Lobo's particular brand of terrorism is more al Qaeda than *revolucionario guerrillera*. Nevertheless, the film spins contemporary terrorism in terms of 1980s politics, as when offering a spokesman for the fictitious Latin American Solidarity Committee, based in Los Angeles, who defends El Lobo's terrorism. The scene seems meant as a slam of such prominent 1980s groups as the Committee in Solidarity with the People of El Salvador, sympathetic to the Salvadoran guerrillas.

The film's climax, in which El Lobo tries to bomb the State Department Annex in Washington D.C., recycles the 1993 bombing of the World Trade Center. An associate of El Lobo drives a white van containing the bomb into the underground parking garage of the Annex, and El Lobo plans to detonate it by remote control. In 1993 Ramzi Yousef drove a yellow Ford Econoline van into the underground parking garage of the World Trade Center, between the Vista Hotel and the North Tower, and detonated the equivalent of 1,500 pounds of dynamite, killing six people and wounding more than 1,000. But the fantasy offered by the movie gives us a hero who thwarts the bombing and kills El Lobo and his associate. As we have seen, a principal comfort offered by Hollywood's action thrillers is the continuing reassurance that government authorities and security officials are acting aggressively to keep ahead of terrorist plots. In Hollywood's version of terrorism, American officials are quick and efficient in their responses. They see the terrorist plots coming. They often engage in physical combat with the terrorists and generally thwart them when the bombs are seconds away from detonation. This, for example, is the scenario of *Black Sunday*. In *Collateral Damage*, El Lobo sets up a decoy bombing of Union Station, but the FBI, CIA, and D.C. police all mobilize quickly and efficiently to track the threat. In *The Peacemaker* (1997), the FBI, FEMA, the National Guard, and the NYPD act in concert and move preemptively to thwart a nuclear bombing of New York City. And on the television show *24*, counterterrorism officials remain aggressively abreast of ever-unfolding attacks.

Reality, thus far, is much less encouraging. American intelligence did not foresee the attacks against the World Trade Center, the embassies in Kenya and Tanzania, and the USS *Cole*. In the years before 9/11, the CIA was on hyper-alert because director George Tenet and the agency's Counterterrorist Center felt very strongly that a massive attack from al Qaeda was imminent. Despite this, Mohammed Atta and his conspirators were able to enter the country and hijack the planes. Moreover, institutional rivalries between the FBI and CIA, and laws governing their investigatory jurisdictions, hindered intelligence analysis before 9/11.[35] On that day the institutionalized tensions between New York City's police and fire departments harmed the abilities of these first responders to communicate with one another about the crisis at the World Trade Center.[36] Each department, for example, operated on a different radio frequency. This disparity between the recent history of terrorism and Hollywood's version of it suggests that a chief function of these films is to first evoke and then to allay public anxieties by portraying, much as did the 1950s science fiction films about giant monsters threatening cities, coolly successful responses by military and security forces to threats against the state.

If the response comes too late, as it does in *The Sum of All Fears,* Hollywood fantasy narratives still work hard to provide reassurance. Released on May 29, 2002, the film gave audiences a younger version of Jack Ryan (Ben Affleck), the hero of Tom Clancy novels who previously had been seen on screen as an older character in *The Hunt for Red October* (1990), *Patriot Games* (1992), and *Clear and Present Danger* (1994). In *The Sum of All Fears,* terrorists detonate a nuclear bomb and destroy Baltimore. Ryan and the intelligence community are aware of the unfolding plot but cannot stop it in time. U.S. President Robert Fowler (James Cromwell) and his entourage are in Baltimore at the stadium watching a football game, and Ryan barely has time to warn the group that the bomb is going to detonate in the stadium. Moments before it goes off, the Secret Service evacuates the President. The film's depiction of the explosion may be symptomatic of the newly sensitive context for such depictions that followed 9/11. Whereas terrorist thrillers before 9/11 positively luxuriated in fireballs and thunderous audio effects, *The Sum of All Fears* portrays the explosion in an oblique and indirect manner. As the President is being evacuated, the action cuts to a downtown hospital where Ryan's lover, Dr. Cathy Muller (Bridget Moynahan), works. Electronic noise suddenly replaces the live feed on a television set behind Muller, and a split second later a shock wave blows out the large window facing her, knocking Muller and her colleagues backwards and out of the frame. The scene then cuts to the President's convoy, heading out of town. The spreading shock wave engulfs the cars and knocks them around like toys. Ryan is in a helicopter nearby, and the shock wave throws it out of the sky. The sequence has shown no fireball, no roiling clouds of flame, no multiple explosions, no imagery of mighty buildings crashing to the ground. The visual lexicon of terrorist thrillers, as it has existed for more than a decade, is largely abandoned.

The film spends rather more time on the aftermath of the explosion, unusual in this genre, but even this attention is sanitized because most of it is concentrated on a rescue mission outside the city for the President. When Ryan does drive into the devastation downtown, the film gives us a few quick shots of burning rubble but no long shots that show the scale of the destruction. Baltimore itself, as a major urban center, remains largely off-camera, as do people. Just as the film hides the scale of property destruction, it avoids a portrait of the massive death and suffering that must have accompanied the blast. There are no burn victims, no dismembered corpses, no dead children, and there is no radiation. Ryan is hit by the explosive shock wave, and he drives through ground zero shortly after the blast. He experiences no radiation poisoning, and apparently neither does anyone else. Cathy Muller survives with barely a scratch, despite all that flying glass, and in the film's final scene, the two of them relax on the grass near the White House, and they joke about getting married. Baltimore may be rubble, but its fate certainly hasn't interfered with the love life of our hero and his girlfriend. The epic slaughter that climaxes the film has left no lingering scars of any kind, neither physical nor psychological.

This portrait of the nuking of Baltimore offers audiences a most perfect expression of their anxieties about weapons of mass destruction. The film evokes these fears and then allays them by suggesting that, should the worst occur, it really won't be so bad. It certainly won't interfere with our hero's wedding plans, and the filmmakers won't do anything as crass as showing thousands of dead bodies. This duplicity at the climax of *The Sum of All Fears* is the most egregious to be found in the cycle of terrorist-thriller films. Moreover, in the Tom Clancy novel that was the source for the film, the villains were a hodge-podge that included German communists, an American Indian, and Palestinians. While the film was in preproduction, the Council on American-Islamic Relations (CAIR) persuaded the filmmakers that they ought not to depict Middle Eastern characters as terrorists. CAIR, the Arab-American Anti-Discrimination Committee, and other groups had been very critical of such depictions in past films including *The Siege, True Lies,* and *Executive Decision*. The film's director, Phil Alden Robinson, agreed with CAIR's recommendation and wrote the organization, "I hope that you will be reassured that I have no intention of promoting negative images of Muslims or Arabs, and I wish you the best in your continuing efforts to combat discrimination."[37] The events of 9/11 rendered this decision controversial, with numerous commentators charging that it represented a form of capitulation that served to disavow the Islamist threat to America.

9/11 also made CAIR newly controversial. Formed in 1994, the group was dedicated to promoting an understanding of Islam amongst non-Islamic publics and to safeguarding the civil rights of American Muslims. After 9/11, critics charged that the organization had financial and personnel ties to terrorist groups, which CAIR has denied. CAIR has been active in many arenas, which includes the media, where it has regularly scrutinized depictions of Arabic and Muslim characters in film and television programming.

The changes recommended by CAIR, and which the filmmakers accepted on *The Sum of All Fears,* helped to make the film especially disconnected from the new context that 9/11 had established. The film proffered an international cabal of neo-Nazis as the villains, a group led by Dressler (Alan Bates), an aristocrat with ambitions for world domination. As Jonah Goldberg observed, "Whereas in real life most neo-Nazis smash cans of beer against their heads while dancing in the woods, in Hollywood's vision they wear perfectly tailored suits and plot world domination from the highest corridors of power."[38] In the film's nonsensical storyline, Dressler explains his objectives. He says that it is wrong to think that, in the struggle between communism and capitalism, fascism was "just a hiccup." The followers of Hitler thrive, he claims, and his goal is to provoke a nuclear war between Russia and the U.S. in which they will destroy each other, after which his Nazis can take over the world. He neglects to mention that the world might be a tad radioactive. While the preproduction plot revisions, therefore, were well intentioned, the resulting storyline seemed especially irrelevant after 9/11. As numerous commentators pointed out, neo-Nazis were the one group that nobody would object to as villains, but they lacked resonance when pitched as terrorists in the contemporary world.

While these attributes of the film—its villains and its envisioning of terrorist violence—work to disconnect it from its contemporary context, one of the narrative events in the depicted Baltimore bombing does resonate unpleasantly with reported events just before 9/11. In the film, President Fowler and his officials evacuate the stadium, but the public is not informed about the threat. The rationale in the story is that there simply is no time to issue a warning, and Fowler says, from the back of his limousine as it rushes away, "Get those people out of the stadium." But, receiving no warning, the fans in the stadium are vaporized. One of the most contentious issues that has surrounded the events of 9/11 is what the government knew or didn't know, and conspiracy theories postulate that the Bush administration had full knowledge of the coming attacks.[39] Unusual items reported in the news have helped fuel these suspicions. CBS News, for example, reported on July 26, 2001, that Attorney General John Ashcroft had stopped flying commercial airlines following an FBI threat assessment.[40] Following 9/11, CBS News anchor Dan Rather is reported to have said that the Ashcroft warnings indicated a high level of concern and asked, "Why wasn't it shared with the public at large?"[41] *Newsweek* reported that a group of Pentagon officials had canceled flights just before 9/11. "*Newsweek* has learned that while U.S. intelligence received no specific warning, the state of alert had been high during the past two weeks, and a particularly urgent warning may have been received the night before the attacks, causing some top Pentagon brass to cancel a trip. Why that same information was not available to the 266 people who died aboard the four hijacked commercial aircraft may become a hot topic on the Hill."[42] In this context, the film's depiction of government officials evacuating from the stadium, while the public is left in the dark about a looming threat, is the single detail in the film that connects most directly with the events of 9/11, as reported, suspected, or theorized. Otherwise, *The Sum of All Fears* locates terrorism in a mostly imaginary landscape.

ISLAMIST TERROR ON FILM

While movie terrorists before 9/11 were a mostly daft lot—loonies, crackpots, and embittered ex-police or military officers—Islamist characters emerged as villains in only a few major productions. The films were heavily criticized by CAIR, and Hollywood thereafter seemed to back away from further depictions of Islamist jihadists. The films were *True Lies* (1994), *Executive Decision* (1995), and *The Siege* (1998). Of the three, *True Lies* is the most simple-minded, offering cartoonish villains in a plot that is a knowing riff on James Bond adventures. A radical Palestinian group, Crimson Jihad, aims to detonate a nuclear bomb in an American city, and it's up to Arnold Schwarzenegger to stop it. The preposterous nature of the film's fantasy is evident in the casual way that the nuclear explosion is portrayed. After Arnold has beaten the bad guys, the bomb explodes out at sea, away from the Florida Keys, and the mushroom cloud furnishes the romantic backdrop for a kiss between hero Harry Tasker (Arnold) and his wife (Jamie Lee Curtis). The portrayal of Islamist terrorists in *Executive Decision* and *The Siege* is more serious. In *Executive Decision,* terrorists hijack an airplane and plan to use it as a bomb, while in *The Siege* a sustained bombing campaign in New York City leads the government to impose martial law, imperiling American democracy. In each case, the storyline resonates in clear and compelling ways with 9/11 and the events that followed. The films, therefore, merit close attention because of their claim to a degree of predictive insight.

As noted earlier, bombings and hijackings overseas against American targets helped to trigger the onset in the 1980s of Hollywood's terrorist thrillers. The subsequent emergence of Islamist movie terrorists in the 1990s seems also to have been connected to key events. As Jack Shaheen has shown, Arabic and Palestinian villains have a long history in Hollywood. But in earlier pictures, such as *Black Sunday* or *Wanted: Dead or Alive,* their grievances and motivations tended to be political (when they were given motivations at all). By contrast, the terrorists in *Executive Decision* and *The Siege* are motivated at least as powerfully by religion, and this was a new element in Hollywood's action thrillers. The timing was significant. The 1993 bombing of the World Trade Center had exposed the workings of a radical Islamist group based in New Jersey, which also had plans to destroy other area landmarks. *Executive Decision* was released just as the FBI and CIA were identifying in secret and classified bulletins an emerging new threat in the form of radical Islam. The FBI's 1995 report was entitled "Ramzi Ahmed Yousef: A

New Generation of Sunni Islamic Terrorists." Yousef was the ringleader of the New Jersey bombers. The report stated that "a new generation of terrorists has appeared on the world stage over the past few years."[43] Rather than being a state-sponsored group, "Islamic extremists arc working together to further their cause," and the groups are "autonomous and indigenous."

The trigger for the reports was the Yousef bombing. It was engineered by a group of radicals in the New York—New Jersey area that had coalesced around the figure of the blind sheikh Omar Abdel Rahman. Rahman's group also planned to bomb a host of area landmarks—the United Nations, the Lincoln and Holland Tunnels, the George Washington Bridge, the PATH train line, and FBI headquarters. In a classic example of blowback, Yousef had learned to make bombs in Afghanistan using materials and resources supplied by the CIA and its Pakistani counterpart, the ISI (Directorate for Inter-Services Intelligence). Yousef, and his uncle Khalid Sheikh Mohammed, had also targeted airplanes. In 1995 Philippine police found their computer files, which described plots to bomb a dozen American airplanes and to hijack a plane and fly it into the Pentagon.[44] The year after Yousef's failed attempt to topple the World Trade Center, Mohammed determined to try again and visited bin Laden in Afghanistan, where he pitched the idea of training pilots to fly airplanes into buildings.[45]

Other incidents in these years included the 1994 hijacking of Air France Flight 8969 by the Armed Islamic Group (GIA), which had formed in opposition to the Algerian government. During a standoff with the French police, the GIA demanded that the plane be fully stocked with fuel, a demand that elicited speculation that the group might attempt to fly it into a landmark building like the Eiffel Tower. The various plots in these years involving airlines and public landmarks led the CIA, in its secret 1995 report, to write about a "new terrorist phenomenon" involving a loose coalition of groups operating independently and transnationally to target the United States. Specifically, the agency warned, "Several targets are especially at risk: national symbols such as the White House and the Capitol, and symbols of U.S. capitalism such as Wall Street. . . . We assess that civil aviation will figure prominently among possible terrorist targets in the United States."[46] This was six years before the attacks of September 11.

The storyline of *Executive Decision* is rooted in this context of plots surfacing in 1994 and 1995 involving airline strikes on public buildings by radical Islamic groups. The film extrapolates from these a scenario in which an Islamist leader, Nagi Hassan (David Suchet), and a team of eight hijackers seize a passenger jet traveling from Athens to Dulles Airport in Washington D.C. As on 9/11, the hijackers terrorize the plane's passengers and intimidate them into submission. As on 9/11, the hijackers burst into the pilot's cabin. And, just as Mohamed Atta announced on American 11, one of the planes that would hit the World Trade Center, Hassan tells the passengers that if they remain calm, no harm will come to them. In his official demands to the U.S. government, Hassan says that he wants to exchange the plane and its passengers for money and the safe release of his boss, the international terrorist El Sayed Jaffa (Andreas Katasulas), who is now in U.S. custody. But this is just a ploy to get the aircraft inside U.S. airspace and over Washington D.C., where he plans to detonate a canister of stolen Soviet nerve toxin, DZ-5, which will kill thousands in the area. It is, thus, a suicide mission, and, in another of the film's details that presage the 9/11 hijackings, Hassan has not informed all of his cohorts about this. Some of them do not know that they are on a suicide mission.

When, after Jaffa is released by the U.S., one of them challenges Hassan and asks whether their mission is now over, Hassan replies, "Allah has chosen for us a task far greater than Jaffa's freedom. We are the true soldiers of Islam. Our destiny is to deliver the vengeance of Allah into the belly of the infidel." It is, thus, a suicide mission to be carried out in the name of Islam rather than for any specific political reasons. When his challenger tells Hassan, "This has nothing to do with Islam. This is not Allah's will. You're blinded by hatred," Hassan kills the man. Although this moment of dissent supplies a point of view that honors Islam and counters the Islamist fundamentalism of Hassan, it carries less weight in the film because the character is incidental to the plot, compared with Hassan's motives which are central to the story. And it was this identification of Islamist fundamentalism with terrorism that worried CAIR and led it to request that Warner Bros. edit offending material out of the film, which the studio declined to do.[47]

While Arabic characters traditionally have furnished convenient villains for Hollywood, as have many non-White ethnic, racial, or religious groups, and while *Executive Decision* is hardly an example of literate, nuanced filmmaking, peopled as it is by stock character types, it is also true that the film was drawing on contemporary events and sensing where a new generation of terrorists was likely to be found. In this regard, writing in *Middle East Quarterly,* Daniel Mandel points out that these portraits correspond to real phenomena familiar to the moviegoing audience and that CAIR's critique amounts to a position that films simply should not portray Islamist terrorism. He writes,

> Verisimilitude is the all-important consideration and by that standard
> Hollywood can be vindicated. Accordingly, objections to the effect that
> Hollywood could not get away with substituting blacks or Jews in these
> movies' hateful roles miss the point. There are simply no Jewish versions
> of Usama bin Ladin or black versions of Sheikh Omar Abdul Rahman.
> Should there ever be, we are likely to see their fictionalized counterparts in
> Hollywood movies.[48]

Hassan's suicide mission, for example, has numerous precedents, as does a scene that occurs near the beginning of the film in which one of Hassan's followers walks into a Marriott hotel in London and detonates a dynamite vest attached to his chest. It shows the type of suicide bombing that came to the fore in the Middle East during the 1990s when Hamas used the tactic with devastating results against Israel. The imagery in the film has a haunting and iconic power because it connects with such brutal directness to the suicide bombers who were even then blowing up buses, pizzerias, and markets in Israel. And yet this kind of imagery—a suicide bombing against a civilian establishment—had not appeared before this in Hollywood's terrorist action films. This is the only such scene in the cycle of pictures released before 9/11. Several scenes in *The Siege* approximate this one, but none show a suicide bombing with such on-camera exactitude. And after 9/11 such scenes have been very rare.

The Tamil Tigers in Sri Lanka, fighting for Hindu Tamil secession from the ruling Sinhalese Buddhist majority, regularly employed suicide bombings (some say the Tigers invented this tactic) and used a female bomber to assassinate the former Indian Prime Minister Rajiv Gandhi in 1991. But the Tigers are not primarily a religious group and, therefore, do not have to wrestle with the issues that suicide poses within a religious tradition. Islamist terrorists do—there is a strong prohibition on suicide in the Qur'an. Thus when Middle Eastern terrorists took up suicide as a weapon—in the 1983 truck bombing of the Marine Barracks in Lebanon and in Hamas' attacks on Israel—self-annihilation had to be reconceptualized as martyrdom, which is an honorable course of action. This kind of revisionist thinking is controversial, as witnessed by the refusal of many Afghani jihadists to undertake the suicide missions against the Soviets advocated by their brethren from Saudi Arabia, Jordan, and Algeria.[49] Thus, in the film, Hassan's challenger might also have responded that suicide is un-Islamic—except that, for Hassan, as for bin Laden and his associate Ayman al-Zawahiri, martyrdom in God's name is a calling. For Zawahiri, suicide bombers represent "a generation of mujahideen that has decided to sacrifice itself and its prosperity in the cause of God. That is because the way of death and martyrdom is a weapon that tyrants and their helpers, who worship their salaries instead of God, do not have."[50]

Thus the film's villain, Nagi Hassan, personifies these trends and embodies what Malise Ruthven has termed "a fury for God."[51] Ruthven notes, "Religious violence differs from violence in the 'secular' world by shifting the plane of action from what is mundane, and hence negotiable, to the arena of cosmic struggle, beyond the political realm."[52] Hassan's irresolute and unshakable demeanor suggests his belief that he is enacting a higher logic; he describes himself as "the sword of Allah." Such rhetoric is very like bin Laden's own:

> Concerning the Muslims, I tell them to trust in the victory of God, and to answer the call of God, and the order of His Prophet, with jihad against world unbelief: And I swear by God, happy are those who are martyred today, happy are those who are honored to stand under the banner of Muhammad, under the banner of Islam, to fight the world Crusade. So let every person amongst them come forward to fight those Jews and Americans, the killing of whom is among the most important duties and most pressing things.[53]

The tone and content of Hassan's remarks also are similar to the notes left behind by Sayyid Nosair, one of Yousef's collaborators in the 1993 World Trade Center bombing. In his journal, Nosair wrote that bringing down the Trade Center would be a means to "break and destroy the enemies of Allah.[54] Thus, when the film's hero, David Grant (Kurt Russell), and a team of commandos succeed in retaking the plane and disarming the bomb, rather than accept defeat and live to fight again another day, Hassan machine-guns the cockpit, killing the pilots and sending the aircraft into a death dive. He will not countenance the loss of his prospect for martyrdom, nor did the hijackers at the controls of United Flight 93, who in their last moments, as the passengers beat on the cockpit door, talked about flying the plane into the ground. Seconds later it did crash, either because of a struggle in the cockpit with the passengers or as an intentional act of suicidal martyrdom by the hijacker pilots.

But *Executive Decision,* which otherwise evokes numerous resonances with the events of 9/11, evades this outcome. David Grant is an amateur pilot, and he improbably gains control of the aircraft and lands it not safely but successfully. Like the other films in Hollywood's terrorist action cycle, *Executive Decision* evokes anxieties in order to allay them. The security forces that David represents carry the day with minimal loss of life except for the terrorists. And, like *Air Force One* and *Passenger 57,* but unlike the events on 9/11, the film offers the comforting vision of heroic combat on board the hijacked aircraft, with our heroes stealthily maneuvering their way through backdoor and below-floor compartments and passageways in order to get the drop on the terrorists and take them out.

Executive Decision was one of three films in this period that seemed especially prescient in envisioning events such as those that culminated on 9/11. The others are *The Siege* and *Fight Club* (though *Fight Club* is otherwise dissimilar in that it does not depict Islamist terrorism). *The Siege* lacks the reassuring emphasis on military derring-do that pervades *Executive Decision* and many other terrorist action films. Indeed, it aims to warn its viewers about several dangers to the republic, only one of which is terrorism. The other danger is the erosion of civil liberties that a war on terror can easily produce. Like many films of the 1990s, *The Siege* builds its storyline from a network of references to contemporary events, and, because this is a more self-conscious film than the others, its orientating references also include classic works of political cinema. Shots of the U.S. Army marching up a street in Brooklyn recall the imagery from Pontecorvo's *The Battle of Algiers* in which the French paratroopers march through Algiers. The title of the film recalls the title of Costa-Gavras' film about the Tupamaros guerrillas in Uruguay, *State of Siege* (1972), and a plot detail—the detention and torture of prisoners held in a sports stadium—recalls a similar practice of the Pinochet dictatorship in Chile as portrayed in Costa-Gavras' *Missing* (1982).

The film's self-awareness may result in part from Lawrence Wright's participation as one of the screenwriters. A journalist and scholar, Wright today is best known for his book, *The Looming Tower: Al-Qaeda and the Road to 9/11* (2007), which won the Pulitzer Prize and the National Book Award. After the book was published, Wright recalled his work on the film. He said that *The Siege*

> anticipated, in certain eerie ways, the attacks on America by Islamist terrorists and the damage that these attacks would cause to our country and

our civil liberties. While researching the film, I had the opportunity to speak to agents in the New York office of the FBI and hear their anxieties about possible strikes against the American homeland. "The Siege" reflects those concerns, which turned out to be so shockingly premonitory. When I watched the attacks on America that Tuesday morning in September, I thought, "This looks like a movie." Then I had the sickening realization, "This looks like my movie."[55]

The Siege constructs its storyline from the history of U.S. involvement in and Afghanistan. It invents a radical Iraqi sheikh, Ahmed bin Talal, who is wanted by the U.S. for launching terrorist attacks on U.S. facilities overseas. These include an actual bombing, the 1996 attack on Khobar Towers, a military complex in Dhahran, Saudi Arabia, housing American soldiers enforcing the no-fly zone in Iraq. News footage of the bombing opens the film, followed by footage of President Clinton responding to the Khobar attack. Clinton says, "The explosion appears to be the work of terrorists, and if that is the case, like all Americans I am outraged by it. . . . Those who did it will not go unpunished." Although this bombing is considered to have been the work of Hezbollah operating with Iranian support, in the film's fictional world it was engineered by bin Talal. In response to the attack and operating outside the law, a prestigious but maverick general, Devereaux (Bruce Willis), engineers the ambush and kidnapping of bin Talal, who is then held in a secret location that is not divulged even to senators and other high-ranking government officials.

It should by now be clear that the model for bin Talal is Osama bin Laden, whom the CIA aimed for years to kidnap from Afghanistan. Here the film grossly simplifies its sources. Bin Talal improbably travels unescorted in a single limousine, making the snatch an easy operation. By contrast, bin Laden never traveled alone, moved frequently, operated within an impenetrable ring of security, and was protected by the Taliban government. Reliable information about his location was rarely available; thus, the CIA could not launch snatch operations without relying on a certain amount of guesswork, and President Clinton settled for firing cruise missiles at targets where he potentially might have been. The film simplifies these realities in order to launch its premise—that the kidnapping of bin Talal triggers a series of terror attacks in Manhattan by jihadists motivated by rage over the kidnapping and by hatred for America.

As a result, three armed men with explosives strapped to their bodies hijack a Brooklyn bus, but make no political demands. When the media cameras arrive, they blowup the bus, killing everyone aboard. The FBI learns that one of the men, Ali Waziri, came to the U.S. from Frankfurt on a student visa and got into the country despite being on a terrorist watch list. These story events are modeled on actual incidents. Omar Abdel Rahman, a ringleader of the 1993 World Trade Center bombing, had been on a terrorist watch list, but the State Department and the CIA nevertheless allowed him to immigrate to the United States in 1990. The ringleader of the 9/11 hijackers, Mohammed Atta, was based in Germany—Hamburg, not Frankfurt—and applied for a student visa in the U.S. Moreover, the CIA knew that two al Qaeda operatives were inside the U.S. in the period just before September 11, but did not report this to the FBI, and these men subsequently participated in the plot.

Covering the bus bombing, a newscaster announces, "Beirut comes to Brooklyn," but, as the film shows, a more accurate description would invoke Afghanistan rather than Beirut. *The Siege* dramatizes the unintended consequences of CIA support for the anti-Soviet mujahideen in Afghanistan, and this focus makes it one of the rare Hollywood films to take the concept of blowback seriously. Late in the film, CIA agent Sharon Bridger (Annette Bening) tells FBI agent Hubbard (Denzel Washington) the truth about a suspected terrorist, Samir Nazhde (Sami Bouajila). Nazhde was on the CIA payroll in Iraq, helping bin Talal to overthrow Saddam Hussein. The Agency was financing bin Talal, but then a policy shift occurred and the Agency pulled out its support. Hussein's forces massacred the rebels. Hubbard presses Bridger about what the CIA had Nazhde doing, and then he guesses the truth—the CIA taught them how to make bombs. "Now they're here doing what you taught them to do," he tells her. These events in the backstory of the film blend the history of U.S. involvement in Iraq and Afghanistan. The CIA had encouraged the Kurds in Iraq to rise up following the Gulf War, and, absent the U.S. support that had been promised to them, they were killed by Saddam's army. The more salient details in the backstory, however, give us the origins of bin Laden and his fatwa against America. The CIA and the ISI poured huge monies into Afghanistan in the 1980s, along with military resources, which helped fuel the rise of a fundamentalist Islamist army and regime, the Taliban. When the Soviets left Afghanistan, so, too, did many jihadists in order to continue their struggle elsewhere. One godless superpower had just been defeated, and now it was the turn of the United States. As the bin Laden figure, bin Talal evokes this history.

In production during 1997, the film sees very clearly the implications of the pro-mujahideen policy in Afghanistan, and it predicts that the fallout from this policy would lead to fundamentalist religious terror on American soil. In response to the kidnapping of bin Talal, suicide bombers blow up the bus and its passengers in Brooklyn and then bomb a crowded Broadway theater. This latter sequence is more horrific than the bombing scenes in Hollywood thrillers have been, which sanitize the violence by avoiding portraits of the aftermath. When Hubbard and Bridger arrive, they see dazed, burned, and bloodied people screaming on the sidewalk. One woman in an elegant evening gown descends a remaining staircase in the ruined building. She looks dazed and then turns to the side, revealing that she is missing an arm. In these respects, the film is more honest about the effects of the bombings that are otherwise so routinely portrayed in Hollywood's action thrillers. The Broadway bombing is followed by a cataclysmic event, which, given the film's general prescience, one might expect to involve the World Trade Center. Instead, One Federal Plaza, housing the FBI and other government offices, is obliterated by a truck bomb. (The model here seems to have been the bombing of the Murrah Federal Building in Oklahoma City.) Six hundred people die, and the bombing campaign creates not only fear and panic but also a political demand that something be done.

And herein lies the second danger that the movie wishes to portray and to warn against. It is an attack on civil liberties, employed as a political response to terrorism and in ways that endanger the democratic principles of the nation. In the film, the FBI's failure to stop the bombings produces a growing conviction amongst the public and in Congress that conventional law enforcement is not enough, that a military solution is necessary. The President declares martial law in New York City, and Devereaux leads a force of 10,000 soldiers to occupy Manhattan, seal off Brooklyn, and conduct house-to-house roundups of Arabic men, who are then detained in a flood-lit sports stadium. What follows in the latter third of the movie is a conflict between two different approaches to terrorism—personified by Hubbard and by Devereaux—in which the problem is viewed as either one of law enforcement or as a war amenable to a military solution. One sequence that skillfully poses the difference in diametric terms shows Hubbard and his men visiting a garage where they arrest Tariq Husseini (Amro Salama), one of the conspirators. Hubbard successfully makes the arrest only to have Devereaux show up with his military force and provoke a firefight in which the army demolishes the garage. In this case, the civil procedures of law enforcement had accomplished the goal quite nicely, without the violence and destruction unleashed by Devereaux.

In contrast to the civil procedures that Hubbard advocates, Devereaux practices torture on his captives. Following the assault on the garage, Devereaux takes Husseini to the stadium, where he is tied naked to a chair in a bathroom in imagery that now evokes the abuse photos from Abu Ghraib prison in Iraq. As Hubbard watches uneasily, Devereaux and his men discuss which method of torture would produce the quickest results—shaking, electric shock, water, or cutting. Hubbard explodes, "Are you people insane? What if what they [the terrorists] really want is to force us to herd children into stadiums like we're doing, and put soldiers on the street, and have Americans looking over their shoulders, bend the law, shred the Constitution just a little bit? Because if we torture him, general, we do that and everything that we have bled and fought and died for is over, and they've won." Devereaux has Hubbard escorted from the room; outside, we hear Husseini screaming. Shortly afterward, Bridger comes out, saying sadly that the man knew nothing. A gunshot then issues from the room. The implications are clear—Devereaux's men have tortured Husseini until they realize he is useless to them, and then they execute him with a gunshot to the head.

Devereaux believes he is acting in the best interests of the country, and he has a measure of political support for his actions. But the film also implies that he is a potential dictator waiting in the wings to seize power. It turns out that Devereaux may have abducted bin Talal to provoke just the kind of crisis that would enable him to use military force against an American city, and from that base to potentially expand his appeal as the country's solution in its period of crisis. As one senator says during the debate over whether to recommend that the President invoke martial law, "You don't fight a junkyard dog with ASPCA rules. What you do is take the leash off your own bigger, meaner dog." Indeed, as Walter Laqueur has pointed out, modern states are always more powerful than terrorists. The question is, to what ends they will resort in self-defense? The most extreme end was represented by the military dictatorship in Argentina, which used terror in the 1970s to combat a guerrilla army seeking its overthrow. The military government detained, tortured, and "disappeared" thousands of Argentine citizens.

In respect of an outcome like this, *The Siege* is heavy-handed and clumsy in its depictions of the threat of military rule in America. The events of 9/11 show how clumsy. The Bush administration did not declare martial law, but it did move aggressively to expand Presidential power and to order warrantless surveillance of American citizens, which, however objectionable, is a more benign response than what *The Siege* shows. And the administration was cleverer than the scenario that the film offers. Instead of rounding up citizens and immigrants and holding them in a public stadium, those detained were declared "enemy combatants" and held offshore and in secret, beyond the reach of courts of law. MSNBC commentator Erik Lundegaard put it well when he observed that the filmmakers "assumed the terrorists would think small (buses, schools) and our reaction would be loud (martial law, herding ArabAmericans into stadiums). Instead the terrorists thought big . . . and our reaction, at least in rounding up suspects, has been relatively quiet and secretive. Put it this way: We're not doing it in a stadium with the lights on."[56]

While the film may veer too far toward melodrama in its depiction of Devereaux and the occupation of Brooklyn, it was shrewdly perceptive in noting that torture would be included in the package of counterterror responses and also in warning that such an outcome would irreparably damage the standing of the United States. One of the reasons for housing "enemy combatants" beyond the reach of the law at Abu Ghraib and other secret prisons evidently was so that they might be tortured or, to put it more euphemistically, be subjected to aggressive interrogation. David Cole and James X. Dempsey write,

> If If there was ever any doubt, it became clear in June 2004 that the torture at Abu Ghraib could not be dismissed as the responsibility of a few bad actors. Two leaked memos, one dated August 2002 to White House Counsel Alberto Gonzales from the head of the Justice Department's Office qfLegal Counsel, and the other dated March 2003 to Defense Secretary Rumsfeld from a "Working Group on Detainee Interrogations in the Global War on Terrorism," made crystal clear that the Bush administration consciously sought out every loophole it could construct in order to justify inflicting physical and psychological pain on captives for intelligence purposes.[57]

The international uproar that followed the release of the Abu Ghraib photographs provides a self-evident illustration of Hubbard's warning to Devereaux. It's very clear how *The Siege* evaluates the question of whether terrorism is best countered through war or through law enforcement. It advocates the latter course of action. Hubbard brings down the last of the terrorists and then obtains a writ from District Court for Devereaux's arrest on charges of the kidnapping and murder of an American citizen (Husseini). Devereaux is led away in handcuffs, and, in the last image, military vehicles leave Brooklyn amid the cheers of a diverse crowd of mixed races, ethnicities, and religions that is meant to personify the best attributes of civic cooperation and mutual respect in American society. Of course, this ending is improbable, offering an unconvincing resolution of a question that is rather more complex than the film acknowledges, namely, how to distinguish the conditions under which law enforcement or military force provides the best response to terrorism.

Despite the clarity of the film's allegiance to civil liberties, an ambivalence about how to cope with terrorism creeps into the movie. When the bus is hijacked, Bridger tells Hubbard to use his snipers and kill the hijackers because they're on a suicide mission and have no intention of negotiating. But Hubbard believes in negotiation, and he tries to talk with the hijackers, hoping to explore with them a way out of the crisis. As Bridger predicted, they blow up the bus. Hubbard is stunned, and during a subsequent hostage crisis—a suicide bomber holds a classroom of schoolchildren captive—Hubbard forgoes dialogue, bursts into the room, and shoots the man dead. Later in the film, when the FBI locates a three-man terrorist cell, Hubbard waits for a warrant before arresting them. Again Bridger warns him he's making a mistake. You're not Sir Thomas Moore, she says, and they have a warrant from God. They're ready to die. The timely arrival of the warrant closes the debate, but in this scene, and the others just mentioned, *The Siege* acknowledges that an effective response to terror may be hampered by legal procedures. The film, though, doesn't venture very sympathetically into this territory, apart from the threads in these scenes. It intends to warn its audience that Islamist terrorism is a new danger to America and that authoritarian political responses, fed by panic and opportunism, may prove equally destructive to the country.

In doing so, the film attempts to reproduce a range of voices and points of view about the nature of religion, Islam, and terrorism. It shows the bombings eliciting a rise in hate crimes and racism directed at New York's Muslim population, and it condemns the blunt racial profiling carried out by Devereaux's troops, who round up all Arabic men of a certain age. It also suggests that religion is used as a tool of manipulation by those who recruit the suicide bombers. In a poignant monologue, Samir recalls how his brother, who loved movies and was not especially religious but lived amid despair in the Palestinian camps, was approached by a sheikh who convinced him that dying for Allah was a great calling and that the martyr would live forever in paradise. His brother subsequently strapped dynamite to his chest and bombed a movie theater. Given the skepticism that Samir shows in this scene toward the political machinations that produce suicide bombers, it makes little sense when he is revealed at the film's climax to be a suicide bomber himself. Although this plot twist diminishes the anguish that he has expressed over the death of his brother, the earlier scene nevertheless remains notable as the only such occasion when Hollywood film of this period attempted a portrait of the material conditions that can produce suicidal violence. At the same time, this portrait fails to account for the prevalence of a bourgeois, professional and technocratic background among many radical jihadists. The four suicide pilots on 9/11, for example, all had pursued higher education at universities. As Malise Ruthven notes, "the overwhelming majority of the leaders of Islamist movements have scientific educational backgrounds and qualifications."[58] She speculates that this technical training contributes to feelings of alienation from Islam and the West that can result in a renewed sense of religious radicalism.

On the other hand, consistent with many other Hollywood films, in *The Siege* the specifics of organizational identities remain vague. Are Samir and his brother Hamas, Fatah, Islamic Jihad, or Popular Front for the Liberation of Palestine? As Jordan Wagge has observed, "most Middle Eastern terrorists in movies are never even assigned organizations, as if just being Middle Eastern or of Middle Eastern descent is enough to make a terrorist."[59]

Finally, through the character of a Lebanese FBI agent, Frank Haddad (Tony Shalhoub), the film attempts to balance out its portraits of the Islamist bombers. Haddad is a patriotic American and a government agent devoted to his job. CAIR and other groups, however, protested that Haddad was in the "one good Indian" tradition of Hollywood stereotyping and that, overall, *The Siege* equated Islam with terrorism. Like *Executive Decision, The Siege* generated controversy of a sort that the film industry thereafter wished to avoid, and one result was the changes in *The Sum of All Fears* that made the villains a group of neo-Nazis. Thus, ironically, as Osama bin Laden and company brought an Islamist attack to America, Hollywood film had begun to reject Islamist villains from the screenplays of movies about terrorism. Within the context of Arabic stereotyping that has pervaded Hollywood film for many decades, *Executive Decision* and *The Siege* may well have seemed like more of the same at the time they were released. But now, with Islamist terror having emerged as a very real phenomenon, these films seem prescient in a way they could not have appeared when released. They are

pulp melodramas, but the scenarios they evoke have achieved some valida-
tion from history. *The Siege* does not equate Islam with terrorism, but it
does portray Islamist terrorism, and in this respect it's a film that seemed to
see what was coming.

After 9/11, Islamist terrorists largely disappeared from studio films. *Iron
Man* (2008), for example, features a sequence set in Afghanistan where hero
Tony Stark, a wealthy American weapons manufacturer, is kidnapped by a
terrorist group that wants him to make weapons for them. But they are
generic bad guys, nonspecific, not identifiable as Islamists. In respect of
Hollywood's turn away from Islamist terrorists as movie villains, Ross
Douthat notes that "an air of omission, even denial" hangs over recent
American film. "Terrorist baddies turn out to be Eurotrash arms dealers
(2006's *Casino Royale*), disgruntled hackers (2007's *Live Free or Die Hard*), a
sinister air marshall (2005's *Flightplan*), or the handsome white guy sitting
next to you in the airport lounge (2005's *Red Eye*). Anyone and anybody, in
other words, except the sort of people who actually attacked the United
States on 9/11."[60]

THE REJECTION OF MODERNITY

During the years that Hollywood was producing its cycle of terrorist thrillers,
the only major act of terrorist violence that occurred on American soil was
the April 19, 1995, Oklahoma City bombing of the Alfred P. Murrah Federal
Building, carried out by Americans who were disaffected and alienated with
their government. It capped a series of violent clashes between the FBI and
militia, splinter or segregationist groups in the mid-West—the 1992 assault
on white separatist Randy Weaver's cabin at Ruby Ridge in Idaho and the
1993 assault on the Branch Davidian headquarters in Waco, Texas. The
government killings of members of the Weaver family and the Davidians
spurred the growth of right-wing militia groups in the mid-West that were
antigovernment and radical proponents of gun rights, fearful that the government would try to confiscate firearms that were in the possession of ordinary Americans. Timothy McVeigh claimed that the attack on the Murrah
building was meant in part as payback to the government for the Waco
assault, and he also cited the need to protect the right to bear arms. "It was
at this time, after waiting for non-violent checks and balances to correct
ongoing federal abuses and, seeing no such results, that the assault weapons

ban passed and rumours surfaced of nationwide, Waco-style raids scheduled for spring 1995, to confiscate firearms."[61] As a result, he said he made a decision to "go on the offensive."

The radical right-wing militia movement is the other category of homegrown enemy identified in Hollywood movies of the pre-9/11 era. Militia groups were not involved in the Oklahoma bombing, but McVeigh is a figure who straddles both categories of homegrown enemy as depicted in Hollywood movies. He was a disgruntled former soldier, and he frequented gun shows, which were a gathering place for militia members, and was motivated by some of their issues, such as the fear of a government conspiracy to seize firearms. McVeigh thus connects the two categories of threat that Hollywood was depicting. Costa-Gavras' *Betrayed* (1988) dramatizes the racial prejudice that animates much of the militia movement but does so in a heavy-handed, almost caricatured manner. *Arlington Road* (1999) weaves a fictionalized version of the Ruby Ridge assault into a story about right-wing militias operating like sleeper cells and infiltrating urban areas, where they wait to unleash spectacular acts of bombing. Michael Faraday (Jeff Bridges) teaches college courses on terrorism; he had been married to an FBI agent killed during the film's version of the Ruby Ridge assault. His grief makes him an easy target for manipulation by Oliver and Cheryl Lang (Tim Robbins, Joan Cusack), a model suburban couple who live across the street, seemingly ordinary people but who are secretly plotting to blow up the J. Edgar Hoover building in Washington D.C. They set Jeff up as a fall guy for the bombing, and when Oliver's mask of suburban gentility is removed, he is revealed to be a ruthless, antigovernment crusader on a religious mission. "Are you happy in your godless suburban life?" he asks Michael, as the film suggests that the bombers are motivated partly by religious fundamentalism. Unlike the terrorist action thrillers in which a hero prevails, *Arlington Road* concludes on notes of maximum paranoia. Racing to the Hoover building to warn the FBI that the Lang group is plotting an attack, Michael realizes too late that the bomb has been stashed in *his* car; he has delivered it. It explodes, destroying the building, and newscasts of the destruction deliberately evoke the imagery of Oklahoma City. The news media report that a federal investigation has concluded that Michael was the bomber and that he was motivated by guilt and rage against the government over the death of his wife. Through this denouement, the film evokes the rich tradition in American history and culture of paranoia and conspiracy. By casting doubt on the conclusion of the federal investigation, the film acknowledges the lingering questions that have surrounded other epochal acts of violence, such as the assassination of President Kennedy, the Murrah bombing, and, by implication for it was two years away, the events of September 11.

The terrorists of *Fight Club* (1999) are not right-wing militia types, but like Osama bin Laden, and the Langs of *Arlington Road,* they are motivated by animosity for the perceived moral bankruptcy of American society and by hostility toward modernity. In this respect, they share the radical Islamist hatred for the materialism of a society of abundance. The protagonist of *Fight Club* is an unnamed narrator (Edward Norton) who is consumed by anguish and despair over the banality and emptiness of his corporate life. He obsesses about filling his apartment with catalog items from Ikea. "I'd flip through catalogs and wonder what kind of dining set defines me as a person," he tells us in sardonic voice-over. He eventually experiences a psychotic break with reality and conjures up a fantasy companion, Tyler Durden (Brad Pitt), through whom he can vent his anger at corporate America and plot revenge. Durden, as the narrator's alter ego, describes the psychological emptiness that modern America creates in its citizens by making them into consumers. "Murder, crime, poverty—these things don't concern me. What concerns me are celebrity magazines, television with 500 channels, some guy's name in my underwear." The things that you own, he says, end up owning you, and he imagines a looming apocalypse. "Martha [Stewart] is polishing the brass on the *Titanic,* and it's all going down."

Durden and the narrator assemble "fight clubs" across the country. These are bands of hostile, angry, disaffected men who feel oppressed in their lives, and Durden offers them a war against America that he defines as a spiritual and righteous action, essentially a jihad. He tells the members of one club, "Advertising has us chasing cars and clothes, working jobs we hate so we can buy shit we don't need. We're the middle children of history, no purpose or place. We have no great war, no Great Depression. Our great war is a spiritual war. Our Great Depression is our lives."

So the fight clubs launch Project Mayhem, an escalating series of terrorist actions directed at corporate property, climaxed by a plot to turn several city blocks into smoldering rubble, what the narrator calls a great "theater of mass destruction." They plant explosives in a dozen financial buildings, to bring about what Durden calls "the collapse of financial history." With this ambition, he reenacts the Galleanists' dreams of destroying Wall Street from the previous century. The film's penultimate imagery shows the demolition and collapse of a group of World Trade Center-like high-rise office buildings, an apocalypse of destruction that is impossible to watch after 9/11 without an almost unbearable sense of foreboding. The destruction that Durden and the narrator unleash, the effort to destroy "financial history" is an effort, like al Qaeda's, to turn back the clock to a precapitalist, premodern era that the terrorists imagine to be more benign and less corrupt. In this respect, what *Fight Club* expresses are the psychological rage and alienation that help to spawn terrorism. If Hollywood's action films, which are fixated on the visual spectacle of outlandish fireballs, give us the externals of terrorism, *Fight Club* maps its interior coordinates.

Its characters are motivated by an alienation from modernity that is similar to the Islamists. Osama bin Laden and other radical fundamentalists are putting into practice the ideas expressed in tracts by Hasan al-Banna and Sayyid Qutb, Egyptian writers who became the intellectual fathers of the radical Islamist insurgency. Both decried the godless modernism of American society and advocated a program of jihad to restore the caliphate, a pure Muslim state. As if furnishing a model for Tyler Durden, al-Banna described how materialism had poisoned Western culture, like "a viper's venom [creeping] insidiously into their affairs, poisoning their blood and sullying the purity of their well-being."[62] And, like Tyler Durden, al-Banna believed the end was coining. The West "is now bankrupt and in decline. Its foundations are crumbling and its institutions and guiding principles are falling apart. . . . The millions of its wretched and hungry offer their testimony against it."[63]

Al-Banna founded the Muslim Brotherhood in 1928, an insurgent, jihad-oriented group that Qutb subsequently joined, following a visit to America in 1949—New York, Washington, D.C., San Francisco, and Greeley, Colorado—which confirmed his antipathy for the unholy, capitalist country. Malise Ruthven notes, "Qutb's visit to the United States deserves to rank as the de-fining moment or watershed from which the 'Islamist war against America' would flow."[64] Qutb wrote that in America "new gods are worshipped, which are thought to be the aim of human existence—the god of property, the god of pleasure, the god of fame, the god of productivity."[65] But in fact a bitter emptiness pursues people there "like a fearsome ghost."[66] Tyler Durden in *Fight Club* is such a ghost, who chases the narrator, in flight from his true inner nature.

The rejection of modernity in *Fight Club* links the film's characters with the Islamist terrorists who would find a way to act on Durden's dream of destroying financial history. But this theme, of hostility toward historical notions of progress, is also one of the founding principles of terrorism in the

Western tradition. The rejection of modernity, so profoundly manifest in Islamist radicalism, has been also a motivating force behind terrorist violence in the West. Martin Miller writes that Western terrorists reject "the moral and legal foundations of the modern state . . . [and aim] to annihilate the implicit social contract that had traditionally defined and bound together Western societies."[67] He continues, "Terrorists are the expression of that part of Western culture that has moved beyond the paradigm of progress that has dominated our thinking since the eighteenth-century Enlightenment . . . they believe that secular evil can be overcome by destroying the value system of progress itself."[68] From this standpoint, bin Laden and his ilk demonstrate the same impulse that has been manifest in Western terrorism, namely, an attack on liberalism and modernity, and Paul Berman has argued that the antiliberal totalitarianism of radical Islam, in fact, has its roots in the totalitarian movements of Western culture.[69]

The efforts of al Qaeda and of *Fight Club's* Project Mayhem to turn back the clock of history share this originating impulse, this antipathy for the materialism of the West and the liberal democracy that proved to be such an engine for industrial development. It is this commonality of intent that helps to make the ending of *Fight Club* so extraordinarily eerie and chilling. The narrator and his girlfriend stand before the window in a high-rise office building. "Trust me, everything's going to be fine," the narrator says as the explosions go off. They join hands and watch as the skyscrapers across from them collapse and fall, gutted by the explosives of Project Mayhem. The last pair of buildings to fall is a replica of the World Trade Center, not as tall relative to surrounding buildings, but sporting the WTC's bland, monolithic exterior and sheared-off, flat top. One tower begins to topple into the other, as if fulfilling Ramzi Yousef's dream, but then they fall straight down as they did on September 11. The imagery so literally maps onto the sight of the World Trade Center's collapse as to become deracinating. It warps the ending of the film. *Fight Club* throughout has been a manifesto for terrorists, but now, at the end, the indulgences that fiction claims for itself mock the physical and emotional realities of a context in which buildings really did fall.

This uncomfortable intersection of fiction and fact, whereby *Fight Club* becomes the harbinger of events that it is ill-equipped morally and politically to handle, furnishes an appropriately telling riposte to Hollywood's cycle of terrorist thrillers. 9/11 killed this cycle of films—its ideological limitations were inadequate responses to the events of that day. This was because the films offered mainly an aesthetic response to terrorism, one grounded not in politics or issues of morality but in cinematic spectacle. Terrorism for Hollywood before 9/11 provided a vehicle for stories in which filmmakers could stage huge explosions, and the viewing position allocated for the spectator was exactly that of the narrator and his girlfriend at the end of *Fight Club,* holding hands pleasurably, secure in the knowledge that they will be fine. "We have front-row seats for this theater of mass destruction," the narrator tells us, implicating the film's viewers in the voyeuristic terms of terrorism Hollywood-style. It's a largely guilt-free viewing zone, from which epic fireballs or the destruction of an urban skyline can be enjoyed for the scale and power of the devastation, and this is why the violence is nearly always sanitized by avoiding the details of human suffering or body mutilations that would accompany such events. As Murray Pomerance wrote, "the image of disaster permits us to stand back from it and gasp, a reaction of such complete uninvolvement, even superiority, that we stun ourselves into guilt by experiencing it as beautiful."[70] And as Susan Sontag pointed out in her classic discussion of 1950s science fiction films, images of disaster in the movies tend to emphasize damage to things rather than to people. This emphasis invites "a dispassionate, aesthetic view of destruction and violence—a *technological* view. Things, objects, machinery playa major role in these films. A greater range of ethical values is embodied in the dÈcor of these films than in the people."[71]

Terrorists, too, take a very detached, distanced view of the people they plan to kill. Moreover, taken in historical terms, terrorism has often pursued violence as theater, with its attendant emotional gratifications. An anarchist in the 1880s waxed lovingly over his weapon of choice:

> Dynamite! Of all the good stuff this is the stuff. Stuff several pounds of this sublime stuff into an inch pipe (gas or water pipe), plug up both ends, insert a cap with a fuse attached, place this in the immediate neighborhood of a lot of rich loafers who live by the sweat of other people's brows, and light the fuse. A most cheerful and gratifying result will follow.[72]

The attacks of September 11 were a political and military action, but they were also, in their audaciously visual staging, an act of theater. Responding in an injudiciously literal way to this conception, the composer Karlheinz Stockhausen called the attacks a "work of art," a phrase that elicited outrage. Terror as theater, though, could have a natural affinity with Hollywood film, and for a decade and a half the industry built ever bigger fireballs to give its audience audacious violence with a rush and minimized the ethical values inherent in so much carnage. As Eric Lichtenfeld wrote, action filmmakers showed "reverence for destruction."[73] The explosions that result when a bus collides with an airplane in Speed look apocalyptic, as does the detonation of an abandoned ship in *Blown Away*. *Broken Arrow* aimed for quantity as well as quality of destruction. It offered viewers four helicopter explosions, one nuclear explosion, one stealth bomber explosion, and one train explosion, all with appropriately lengthy fireballs. During the helicopter explosion, the same footage is replayed twice, captured by multiple cameras, so that the chopper explodes several times. Once simply is not enough when it comes to the voluptuous pleasure of big things going bang. Travolta as the villain watches the explosions and shouts enthusiastically, "God damn! What a rush!," an outburst meant to personify the joy that the movie's audience was intended to take at the fireballs. Novelist James Hall suggested that, in fact, Hollywood had a formula for the preferred number of fireballs in an action movie. "Just before Sept. 11 changed storytelling in America forever, my Hollywood agent explained that my new novel was doomed in movieland because it lacked sufficient 'explosive moments.' It was exactly nine fireballs short of the prevailing formula.[74]

9/11 rang down the curtain on Hollywood's theater of mass destruction, at least for a little while. Hall was wrong. It didn't change storytelling in America forever. But now filmmakers had a real event, at home, to which they could respond if they so chose. The World Trade Center had collapsed. A section of the Pentagon was incinerated. A plane full of passengers had smashed into a field in Pennsylvania before it could strike its target. Death and destruction at home were no longer a popcorn dream. The next chapter shows how Hollywood responded and adapted to these events.